Genealogies of Fiction

Genealogies of Fiction

WOMEN WARRIORS AND THE DYNASTIC
IMAGINATION IN THE *ORLANDO FURIOSO*

Eleonora Stoppino

FORDHAM UNIVERSITY PRESS *New York* 2012

THIS BOOK IS MADE POSSIBLE BY A COLLABORATIVE GRANT
FROM THE ANDREW W. MELLON FOUNDATION.

Library of Congress Cataloging-in-Publication Data

Stoppino, Eleonora.
    Genealogies of fiction : women warriors and the dynastic imagination in the
Orlando furioso / Eleonora Stoppino. — 1st ed.
        p. cm.
    Summary: "Genealogies of Fiction is a study of gender, dynastic politics, and
intertextuality in medieval and Renaissance chivalric epic, focused on Ludovico
Ariosto's Orlando furioso. Relying on the direct study of manuscripts and incunabula,
this project challenges the fixed distinction between medieval and early modern
texts and reclaims medieval popular epic as a key source for the Furioso. Tracing the
formation of the character of the warrior woman, from the amazon to Bradamante,
the book analyzes the process of gender construction in early modern Italy. By reading
the tension between the representations of women as fighters, lovers, and mothers,
this study shows how the warrior woman is a symbolic center for the construction
of legitimacy in the complex web of fears and expectations of the Northern Italian
Renaissance court"— Provided by publisher.
    Includes bibliographical references and index.
    ISBN 978-0-8232-4037-1
    1. Ariosto, Lodovico, 1474–1533. Orlando furioso.   2. Ariosto, Lodovico,
1474 1533—Characters—Women.   3. Ariosto, Lodovico, 1474–1533. Orlando
furioso—Sources.   4. Women in literature.   5. Amazons in literature.   6. Sex role
in literature.   7. Genealogy in literature.   8. Intertextuality.   I. Title.
PQ4572.A3S76 2012
851'.3—dc23
                                                                      2011037016

Printed in the United States of America

14 13 12   5 4 3 2 1

First edition

per Manuel

CONTENTS

FIGURES

ACKNOWLEDGMENTS

I have incurred great debts of gratitude in the years of work on this book. I would like to thank, first and foremost, Albert Russell Ascoli and Cesare Segre, who have guided me on different but intertwining paths of research and intellectual rigor.

Dennis Looney, Ronald Martinez, and Kasey Evans gave fundamental suggestions to improve the manuscript and saved me from many errors; those that remain are, of course, my own. Helen Tartar and Tom Lay have been impeccable editors, and it has been a pleasure to work with them, as well as with Tim Roberts, my managing editor. I would also like to thank Candace Hyatt. Many colleagues and friends read and commented on parts of the manuscript at various stages, and I thank them all: Steven Botterill, David Hult, Sergio Zatti, Monika Otter, Stefano Jossa, Rebecca Manley, Andrew Jainchill, Armando Petrucci, Manuel Rota, Marco Ruffini, Andrea Canova, Veronika Fuechtner, Colleen Boggs, Michael Cole, Ippolita di Majo, Wendy Heller, Monique O'Connell, Daniel Javitch, Estelle Lingo, Maude Vanhaelen, Morten Hansen, Lilya Kaganovsky, Rob Rushing, Renée Trilling, Marcus Keller, and Areli Marina.

This work would not have been possible without the generosity of Anna Montanari, whom I thank deeply. I would also like to acknowledge the support and friendship of many others who have accompanied my life and my work during these years: Regina Psaki, Maria Luisa Meneghetti, the late Ruggero Stefanini, Franca Nardelli, Domietta Torlasco, Peggy McCracken, Sharon Kinoshita, Elissa Weaver, Deanna Shemek, Antonia Tissoni Benvenuti, Cristina Montagnani, Françoise and Joe Connors, Michael Rocke, Madeleine Viljoen, Annalisa Izzo, Susan Gaylard, Angela Capodivacca, Silvia Valisa, Barbara Spackman, Graziella Parati, Keala Jewell, Nikhil Rao, Miguel Valladares and Paula Sprague,

Ora Gelley, Nancy Canepa, Beppe Cavatorta, Anna Minardi, Nancy Castro and Gillen Wood, Ericka Beckman and Marcelo Bucheli, Michael Rothberg and Yasemin Yildiz, Dara Goldman, Bob LaFrance, Heather and Vernon Minor, Harry Liebersohn and Dorothee Schneider, Jim Hansen, Paula Mae Carns, Javier Irigoyen García, Luisa Elena Delgado, Mariselle Meléndez, Silvina Montrul, Diane and Antonino Musumeci, and Giuseppe Sangirardi.

A number of institutions provided support for the conception, research, and production of this study: the University of California at Berkeley, Dartmouth College, the University of Illinois, the Research Board at the University of Illinois, the Hewlett International Travel Fund, Villa i Tatti (the Harvard Center for Renaissance Studies), the American Council of Learned Societies, the Mellon Foundation, and the Centro Studi Rinascimentali of Ferrara.

I am grateful for the opportunity to work at a number of libraries, whose staff made it possible for me to gather the documents necessary for the completion of this book: my own home library at the University of Illinois, the Rare Book and Manuscript Library and the staff of the Interlibrary Loan Office in particular; the Biblioteca Nazionale Braidense, Milan; Biblioteca Trivulziana, Milan; Biblioteca Nazionale Centrale of Florence; Biblioteca Mediceo Laurenziana of Florence; Biblioteca Riccardiana, Florence; Berenson Library at Villa I Tatti, Florence; Biblioteca della Cassa di Risparmio di Firenze, Fondo Ridolfi, Florence; Biblioteca Apostolica Vaticana, Rome; Biblioteca Casanatense, Rome; Biblioteca Corsiniana, Rome; Biblioteca Universitaria, Pavia; Biblioteca Estense, Modena; Biblioteca Comunale Ariostea, Ferrara; Biblioteca Palatina, Parma; Biblioteca Statale, Cremona; the Pierpont Morgan Library, New York; the Wellesley College Library, the Houghton Library at Harvard University, the Beinecke Rare Book and Manuscript Library at Yale University, and the Rare Book and Manuscript Collection of the Van Pelt Library of the University of Pennsylvania.

Finally, my deep thanks to my family: to my father, Mario Stoppino, who loved Ariosto and would have been happy to see this book; my mother and sister, Rachele Corsico and Lidia Stoppino; all the friends and family in Italy, from Bergamo to Pavia to Pieve Albignola. And, of course, Leo.

This book is for Manuel Rota.

Introduction

Delle idee, non ho paura; bensì, la dove si tratta di scienza, ho paura
di ciò che senza essere idea se ne dà l'aria, ho paura delle concezioni
subiettive; ho paura di quel fenomeno per cui nelle nubi ci accade di
veder draghi, giganti, eserciti, castelli, che, vissuti un momento nella
nostra fantasia, bentosto si trasformano e si dissolvono.

[Ideas I do not fear; rather, when it comes to science, I fear what
pretends to be an idea; I fear subjective conceptions; I fear the phenomenon that makes us see dragons, giants, armies, castles in the
clouds—all things that, having lived for a moment in our fantasy,
soon change and disappear.]

— PIO RAJNA

When Ludovico Ariosto wrote the *Orlando furioso*, at the beginning of the sixteenth century, the northern Italian court of
Ferrara was a vital center of humanistic and chivalric culture,
and its lords, the Este, were enjoying unprecedented political
prestige. In the city that had nurtured learned humanists such
as Guarino da Verona and Tito Vespasiano Strozzi, Matteo
Maria Boiardo's *Inamoramento de Orlando* had established a
new point of reference for chivalric poetry. At the same time,
three important marriages—that of Ercole d'Este to Eleonora
d'Aragona (1473), of Isabella d'Este to the Marquis of Mantua Francesco Gonzaga (1490), and of Alfonso d'Este to Lucrezia Borgia (1501)—were both a symptom and the cause of the
rise of this small northern court on the political scene of Italy.
These marriages also marked a new trend in the court's history.
For the first time, prestige and power were concentrated in the
hands of the wives: women were acquiring a space within the
dynastic structure of power.

These women relied on narratives of legitimation specifically
tied to the culture of Ferrara in order to acquire and maintain

power. On the political front, after centuries of illegitimate Este
rule, with Ercole d'Este the family started to focus its attention
on legitimacy, and therefore on women's ability to either preserve
or destroy it. The extreme visibility of figures such as Eleonora,
Isabella, and Lucrezia both resulted from and perpetuated the
Este concentration on female dynastic power. Such power was already present, in the form of chivalric narrations, in the texts that
the court (and especially Isabella d'Este) avidly consumed. These
readings were not just the lofty poems by Boiardo and Strozzi but
also popular narratives of giantesses and battles, and serial adventures of Saracen princesses and their conversions. These were
the stories that gave the court—and Ariosto—images of women
in power.

Still, scholars have not established a connection among
chivalric culture, the dynastic system, and gender relations in
the analysis of the Renaissance chivalric epic in general and
Ariosto's *Orlando furioso* in particular. Ariosto's brilliant
adaptation of medieval romance, even if recognized and celebrated, is often difficult to follow, since the chivalric material
he refers to is less well known than are his classical sources;
with few exceptions, critics still dismiss the dynastic elements
in the *Furioso* as empty praise; finally, the discussion of gender and women's position in the poem has been in most cases
relegated to a specific debate over Ariosto's real or supposed
feminism.

The purpose of this book is to demonstrate the intrinsic
connections among these three apparently distinct systems—
chivalric culture, the dynastic system, and gender relations—
and to define them as instances of genealogy. Genealogy does
not exist as a single monolithic process, either as a historical
phenomenon or as an explanatory tool. *Genealogies of Fiction* explores the intersection of different yet related genealogical systems: intertextuality, political dynasty, and gender
(intended as the construction of gender distinctions). The book
addresses genealogy as an interpretive tool, as a dimension of
history, and as a defining feature of cultural production, thus

casting new light on a crucial aspect of medieval and early modern studies.

Genealogical thinking is deeply embedded in sixteenth-century Ferrarese culture and in Ariosto's work. Boccaccio's *Genealogie deorum gentilium*, a text that was very dear to the Italian Renaissance, expresses this fascination with genealogical trees and their interpretation as forms of writing:

> In the beginning of each book I decided to have a tree, which would have the father of the dynasty at its root, and in its branches the entire progeny, according to the order of its descent, so that you may see in them all the characters and their order as described in the book that follows. You will also find the books distinguished by rubrics, which expand in a larger description what you have read as a name only in the leaves of the tree.[1]

The conceptual overlap of trees as images and writing in the *Genealogie* is striking: what you *see* in a depicted tree on the page becomes expanded in written rubrics and in the text itself that you *read*. Boccaccio's use of the tree both as a figure of generation and thought and as the image of writing is so constitutive of his work and its reception that the manuscripts of the *Genealogie* kept the trees as a very stable component of the text.[2] And even after the advent of print, the very successful 1494 Venetian edition of the book reinstated the trees after an initial disappearance in its printed history.[3]

As a real-life counterpart to the trees of Boccaccio's pagan gods, the medallions of the lords of Ferrara, their sons, daughters, and wives, decorate the pages of Pellegrino Prisciani's *Annales Ferrariae* and of the *Genealogy of the Este Princes* (*Genealogia dei principi d'Este*).[4] They testify to a culture for which the genealogical tree represents not only succession and generation but also communal representation and self-conception.[5] In both texts, however, there is an element that sets them apart from the Boccaccian model of genealogy: the Este women—daughters, sisters, and wives—are a constitutive part of the trees.

   The homologies between historical, rhetorical, and gendered
genealogical forms in Ariosto and the culture of his times appear
clearly once we revisit these structures of power from the point of
view of their female components. At the core of the genealogical
system of transmission of political power is the question of legitimacy. Within any genealogy, women both guarantee and, consequently, threaten the legitimate line of succession. In the case
of the Este, the tension over legitimacy is such a commonplace
of dynastic history that it is almost taken for granted. From the
popular song commemorating the licentiousness of the most important lord of the family, Niccolò III ("On this side of the Po and
on the other, they all have Niccolò as a father"),[6] to the spiteful
but truthful observations of Pope Pius II,[7] to the loss of the duchy
of Ferrara by the Este in 1597 because of a lack of legitimate
heirs, the history of Ferrara under the Este is a story of legitimacy
and bastardy.[8] To our knowledge, which may indeed be limited,
Niccolò had twenty-nine sons and daughters, only five of whom
were legitimate.[9] Among the lord's bastards are two of the most
important Renaissance lords of Ferrara, Leonello and Borso,
who ruled from 1441 to 1450 and from 1450 to 1471, respectively. And the history of the duchy is punctuated by scandals,
conspiracies, and murders that all point conspicuously to fears
and threats of illegitimacy. The story of Niccolò's illegitimate
son Ugo and his young stepmother Parisina Malatesta, killed
because of their illicit love, brings together, in overstated terms,
the contradictions between accepted male-generated illegitimacy
(Niccolò's son Ugo) and the female threat to legitimacy (Parisina's
desire for another man). Once the first and only legitimate heir
of Niccolò to become duke, Ercole, comes into power in 1471,
the pressure on legitimacy increases: Ercole takes measures to
omit his own illegitimate children from the hereditary axis, and
representations like those of the *Genealogy*'s trees, which depict
"natural" offspring and "natural and legitimate" offspring side
by side, become impossible.[10] This ideological shift has enormous
consequences for the female side of the dynasty. Since legitimacy
is perceived as a necessity, the wives simultaneously become more

powerful (only their sons will inherit power) and more subject to strict control (their sons *must* be legitimate).

Ariosto becomes explicitly part of this history with the epithalamium for the first legitimate ruler's son, Alfonso, and his disgraced bride Lucrezia Borgia, the daughter of a pope. For the nuptials, the young poet writes a classically inspired text that celebrates the greatness of Ferrara in its alliance with the Roman family, and frames the bride's arrival as the sign of a *translatio imperii* of sorts. The poem, which will be the focus of my last chapter, uncovers some of the central elements at stake in the genealogical perception of the dynasty and its poetry: hypergamy, exogamy, mixed lineages, and the crucial place of gender in their formation.

My guiding thread is a consideration of the character Bradamante, who triggers genealogical reflections in numerous ways. Bradamante is a woman warrior; one of the protagonists of the *Furioso*; and, with Ruggiero, the destined founder of the Este dynasty, for whose scions (Cardinal Ippolito and Duke Alfonso) the poem was written. From her first appearance in canto I, when she defeats an unwitting knight and leaves him to contemplate his humiliation at the discovery of her true gender, until her marriage to Ruggiero at the end of the poem, Bradamante remains at the center of the meandering plot of the *Furioso*, embodying the qualities of courage and moral consistency that so many of her fellow knights lack. What is more, Bradamante is given a remarkably specific function in the poem: she is the sole addressee of its central prophetic sequences. Prophetic communication, a hallmark of epic texts from Homer to Virgil to Boiardo, is in the *Furioso* directed for the very first time to female ears and eyes. This break with the tradition signals the relevance of the character and at the same time marks her as a privileged "inside reader" of the text.[11]

The sections of the poem where Bradamante is literally depicted as an interpreter—be it the Rocca di Tristano episode in cantos XXXII–XXXIII or the final contemplation of Cassandra's pavilion in canto XLVI—reveal one of the central themes of the poem: the dynastic, genealogical narrative that will bring about the foundation of the House of Este. Her character is also the key to the two additional genealogical dimensions of this study. The *Furioso* is constructed through carefully interwoven textual models of different periods and genres (medieval, classical, and humanistic): the character of Bradamante, in turn, is constructed through a succession of texts that frame her as a warrior woman. Breaking away from the traditional analysis of the warrior woman as simply a topos, I consider Bradamante in the context of the intertextual pattern specific to the chivalric epic, which constructs characters across different texts. I then analyze how this textual production is, in and of itself, a genealogy of gender. Luce Irigaray argues for a need to recover a "genealogy of the woman, which has been collapsed inside the man's."[12] Further elaborated in feminist and then gender studies, the concept is explained by Judith Butler:

> To expose the foundational categories of sex, gender, and desire as effects of a specific formation of power requires a form of critical inquiry that Foucault, reformulating Nietzsche, designates as "genealogy." A genealogical critique refuses to search for the origins of gender, the inner truth of female desire, a genuine or authentic sexual identity that repression has kept from view: rather, genealogy investigates the political stakes in designing as origin and cause those identity categories that are in fact the effects of institutions, practices, discourses with multiple and diffuse points of origin.[13]

Femininity and masculinity are constructed differently in different eras, and literary texts participate in this process of creation. Through textual representations of women and men, we can grasp the elements of this formation over time. Texts add a genealogical dimension to gender analysis because they are built through incorporations of other texts: they are constructed by layered representations of genders.

The study of the construction of gender in a Renaissance text and in its models is, in a sense, a "micro-genealogy," one that concerns itself almost exclusively with literary representation and the realm of discourse. The *Furioso* constitutes a challenging subject for such an analysis, given the proclaimed interest of its author in what he sees as the unfair discourse concerning the female sex. In many prologues, Ariosto complains that poets have been unfair to women, preventing them from reaching the same degree of fame as men (see cantos XX, XXXVII, and, more ambiguously, XXVI and XXVII). This complaint is strictly connected to the idea that poetry and praise are deceptive instruments in the hands of those who hold political power, and that fame is governed by such instruments.[14]

Through these two genealogical processes, the textual and the sexual, *Genealogies of Fiction* reconsiders the political themes of the *Furioso* and shows how Ariosto is building a different, more literal kind of genealogy: a gendered dynasty. His text portrays gendered characters and uses them instrumentally to discuss the functioning, and malfunctioning, of the dynastic pattern and thus implicitly challenges the Estes' matrimonial policy. Genealogy, R. H. Bloch has argued, is the symbolic structure that defines the Middle Ages: a genealogical structure of society is consistent with a literary and grammatical discourse based on an etymological pattern. Although one could object to such a linear correspondence between different semiotic systems, Bloch's main claim still voices one of the important historical challenges to the study of literature: is it possible to find homologies between a formal narrative structure and the symbolic structures of a society? Is it possible, for instance, to link the genealogical structure of a noble family in fifteenth- and sixteenth-century Italy to the literary conventions of the chivalric poem?

I answer this question by bringing together three different sets of genealogical practices (the textual, the sexual, and the dynastic) and analyzing them together over the course of the book. Considering the problem of literary models in the *Orlando furioso*, I reevaluate the presence of the Romance epic and chivalric tradition within Ariosto's poem. In the course of this analysis, I consider French prose romances, Italian reelaborations of them, and late medieval *cantari* and *poemi cavallereschi*, most of which still lack modern editions. My readings demonstrate that these medieval intertexts play a key role in shaping Ariosto's poem as a dynastic text. Furthermore, I show that the dynastic discourse, articulated through the rewriting of Romance intertexts, is deeply rooted in the attempt to establish female genealogies. Ariosto uncovered a critical blind spot, a site of tension in the political world in which he lived: the role of women in the foundation and perpetuation of a dynasty. The insertion of women into the representation of political genealogy results in the loss of a vertical, linear descent. Lineages become horizontal and conflicted, and they reveal hidden fears: the uncertainty of legitimacy and the danger of competing loyalties (to the father and to the husband).

Like quicksilver, the different forms and traditions collected in the poem come together and separate in a continuous movement: it is almost impossible to see the junctions, to find points of discontinuity. This body of "sources," models, and intertexts, woven together by the poet in a web, constitutes a labyrinth of references within which critics have attempted to find their way from the sixteenth century onward. The most important critical work, in this respect, is arguably Pio Rajna's monumental *Le fonti dell'*Orlando furioso, first published in 1876: itself a labyrinth of meticulous identifications, both of medieval and of classical "sources." Rajna's expositional strategy consists of narrating the poem's multiple tales one by one, from beginning to end, and thus out of their original sequence, following his own *entrelacement*, often driven by the desire to complete a story. By doing so, he runs the risk of neutralizing the complex organizing strategy enacted by Ariosto on his models. In providing an immense number of references to texts that Ariosto knew or might have known, Rajna makes a claim to the objective judgment of erudition. In reality, though, his work is based on clear assumptions about artistic values. Originality is for him the central quality for the work of art. Even more important, Rajna assumes that he and the poet share a hierarchical vision of literary texts, one that situates medieval texts well below the classics. Following this view, the medieval and late medieval models have consistently been interpreted as merely raw "matter," dear to the aristocratic atmosphere of the Este court, renewed and infused with meaning by the classical "forms" of the humanistic era.[15] In addition, the dynastic excursuses have been ascribed essentially to the "epic" dimension of the poem, that is, the linear, centripetal narration of classical derivation. These narrations, however, prove to be built on more complicated foundations than Rajna believed: they are permeated by details that are incongruent with their alleged classical model.

The study of intertextuality in the *Orlando furioso* has at its core the dichotomy of the medieval versus the classical "source." Critics have tended to link the different nature of the intertexts, as Albert Ascoli has observed, with the bipolar character of the poem, which is epic and romance.[16] In this context, the coexistence of romance and classical models has often been interpreted as a sign of ironic treatment of the latter.[17] Moreover, such dichotomy has often hidden a third fundamental term in the construction of the poem: the humanistic source. Critics have often disregarded the presence of humanistic texts in the *Furioso*, and they have seldom studied the poem in the context of the humanistic debate on imitation.[18] Daniel Javitch, focussing on classical sources or their medieval rewriting, has cast light on some of Ariosto's imitative strategies. *Imitatio* in Ariosto, Javitch argues, is based upon the accumulation of sources, that is, on the imitation of imitation. It is through the use of texts which imitated other texts that Ariosto realizes the particular effect of echoes and distantiation so typical of his poetry; and such strategy, Javitch argues, is not aimed at establishing competition between texts: Ariosto builds textual genealogies in order to free his writing from competitive pressure, and to show that there is no "definitive" or "better" version of a given *topos*.[19] Javitch's position offers an innovative explanation for the "ironical" strategy praised in the *Furioso* for centuries. In my reading of the poem, I try to combine this important achievement with Ascoli's interpretation of Ariosto's masterpiece as a text "of crisis." In the poem, according to Ascoli, the *entrelacement* technique functions as a site of conflict and redefinition of different intertexts.[20] The relevance of hierarchy in the organization of intertexts, as it appears from a survey of Ariosto criticism, is crucial not only to the positivistic collection of sources undertaken by Pio Rajna but also to contemporary studies of the *Furioso*.

Cesare Segre, in a fundamental study dedicated to "Intertestualità e interdiscorsività nel romanzo e nella poesia," surveys different kinds of research on the literary sources of the *Furioso*, linking them to the two main aspects of a text, semiotic and linguistic.[21] Referring to the concept of intertextuality as elaborated by Julia Kristeva on Bakhtinian linguistic theories, Segre points to the double nature of the texts, which are "linguistic products" and, at the same time, "semiotic products" (1984, 107). The distinction assumes great relevance, Segre argues, for the analysis of the sources, where we have studies on the linguistic aspects and studies on the elements of the plot. These two tendencies are clearly at play in *Furioso* criticism, as well as in the sharp divide between philologists and literary scholars on one side, anthropologists and comparatists on the other:

> La tradizione comparatista, col suo massimo campione
> nel Rajna, si concentra su genealogie tematiche. L'influsso
> diretto, che non sta comunque al centro dell'interesse, è in-
> dividuato, quando lo è, su basi quantitative (serie ampie di
> particolari comuni) e culturali (conoscenza probabile di un
> dato testo da parte dell'Ariosto). La tradizione letteraria
> è rappresentata principalmente dai commentatori ed eru-
> diti, specie del Cinque e Ottocento (sino a Romizi), con i
> loro raffronti puntuali. Il fatto che le due tendenze abbiano
> rivelato fonti di diverso ambito (la tradizione cavalleresca
> francese, italiana e spagnola la prima; testi classici, e testi
> italiani della tradizione poetica illustre la seconda) segnala
> forse anche differenze di utilizzazione da parte dell'Ariosto.
> (1984, 108)
>
> [The comparative tradition, featuring Rajna as its cham-
> pion, focuses on thematic genealogies. The direct influence,

which is not at the center of attention, is dependent upon
quantity (extended series of common details) and culture
(the likelihood that Ariosto knew a certain text). On the
other hand, the competing critical tendency, the literary
tradition, featuring commentators and erudite scholars, especially from the sixteenth and nineteenth centuries (until
Romizi), focuses on specific connections between intertexts.
These two critical tendencies have revealed different kinds
of sources: the former has found points of contact with the
French, Italian, and Spanish chivalric tradition, while the
latter has found classical texts and Italian texts of the lyric
tradition. This divergence probably signals the different uses
Ariosto made of his sources.]

Whereas criticism has reached a high degree of sophistication in
analyzing the classical intertexts,[22] there is no specific method
to record and analyze the passage from the medieval text to the
Furioso.[23] The central question, then, has historically been to
establish hierarchies: "cultural" hierarchies, organizing texts of
different times and cultures ("classical" and "popular" texts,
for instance), and hierarchies endorsed and produced by the author himself, through the use of the *entrelacement* technique. It
has never been thoroughly investigated whether different hierarchies correspond or diverge, or even if they demonstrably exist
in the text. My book preserves Segre's idea—that Ariosto uses
different models in different ways—as the fulcrum of analysis,
but also as the hypothesis in need of verification. That is to say,
if we expect to find different strategies of imitation for the medi-
eval/popular text and the classical/learned text, it is very likely
that we apply a stylistic analysis when we find the latter and a
thematic one when we find the former, thus fulfilling our own
prophecy. However likely it be that these guidelines, established
by centuries of study, are generally correct, this book will be a
continuous effort to mix different approaches on different texts,
making them collapse on each other, to open a space for the
possibility that hierarchies of models are consciously built and
exploited by Ariosto himself.

If the use of the medieval or chivalric intertext is structurally different from the one Ariosto reserves for the classical "source," it is crucial to verify the possibility that we can instead use the same global method for the study of all intertextual phenomena in the poem. What follows is a basic outline of elements, or tools, I shall use throughout my work to conduct such a study: global intertextuality (the study of the relation between text and intertext, but also between different intertexts); the combination of intratextual and intertextual analysis;[24] the study of the intertext in its entirety, as to verify the presence of textual "stickiness," or *vischiosità*;[25] the verification of the typologies of use of the intertext (whether the motifs, the lexicon, the stylistic formulae are used, and to what extent), and study of their interactions. Thanks to the toolbox of intertextual analysis, I propose that we read in the *Orlando furioso* a different epic dimension, not alternative to but concurrent with the classical one: the structure of narrative generated in the Romance epic tradition. Although this book attempts a global interpretation of one aspect of the poem through its sources, and finds in genealogy the unifying thread of such interpretation, its goal is not an exhaustive collection of all the sources and intertextual processes of the episodes considered. The intertextual game, which is an inexhaustible source of pleasure in reading Ariosto's text, is not one of the aims of this book.

The choice to study the textual genealogy of dynastic episodes leads to a fundamental question: whose destiny does the poem tell? Whose future and past are told in the ekphrastic scenes I mentioned above? On one hand, the answer is immediately clear: the Este. The Este family is the fulcrum of the dynastic prophecies, and—as I demonstrate—becomes the point of mediation and negotiation between the classical and the medieval poetics in the genealogy of the *Orlando furioso*. Within the text, on the other hand, the principal and usually the only addressee of the prophecies is the heroine Bradamante. My work explores the reasons for Ariosto's extraordinary choice to stage a woman as the depositary of dynastic prophecies. If, as my reading suggests, Ariosto attached a profound importance to the role of women in perpetuating a dynasty, this female-based dynastic discourse must be considered in relation to the larger discourse on the treatment of gender and female subjects in the poem, as well as to the historical and social practice of marriage and dynastic perpetuation in late fifteenth- and early sixteenth-century northern Italy.

The central feature of predictive scenes in the *Furioso* is their aim: they consistently and systematically provide, to the readers and the characters alike, insight concerning the future of the dynasty to be founded by Bradamante and Ruggiero. The dynastic theme is the strand of the poem that more than any other has been subjected to stereotypes and fixed interpretations. On the one hand, positivists such as Rajna have branded these parts as boring and utterly insincere;[26] scholars of Ariosto's classical imitation have only focused on the Virgilian model of the prophetic scenes, to the detriment of their rich medieval texture.[27] The medieval intertexts find no place in this discussion: the syllogistic reasoning entails that, since the dynastic-prophetic episodes of the poems are epic, and the epic is a classical form of poetry, then these episodes must derive from classical sources. These critics assume that the non-Latin models must be relevant for the romance part of the poem, the one devoted, for instance, to Orlando.[28]

Finally, the lack of interest in the medieval intertexts is paired with a surprising one-sidedness in the consideration of the characters playing a central role in the dynastic narrative and in the prophetic sequences. Scholars have focused either on Ruggiero, or, in some cases, on the "dynastic pair," against all the evidence that puts Bradamante at the center of the genealogical discourse. Critics have been reproducing the partilineal usage: it must be him, it must be Ruggiero. A series of facts complicates the barely more acceptable, but still preconceived idea of the "dynastic pair": prophetic knowledge on the future dynasty is not shared between the two characters; rather, Ariosto assigns to Bradamante the role of the founder, while Ruggiero is shielded from it (in part to protect him from his destiny,[29] in part because of his own racial and religious inadequacy). The choice of Bradamante as an addressee is grounded on a textual strategy constructing a new system of communication and exchange, opposed to the classical epic dynastic knowledge, passed from father to son.[30] An analysis of the *Furioso* as a dynastic text needs to focus on Bradamante, and not Ruggiero, as the central character.

The intertextual pattern of the prophetic scenes retrieves a hidden dimension in the text. The prophecies of the *Furioso* are not completely centripetal,[31] nor linearly directed toward the dynastic realization of the union of the couple (and ultimately toward Ruggiero's death). Their circulation escapes the logic of commodity exchange, since it responds to the logic of the gift exchanged between female hands. Moreover, their medieval subtexts link them to a particular genealogical movement, antithetical to the patrilineal structure of the dynasties.[32]

The study of aspects of Ariosto's poetics (*imitatio, entrelacement*, the use of different intertexts and their status in the narration) becomes inextricably linked with the ideological framework of the poem. In this respect, my study follows a line of research sketched by Fredric Jameson, which searches in discursive practices forms of potential resistance internal to the text. The coexistence of multiple models in Ariosto's text can be read as an instance of what Jameson terms the political unconscious.[33] In analyzing Ariosto's construction of gender and genre, I make use of the tools provided by anthropology for the study of literary texts. In particular, feminist revisions of the field have brought important new contributions to areas of interest to my topic, such as kinship theory and gift theory, subtly reframed by Marilyn Strathern. The debate on women as either gifts or gift-givers is crucial for a text like Ariosto's, where the figure of the woman-patron coexists with the figure of the woman as object of exchange (as seen, for instance, in the problematic status of Angelica, as well as in the extraordinary "ode to female patronage" represented by the fountain description in canto XLII). The study of the role of women within the dynamics of dynasty can enhance our understanding of the specific practices of the Este family. Historians have observed that the little court pursued a very aggressive marriage strategy; likewise, literary scholars have no-

ticed that the Este, probably more than any other comparable
family in late medieval and early modern northern Italy, had a
strong investment in the mythological discourse on their origins.
Genealogies of Fiction links these two sets of practices to the poetic strategy pursued by Ariosto in the *Furioso*.

The book is structured around the figure of Bradamante, and
it explores her figure within the chivalric tradition and in the *Furioso*. The construction of Bradamante is followed through its
textual refractions, be they the traditional characters who bear
her name (Bradiamonte), the characters who share fundamental
characteristics with her (the Amazon), and finally the characters
who interact with her in a dynamic exchange of roles (Melissa,
Marfisa, Lidia). Each chapter has at its center one of these figures.

In chapter 1, "Marriage by Duel: Genealogies of the Warrior Woman," I focus on Bradamante as a woman warrior. In
this analysis, I explore the intersection of literary and historical
genealogy from two perspectives. From the perspective of intertextuality, I survey the presence of Bradamante as a character
in the tradition of the *cantari* and *poemi cavallereschi*; from a
political point of view, I consider these texts as the site of definition of gender within a genealogical structure. I suggest that the
tradition of the *cantari* and *poemi* works as a "political unconscious" for the dynastic epic Ariosto attempted to construct. The
principal texts considered are: *Historia di Bradiamonte sorella
di Rinaldo* (Story of Bradiamonte, Sister of Rinaldo) (Brescia,
1490) and the *Inamoramento de Carlo Magno* (The Falling in
Love of Charlemagne) (Venice, 1481). The reelaboration of these
intertexts in the *Furioso* results in the construction of a genealogy of gender, problematically inserted within the genealogy of
the dynasty.

Chapter 2, "An Amazonian Past: Female Rule and the Threat
of Illegitimacy," surveys the descriptions of Amazonian societies
in the Italian epic tradition preceding Ariosto. It analyzes the figure of the Amazon and its Ariostean incarnation, Marfisa. Look-
ing at Virgil, Pulci, and Boiardo, but also at anonymous epic poems and travel narratives such as Marco Polo's *Devisement du*

monde, this chapter posits Amazonian societies as necessary narrative and ideological preludes to the construction of the female warrior in Ariosto's poem. This section contextualizes within the culture of Herculean Ferrara the revival of the Amazon imagery, and shows it to be the product of a society obsessed with illegitimacy. The analysis of these imagined Amazonian communities moves between a broad overview of the chivalric genres in Italy and the close textual analysis of specific episodes. In the *Furioso*, the crucial episode is the adventure of the woman warrior Marfisa in the land of the "femine omicide" (canto XX).

Chapter 3, "The Paradox of Helen: Genealogies and Textual Hierarchies in *Orlando furioso*, Canto XXXIV," centers on the figure of Lidia and the violence of dynastic foundation. It considers a particular case of intertextuality in the *Furioso* and defines *entrelacement* as the principle by which models are organized and brought into conflict. The Lidia episode (canto XXXIV) reveals a complex web of references, in which a classical model (the *Aeneid*) is revitalized and reformed through a medieval intertext (the *Cantari di Febus il forte*, an Italian translation of a French prose romance). In this chapter, genealogy is considered as the literary technique that allows Ariosto to create a text that has multiple and conflicting meanings inscribed in itself, intertextual layers that acquire significance when read simultaneously. In the episode of Lidia, this particular use of *entrelacement* (realized at the intertextual level) allows Ariosto to expose the violence hidden in the social and literary narrative of marriage alliances.

Genealogy as transmitted through prophetic knowledge is the subject of chapter 4, "The Poem as a Prophecy: Gendered Gifts in the *Orlando furioso*." Melissa the sorceress and the prophecy as a gift are at the center of this section. By analyzing the most important dynastic passages of the *Furioso* (cantos III, XLVI) in relation to the classical *topos* of the prophecy and to the medieval figure of Merlin, it is possible to uncover a narrative model that structures the circulation of prophecies in the poem: the model of gift giving. The figure of Melissa, read against the medieval literary figures of the sorceress and of the sibyl, embodies the altruistic yet ambiguously unstable economy of the gift. The close reading of literary parallels such as Giovanni Gherardi da Prato's *Paradiso degli Alberti* integrates a reflection on the possible connections between the utopian model of the gift and the emblem of the bees that adorns the first two editions of the poem.

Chapter 5, "Externi Thalami: The *Orlando furioso* as a Nuptial Epic," returns to the central figure of Bradamante, focusing on the anthropological models of endogamy and exogamy in relation to the Este politics of marriage as represented by Ariosto in the Rocca di Tristano episode (cantos XXXII and XXXIII). A complex section, interweaving different passages from the *Tristan en prose* and various traditions deriving from it, the Rocca di Tristano episode offers a privileged angle to consider both Ariosto's view of the politics of marriage and his strategy of revision of the poem for the 1532 edition. Ariosto's conflicted representation of exogamy is apparent not only in the poem but also in his works more strictly related to the Este court, such as the wedding oration for the arrival in Ferrara of the infamous Lucrezia Borgia in 1501. This chapter provides a rich historical background for the poet's uncertain attitude, analyzing wedding rituals and practices alongside their literary reincarnations.

CHAPTER ONE

Marriage by Duel

Genealogies of the Warrior Woman

When the warrior heroine Bradamante appears for the first time in canto I of the *Orlando furioso* as an unknown white-armored knight, the effect may be lost on modern readers. The drama that her arrival achieves is not the same for us as for Ariosto's contemporaries, because *we* can wonder who the knight is, even after we find out her name, while *they* were already familiar with Bradamante. For them, this momentous appearance was the continuation of a story told many times before. The history of chivalric characters is by default multitextual. Their personalities and choices were determined not only by the elements of a single text but also by those of a textual constellation, a whole system of poems belonging to the same tradition. The characters in these poems were also, for the early modern public, constellations of literary memories.

Readers and audiences approached these texts with a series of expectations.[1] In order to decode and understand what a character was doing at a given time, the audience needed to know what he or she had done in previous narrations.[2] Only this systemic nature can account for the disruptive power of placing the serious and intransigent Count Roland, Orlando, at the mercy of love or, even more powerfully, of folly. Multiple authors and multiple texts narrated the adventures of the same characters, thus creating a "chivalric intertextuality."[3] A multiplicity of sources, spanning anonymous and authorial works on the same subject, produced a built-in effect of familiarity and novelty that single authors could exploit for their own narrative purposes.

Systemic consistency offers the most important logical proof of the centrality of this tradition to both Ariosto's and Boiardo's poems. Boiardo and Ariosto narrate their stories—the intricate, complex adventures lived by Orlando and Bradamante, Rinaldo and Astolfo—preserving the coherence of the characters' lives as narrated in previous stories. Since Princess Dandolia rescues Rinaldo in the *Inamoramento de Carlo Magno* (1481), for instance, Ariosto has the option to allude to this event as if it were part of the life experience of that character, and he does. Boiardo's and Ariosto's consistency with the versions of the dozens and dozens of anonymous poems is clear evidence of the common knowledge the two poets shared with the consumers of epic-chivalric poetry of their times.[4]

This overabundance of material that made up a common set of intertextual references lost its grip on audiences by the time the chivalric epic became a strictly authorial endeavor. Historically and literarily, Ariosto is in a liminal position in the transition between authorial control and systemic consistency; paradoxically, it is precisely Ariosto's success as an author that obscured the previous tradition. In the *Furioso* and in earlier texts, characters respond less to the internal logic of the text than to the global, multilayered logic of the corpus. It is therefore essential to explore the versions of characters and their stories, various and at times contradictory, that Ariosto, and Boiardo immediately before him, had at their disposal as they conceived their poems. The recovery of chivalric intertextuality provides a more faithful hermeneutical approach to these texts than does an insular, authorially based methodology.[5]

The corpus of epic chivalric literature that precedes the *Furioso*—with the obvious exception of Boiardo and, partially, of Pulci—has been for centuries like the scruffy relative no one wants to invite to the party. Already at the beginning of the sixteenth century, this material was so well known that Teofilo Folengo, in his *Orlandino* (1526), could make fun of the connoisseurs of the genre and their pretenses:

> Son certi pedantuzzi di montagna,
> Che poi ch'han letto Ancroia ed Altobello,
> E dicon tutta in mente aver la Spagna,
> E san chi ancise Almonte o Chiariello,
> Credono l'opre d'altri sian d'aragna:
> le sue non già, ma d'un saldo martello. (*Orlandino*, l.29)

> [There are some rustic bookworms, who, because they have read the *Ancroia* and the *Altobello*, and claim that they know the *Spagna* by heart and who killed Almonte and Chiariello, think that others' works are just cobwebs, while their own are made with a solid hammer.]

The legions of Altobelli, Ancroie, Danesi, Falconetti, Guidoni, Rovenze, the series of *innamoramenti* and adventures, the interminable sieges and battles, the implausible deeds of magicians and sorceresses, the sequential love stories of the permanently disgruntled Rinaldo and the never-ending Spanish wars narrated by the *Spagna,* have not had very good press.[6] These poems tell the stories of the knights and ladies of the cycle of Charlemagne, but can also be centered on Arthurian, magical, or religious topics. The texts that preserve this overabundant material are either *poemi* and *cantari*, poems in octaves of variable length, or prose compilations, like the aptly called *selva dei Rinaldi*, the forest of Rinaldo's adventures.[7] These texts were too popular, too serial, too trivial to be taken seriously by scholars: hyperbolic and repetitive, they seldom acquire any reputation for aesthetic value. Their circulation, caught between the end of the manuscript era (the forest of Rinaldo's adventures, for instance, belongs to this category) and the early flourishing of print, make it extremely difficult to reconstruct filiations and standardized versions. They are, in fact, hybrid texts, situated between low and high culture, between novella and epic poem; they are unstable texts, often anonymous and transmitted orally.[8]

Ariosto's poem is fully part of this corpus of texts that demand to be read as a constellation, but its enormous success has obscured them. The poem's instant acquisition of "classic" status made of it a *unicum* in the perception of its posterity, and erased the intertextual threads linking it to its forebears.[9] In order to understand the profound impact of the poem on the corpus to which it belonged, consider the story of the titles of some texts surrounding the *Furioso*. As a genre made even more popular by the advent of print, chivalric poems between the fifteenth and the sixteenth century were extremely susceptible to the laws of the market, and their titles changed according to the most fashionable trends. It is now established fact that the title Boiardo gave to his poem was *Inamoramento de Orlando*, in line with the most famous poems of his time, such as the *Inamoramento de Carlo Magno* and the *Inamoramento de Rinaldo*.[10] But fame retroactively renamed his poem *Orlando innamorato*, modeling the title on the more famous *Orlando furioso*. This simple example attests to the uniqueness of the *Furioso* and at the same time identifies it with the larger constellation: like the most famous examples of its genre, it inspired a series of namesakes, yet it turned into something so radically different—a fully authorial work—that it obscured the conditions of its own production.

Chivalric intertextuality is particularly relevant for a character like Bradamante, because only in constellation with her previous incarnations does Ariosto's manipulation of the preexisting literary material reveal the ideological and political function of the character in the *Furioso*. The intertextual nature of Bradamante's character is specifically connected to her gender and her role in the power relations of dynastic formation. This chapter is an analysis of the epic-chivalric character in its multitextual nature, dedicated to revealing how Ariosto exposes and negotiates the contradictions and difficulties of founding a dynasty on a female character.[11]

Bradamante's history before the *Furioso* can be traced following the characters of the same name in the preceding tradition, as well as the characters that share the same narratological traits. Both approaches are valuable, but neither is sufficient in itself. A global reconsideration of the character of Bradamante as a woman warrior within the poem is necessary in order to shed some light on its traits, both specific and general. The most obvious point of departure is the first poem titled for the heroine herself, the *Historia di Bradiamonte sorella di Rinaldo*. This *cantare* reveals a constitutive trait of the figure of Bradamante, the theme of the "marriage by duel," in which a woman warrior subordinates her transformation into a bride to her defeat on the battlefield. This element and its variations in the tradition allow us to trace Ariosto's narrative choices.

DISAPPEARING WOMEN: SONS WHO ARE MAIDENS

The *Historia di Bradiamonte sorella di Rinaldo* is an anonymous *cantare* printed for the first time in Florence in 1489, and it features the same heroine that Boiardo and Ariosto present as the co-founder of the Este dynasty.[12] In this text, the most prominent features of Bradamante as a female warrior are inscribed; the name of the heroine is the same; the connection is explicit: we could call it an intertext "in the first degree."[13] In this *cantare*, one of the first descriptions of Bradamante, or Bradiamonte, inserts her among the sons of the noble Amone. "And the fifth son was a maiden" is the sentence from the *Historia di Bradiamonte* that brings her to the forefront of the narrative. This is not, however, what we read in the version of the text printed in Brescia in 1490. The author devotes the third through the fifth octaves to the description of Amone's offspring, that is, Rinaldo, Bradiamonte, and their brothers. The first to be mentioned is Alardo, second comes Rinaldo, third and fourth Guicciardo and Ricciardetto. And then, right at the beginning of the fifth octave, in a prominent position, the narrative voice hesitates: "El quinto figliol *fu duna* donzella," "And the fifth was the son of a young lady." The text ought to say "And the fifth son was a maiden," "Ed il quinto figliol *fu una* donzella," who is then revealed as the beautiful and valorous Bradiamonte. That little *d* between *fu* and *una* changes the whole meaning: Bradiamonte becomes the mother of the fifth son of Amone, instead of being his daughter-son, the fifth knight who happens to be a lady.

This is a small mistake, so small that the modern editor refuses to see it, and corrects it without even acknowledging it in the apparatus.[14] Throughout the whole text, it is clear that Bradiamonte is the daughter, Rinaldo's sister, the "son who was a maiden." But it is not an innocent mistake, or a misprint: it probably signals that the compositor of the printed text was expecting a mother, not a son-maiden. Moreover, it seems to be more acceptable for the compositor that the fifth son be illegitimate ("and the fifth was the son of a young lady called Bradiamonte, who never wanted a husband"), than that a son be a maiden.[15] This insignificant *d*" reveals a whole constellation of gender ideologies: Bradiamonte should be the mother of a knight, rather than a knight herself. On the other hand, the threat that the mother poses to the legitimacy of a dynasty is exposed: if Bradiamonte is the mother of the fifth knight, he is an illegitimate son, a bastard. The unconscious movement enacted to protect the text from a menace—a maiden-knight—results in the exposure of a different fear, illegitimacy.

This particular mistake reveals one of the core meanings of the character Bradamante. Specifically, the error casts light on the issue of dynastic generation and the role of women therein. Though it is true that Bradamante is already a central character in Boiardo's *Inamoramento*, it is Ariosto who revitalizes the contradictions and conflicts embedded in her figure. In the poem, she is Rinaldo's sister, a warrior on the side of Charlemagne, as well as the destined founder (with Ruggiero) of the Este dynasty, the rulers of Ferrara in Ariosto's time, and his patrons. Within the poem, her role is marked by an unprecedented element: she is the addressee of all prophetic sequences that reveal the future of the Este.[16]

In this respect, Ariosto renovates an extant tradition from within. The Virgilian model of the prophecy showing the future descendants to the founder of a dynasty had never before been directed to a woman. In this case, consistently, the founder of the dynasty is Bradamante. In canto XLVI, at the end of the poem, she is the only one who understands the stories depicted on the magic pavilion provided for her wedding, because she is the only one, Ariosto says, who knows the whole story.[17] The combination of intertextuality and genealogy signals the ideological importance of the figure of Bradamante in the economy of the *Furioso*.

Ariosto's Bradamante has been interpreted as a figure torn between independence and dynastic destiny. She has been seen as the autonomous woman, able to look out for herself and situate herself in the world on the same level of the knights she so often defeats.[18] When she appears in the first canto, she is presented as a powerful figure, swathed in shining white armor, unsaddling Sacripante without revealing her identity. In the final part of the poem, however, where the dynastic conclusion claims its due, and the marriage with Ruggiero becomes necessary to give birth to the Este lineage, critics have seen a "closure" of Bradamante's independent role. In her submission to bridal duties, in her abandonment of the battlefield, they have read compliance with "bourgeois values,"[19] or "the law of the father."[20] This ideological movement would correspond, on the literary side, to a complete alignment of the poem with the Virgilian, classical epic ending, as opposed to the openness of the preceding romance adventures.[21] The rich layers of textual references to the late medieval intertexts represented by the *cantari* and *poemi cavallereschi* contradict this view. Not only is the presence of these texts pervasive in the construction of Bradamante as a character but it also appears to increase with the poem's third and final revision of 1532.

MARRIAGE BY DUEL: BRADIAMONTE AND ATALANTA

Intertextual analysis provides new means to analyze the figure of the warrior woman. In turn, the analysis of the figure of the war-

rior woman sheds light on Ariosto's strategic use of intertextuality in the construction of his own ideological project. In the case
of the theme of the marriage by duel, added to the 1532 edition
of the *Furioso*, Ariosto's woman warrior reveals itself as the last
incarnation of a genealogy of preexisiting literary figures and,
through the theme of marriage, as the origin of a specific historical genealogy: that of the Este family.

In the 1532 edition of the *Furioso*, Ariosto includes a new episode in the last three cantos, one that complicates and defers the
end of the poem: the wedding of Ruggiero and Bradamante. In
this episode, Bradamante's parents want her to marry the son of
the Emperor, Leone. To avoid being married to Leone and maintain her fidelity to Ruggiero, Bradamante asks for a particular
condition: to be married only to the knight who is able to defeat
her in battle.[22]

> Il don ch'io bramo da l'Altezza vostra,
> è che non lasci mai marito darme
> (disse la damigella) se non mostra
> che più di me sia valoroso in arme.
> Con qualunche mi vuol, prima o con giostra
> o con la spada in mano ho da provarme.
> Il primo che mi vinca, mi guadagni;
> chi vinto sia, con altra s'accompagni. (*OF* XLIV, 70)

> ["Here is the (gift)[23] I crave, your Majesty," requested the
> damsel. "Permit no husband to be bestowed upon me until
> he has demonstrated greater prowess at arms than I possess.
> I must make trial of whoever would have me, either with
> lance or sword: let the first man to defeat me win me; let the
> defeated seek other brides."]

As Pio Rajna first indicated in *Le fonti dell'*Orlando furioso,
the *cantare Historia di Bradiamonte* provides one of the literary
models for this element, which we can call "marriage by duel."[24]
When we combine the analysis of this intertext with a second,
classical intertext—Ovid's tale of Atalanta—we can also debunk
the traditional hierarchy between medieval and classical texts
that consigns the *cantari* to irrelevance. The classical source and

the *cantari* work both together and against each other to create a new force field that becomes Ariosto's Bradamante.

Rather than proceding sequentially, I will focus first on the *Historia di Bradiamonte sorella di Rinaldo*, the source chronologically closest to the *Furioso*. The *Bradiamonte* is an anonymous *cantare*, so popular that it had at least twenty-two editions in the early Renaissance.[25] The plot of the brief poem revolves entirely around the theme of marriage and is easily summarized: the pagan king Almansor falls in love with Bradiamonte, sight unseen, and challenges her to a duel whose prize is her hand; defeated, he is attacked by the Christian army. The action starts when the pagan king Almansor asks his jester, as a man who has traveled, to tell him who is the most beautiful woman in the whole world. When the jester answers, Almansor immediately falls in love with the woman, and decides to leave for Christendom with his army, to win the hand of the Christian Bradiamonte. Bradiamonte's distinguishing feature is that she is a warrior, and will accept as her groom only a man able to defeat her:

> El quinto figliolo fu una donzella
> che fu chiamata per nome bradiamonte
> che fu honesta costumata e bella
> e porto larme indosso e lelmo in fronte
> ne homo non curo sopra la sella
> de gagliardia hera fiume e fonte
> e mai nel mondo non volse marito
> se non chilabbateva sopra el sito. (*Bradiamonte*, c. iv)[26]

> [And the fifth son was a maiden, called Bradiamonte, who was honest, virtuous, and fair; and she wore arms and a helmet on her head, and she did not fear any man in battle; she was the beginning and the end of courage, and she never wanted a husband, apart from the one who could defeat her (on the spot).]

From the beginning, the question of feminine beauty and military strength appear as the fulcrum of Almansor's desire.

The anonymous author made sure that both traditional female beauty and warlike courage and roughness shine through

the jester's description of Bradiamonte. An eyewitness to her surprising qualities, the jester is ready to swear that she is not intimi-
dated by men ("not even a chestnut's worth"):

Recontar non potria la sua belleza
non vol marito se non chi la guadagna
la magna donna di gran gentileza
volentiera giostra sopra la campagna
pero che lha in lei tanta gentileza
verun baron non teme vna castagna
quella e piu bella ch habia mai veduto
ate lo dico o signor mio saputo. (*Bradiamonte* c. 3r)

[I could not recount her beauty: she does not want a husband unless he wins her over; the great woman of great
courtesy takes pleasure at jousting in the field, and since
she has great courtesy in her she does not fear any man, not
even a chestnut's worth. She is the most beautiful I ever saw:
this I tell you, my learned lord.]

Thus, both erotic desire and military pride establish Bradiamonte
as a challenge for the pagan king Almansor. Almansor reaches
Paris with his army, Bradiamonte kills him during the duel that
should bring about their engagement, and the Christians attack
and defeat the pagans. Christians prove to be treacherous in this
second part of the poem: Almansor comes in peace, to form an
alliance with Charlemagne, probably through the marriage; once
he is killed, the Christians seize the occasion to wage war against
an army without a leader and far from its territory.

It is this fierce and dangerous woman that Boiardo chose from
the *cantari* as the future wife of Ruggiero and founder of the
Este dynasty. Thus, Ariosto inherited the character with all its
complicated history. Instead of downplaying Bradiamonte/Bra-
damante's fierceness, Ariosto decided to recover her distinguishing feature: she will marry only the man who defeats her.

In this metaliterary game, it is as if Bradamante could read her
own adventures and choose a rule of conduct suggested by her
position in the literary tradition. Ariosto could have chosen any

number of devices to avoid Bradamante's marriage to Leone. The *cantare*, however, provided a readymade justification of Bradamante's opposition to her parents' dynastic desires. The theme of the marriage by duel and the need to challenge Bradamante not only provides dramatic tension but also resonates with a long history of women warriors.

The similarities between the *cantare* and the addition to the *Furioso* are numerous, and involve both structural elements and formal choices. Bradamante's declarations recall Bradiamonte's words, where the conditions of the duel are posed:

> Rispose Bradiamonte o signor mio
> sel sarracino vol con meco giostrare
> et sel me vince al nome de dio
> per mio marito lo vogliare
> ma se lui perde ce vadagnero io
> fase nel campo del so thesor portare
> dodeci some che stia al parengone
> et quello voglio per viua resone. (*Bradiamonte* c. 7v)

> [Bradiamonte replied: "My lord, if the Saracen wants to joust, and if he wins me (over), in the name of God, I will want him for husband; but if he loses, I will have my gain: make him bring part of his treasure to the battlefield, twelve pounds at least, and I want that amount as a ransom.]

In both texts, the conditions are succinctly summarized in few lines. "Il primo che mi vinca, mi guadagni:/ chi vinto sia, con altra s'accompagni" corresponds to lines 3–5 in the *cantare* ("et sel me vince al nome de dio/ per mio marito lo vogliare/ ma se lui perde ce vadagnero io").

Despite this structural and poetic proximity, however, Ariosto abandons some of the themes of the *cantare*. One of these features is the element of the ransom: a typical sign of the attention to objects and values in the *cantari* tradition. More important, Ariosto downplays the dichotomy between Christian and pagan, which is central to the ideology of the *cantare*. Bradiamonte's suitor and adversary is emphatically identified as a "Moor" or Saracen. When Bradiamonte sees his face for the first time, she remarks that it looks like charcoal ("che hauia el color di carbon spento"), and is upset by the fact that he, who seems a devil ("veder me pare el diauol dalinferno"), aspires to her "sovereign body." The contrast between Bradiamonte's whiteness and Almansor's blackness is so striking that the Saracen himself, having seen her face, addresses her as "madona nata in paradiso" (my lady, you who were born in heaven). These religious elements, whose role should not be overemphasized, but whose presence is evident in the *cantare*, must have appeared irrelevant to Ariosto.[27]

These elements of the representation of otherness, which verge on the grotesque in the *cantare*, are in fact completely absent from the episode in the *Furioso*. Ariosto's decision to deemphasize the racial elements in Ruggiero is part of the normalization of the character. Ruggiero's otherness is completely erased, unlike that of other Saracen characters such as Rodomonte. Not only is Ruggiero baptized when he promises his love to Bradamante but his ancestors are at least in part Christians.[28] The normalization undergone by Ruggiero, which renders him suitable for dynastic purposes, had already affected the other protagonist, Bradamante. In her first literary appearances, Bradamante is in fact the daughter of an Arab king; she later becomes the illegitimate daughter of Amone, Rinaldo's father, and of a pagan princess, and is finally and completely legitimized and Christianized by Ariosto.[29]

The most striking difference between the *Bradiamonte* and the *Furioso* is a crucial element of the plot: the woman warrior is *defeated* in Ariosto's poem.[30] The reasons for this difference are both ideological and narrative. At the ideological level, Bradamante's defeat is central to the process of her normalization: the woman warrior, defeated, becomes just a woman. At the narrative level, this central difference signals the presence of another intertext besides the *Bradiamonte*. As I have already intimated, this other intertext is the myth of Atalanta, a story that may have influenced the medieval Bradamante tradition. In the *Metamorphoses*, Atalanta is the daughter of Schoeneus, king of Boeotia. Because of a prophecy, she decides never to marry, and to propose

to her suitors a challenge: if one of them is faster than her in a
race, she will marry him; but all those who are defeated will die.
The young Hippomenes, struck by her beauty, decides to challenge her, and implores Venus to help him. The goddess, moved
by his prayers, gives him three golden apples. During the race,
Atalanta, who is already in love with Hippomenes without knowing it, stops to collect the beautiful apples that he drops in front
of her, and is defeated. The myth ends tragically when the couple
arouses the rage of Venus, who turns them into lions.

The structure of the engagement challenge posed by Atalanta
is mirrored by the Ariostan Bradamante:

> Territa sorte dei per opacas innuba silvas
> vivit et instantem turbam violenta procorum
> condicione fugat: "Nec sum potiunda, nisi" inquit
> "victa prius cursu. Pedibus contendite mecum:
> praemia veloci coniunx thalamique dabuntur,
> mors pretium tardis. Ea lex certaminis est." (*Met.* X,
> 567–72)

> [Atalanta was frightened by the god's oracle, and lived un-
> wed in in the shady woodlands, ridding herself of her insis-
> tent suitors by imposing harsh terms upon them. "No man
> may have me," she said, "unless he first defeats me in a race.
> Compete against me, and the one who is swift of foot will
> have my hand in marriage as his prize; but death will be the
> reward of those who are left behind. Let us race on those
> conditions."][31]

In both texts, the woman's declaration of her conditions is followed by the alternatives facing the suitor: win or be defeated in
battle for Bradamante, win or die for Atalanta. The element of
death is transferred, in the *Furioso*, inside the challenge itself: the
battle between the woman and her suitor could be deadly.[32]

The defeat of both Atalanta and Bradamante contains elements of ambiguity, insofar as it represents a form of choice. Ovid's heroine is defeated because of her feminine vanity (her desire
to possess the apples, the narrator says), but also because of her

love for Hippomenes, which has undermined her determination to win. Bradamante is fighting to win in order not to marry Leone, but she is unknowingly facing her beloved. Thus, for the reader, who is aware of the situation, her defeat realizes her desire *beyond and against her own will*. Both defeats, however, seem to represent the submission of the woman to the man, and to realize the male fantasy of domination suggested so often in battles involving warrior women.[33] For instance, in the *cantare*, Almansor resorts to heavy innuendos in his awkward attempt to seduce his opponent:

> El resto del bastone getto via
> trasse del fianco la tagliente spada
> disse la donna per la fede mia
> ora seremo . . . di pari sopra la strada
> che torto me facea tua signoria
> hauer teco il bastone a la contrada
> rispose el pagano la dona vol di quello
> pero lo porto meco ite fauello. (*Bradiamonte* cc. 12r–12v)

> [And he threw away the remaining part of his club, and took off his sharp sword, and the woman said: "In faith, now we'll be even on this terrain: your superiority was unfair, since you had your club with you." The pagan replied: "It's the woman who wants it, that is why I take it with me, I tell you."]

The identification of combat weapons with sexual organs confirms the gendered subtext of the episode.[34]

Apparently, then, Ariosto's appropriation of the Ovidian ending reveals an end to the heroine's autonomy. But upon closer inspection, this proves to be the case for Ovid's Atalanta but not for Ariosto's Bradamante. Atalanta loses her autonomy through marriage. She becomes something other than what she was, as the oracle had prophesied ("teque ipsa viva carebis," you shall be absent to yourself in life). Bradamante too has sworn to stay true to herself, precisely through the stratagem of the marriage by trial ("—Ruggier, qual sempre fui, tal esser voglio/ fino alla morte, e più, se più si puote," XLIV, 61, 1–2). As Albert Ascoli has shown, however, this decision becomes, in the final cantos of the *Furioso*, a movement toward the ability to choose which loyalties to honor and which to abandon.[35] Only by being inconsistent in the eyes of those who judge her will Bradamante remain faithful to herself:

> Basti che nel servar fede al mio amante,
> d'ogni scoglio più salda mi ritrovi,
> e passi in questo di gran lunga quante
> mai furo ai tempi antichi, o sieno ai nuovi.
> Che nel resto mi dichino incostante,
> non curo, pur che l'incostanzia giovi:
> pur ch'io non sia di costui torre astretta
> volubil più che foglia anco sia detta. (*OF* XLV, 101)

> [If I prove firmer than any rock in keeping faith with my lover, if in this I surpass every woman that ever lived, that is enough for me. If in all things else I be called inconstant I do not care—so long as I gain from my inconstancy. So long as I be not obliged to accept this man, let them call me wayward as a leaf.]

Thus, Ariosto transforms his character within the tradition, simply emphasizing or deemphasizing particular elements of its previous incarnations.

How do we account for this evolution of Bradamante's character? The answer lies in the study of the *cantare* as a model for the added sequence in the 1532 edition. In particular, it is the political character of the *Historia di Bradiamonte* that allows the transformation of Atalanta's loss of autonomy as she enters the private sphere into Bradamante's inauguration as founder of a dynasty. The *Historia di Bradiamonte* is a political fiction. Almansor clearly comes in peace, proposing an alliance.[36] Bradiamonte's fighting body represents the refusal of the Christian kingdom of Charlemagne to participate in this alliance. It is not a coincidence that a war is immediately waged against the Saracens, with the explicit intent to catch them unaware, when they are not expecting it.[37]

It is clear that Bradiamonte, as a woman warrior, plays a merely representational role,[38] especially when we consider that the second half of the poem, devoted to the war between pagans and Christians, sees her only as a secondary figure. It is this political fiction that Ariosto has in mind when he rereads the nonpolitical tale of Atalanta. Whereas Atalanta loses herself by entering the private sphere, Bradamante finds a voice by entering the public sphere. As the emblem of the refusal to intermarry and forge political alliances, Bradiamonte in the *cantare* is fixed in the repetition of endless defenses of her body and her territory. In the last version of the *Furioso*, Ariosto represents the female founder of the Este dynasty as *choosing* to found the dynasty itself.[39]

The construction of a female genealogy within the *Furioso* is based upon a genealogy of texts, a sequence of texts representing women as controversial political subjects. The recovery of the late medieval intertexts as models for the *Furioso* reveals their survival in the poem as a political unconscious.[40] The *cantari* are a necessary pre-text for Ariosto: by recovering the stories that had for centuries been the subject of popular narrations, widely circulated both in the courts and in the piazzas, Ariosto could either follow Boiardo, and expunge the political issues embedded in these texts, or appropriate them and negotiate their violent contents. Ariosto follows this second path, and his reflection on the role of women makes the pre-texts of the chivalric tradition all the more significant. There is progress and circularity in the story of Bradamante: the particular narrative that distinguishes her in the tradition becomes, in the last version of the *Furioso*, the very device she uses in order to control her marital destiny. The miswritten words of the *cantare* prove to be prophetic: Bradamante *is*, in the end, both knight-daughter and mother-bride of a knight.

PREGNANT WARRIORS: GALIZIELLA

In the *Historia di Bradiamonte*, the pregnancy of the female warrior emerges from the mistake in the printed text. Almansor, the male protagonist, certainly wants to conquer Bradiamonte because of the challenge she poses, but marriage and generation are his ultimate goal. The fact that the warrior must become a bride and the bride must generate the strongest possible off-spring seems crucial to the narrative of the marriage by duel. Galiziella, one of the characters of the Aspramonte cycle, pro-vides a model of a woman warrior who successfully generates strong offspring (Ruggiero himself) after a marriage by duel. Ariosto relies on this preexisting literary figure for many crucial features of his Bradamante. Galiziella, a daughter/mother like Bradiamonte, also accepts a husband on the basis of his supe-rior prowess in battle. The following analysis of the character of Galiziella identifies the woman warrior and her pregnancy as topoi in both the anonymous and the authorial tradition preced-ing the *Furioso*.

The *Aspramonte* is not an anonymous *cantare*, but rather a prose epic with a well-known author, Andrea da Barberino.[41] In his text, Andrea inserts a female warrior, Galiziella, who is at the center of a relatively short but important subplot in the economy of the *Aspra-monte*. It is likely that the *Bradiamonte* had the *Aspramonte*, or a text derived from or parallel to it, as its source. The *Aspramonte* can thus be considered both a first degree intertext, since it is directly im-itated in the *Furioso*, and a second degree intertext, indirectly pres-ent through the influence of the *Bradiamonte*. Bradamante's des-tined husband, Ruggiero, is the son of Galiziella, thus showing again the double genealogy of texts and their characters.

As far as we know, Galiziella appeared for the first time in the cycle of poems that include Barberino's *Aspramonte*.[42] Pio Rajna claims that she does not exist in the French sources used by Andrea (1975, 49); Barberino himself, however, declares that he is using different—and contrasting—texts as the basis for her story.[43] In the *cantari d'Aspramonte*, Galiziella's story is similar to that recounted in the prose *Aspramonte*, which succeeds them chronologically.[44] If we compare Andrea's *Aspramonte* and the *cantari* to the French predecessors, we find that the story of Gali-ziella seems to be an addition of the Italian tradition.

The plot of the *Aspramonte* is linear. The text relates the Italian campaign undertaken by Charlemagne against the Saracens, culminating in the battle over Risa (Reggio). In Risa, the Christian lineage of Riccieri (the future Ruggieri, ancestor of the Ariostan Ruggiero) faces the pagan forces of King Agolante. Following a dispute between his son and a jester about the greatness of Charlemagne, Agolante plans to attack the French emperor.[45] He sends his faithful servant Subrino to spy on the Christian kingdoms of the west for five years. Upon Subrino's return, Agolante decides to invade Christendom. Coming from Feminoro, the land of the Amazons, a bastard daughter of Agolante named Galiziella arrives: "E in questo tempo giunse Galiziella figliuola dello re Agolante; ma era bastarda; e veniva del regno Feminoro con cento damigelle" [At that time Galiziella, the daughter of King Agolante, arrived; she was a bastard, and she came from the kingdom called Feminoro with a hundred maidens].[46] Thus, from her first appearance, Galiziella is introduced as an exotic figure whose lineage is uncertain and whose presence is threatening.

Galiziella is immediately introduced as a woman warrior, more at ease on the battlefield than in traditional female spaces. Almonte, the king's son and Galiziella's half-brother, realizes that his half-sister would rather be fighting in a tournament than sitting as a spectator on a balcony, and arms her "with his own hands." The queen mocks her, but Galiziella, in her white armor, ends up being the winner, obtaining the favor of both her half-brother and the queen. It is precisely her victory in the tournament, however, that highlights again her status as a bastard:

> [Almonte] pregò la reina che, perch'ella fosse bastarda, le facesse onore come a propria figliola. . . . Quando Galiziella fu dinanzi dalla reina, e la reina l'abbracciò e feciela realemente rivestire, e disse: "O franca Galiziella, da ora inanzi voglio che tu sia mia figliuola, e giuroti che alla tornata che noi faremo di Franza (ché con la grazia degli iddei noi l'acquisteremo), che io ti farò portare corona." (*Aspramonte* IX, 45)

[Almonte asked the queen to honor her as a daughter, even
though she was a bastard. When Galiziella arrived in the
queen's presence, the queen embraced her and had her re-
gally clothed, and she said: "Oh noble Galiziella, from now
on I want you to be my daughter, and I promise that when
we return from France (which we shall conquer, the gods
willing), that I will make you a queen."]

Thus, through her status as a warrior, Galiziella seems to be able
to achieve a new form of legitimacy for herself, entailing a unique
kind of feminization. Almonte, in fact, praises her, and makes
her promise that she will never accept as a husband anyone who
cannot defeat her, so as to avoid the improper condition of being
married to someone weaker than she is: "Ma io ti priego che tu
non tolga per marito se tu non truovi barone che ti abatta da cavallo, imperò che si disdice che una femmina abbia uno marito
che possa meno di lei; e però, se niuno barone t'abatte, quello sia
tuo marito" [But I beg you not to take anyone as a husband, unless you find someone who can unhorse you; since it is not proper
that a woman have a husband weaker than she; and therefore,
if anyone defeats you, let that man be your husband] (45). Being
a warrior, being legitimate, and being female are explicitly presented as contradictory qualities in the text.

For a short time, after the tournament, the tension among
these three elements seems to be resolved. Galiziella lives hap-
pily at the court of her father, where she enjoys everybody's
respect and love. The king grants her every wish, so much so
that she plays the role of political intermediary when the Spanish king Galafro wants peace with King Agolante. On this occasion, she is moved to pity for Galafro when he presents her
with a splendid sword (the famous Durindarda, soon to become Orlando's sword). Galiziella then gives the sword to her
half-brother Almonte as a gift before the onset of the campaign against the Christians.[47] As a go-between between the
Christian and the Muslim world, Galiziella is also a figure in
between all the spaces of chivalric legitimacy: she is a woman
and a warrior, someone who can herself wield a sword and a

sister who can give it to a male warrior, an illegitimate and a legitimized daughter.

The development of the plot of the *Aspramonte* inevitably leads to a duel where Galiziella's double nature is unveiled and, through defeat, her female identity is brought to light. When the news reaches the queen's pavilion that Riccieri, the Christian champion, has defeated Almonte, Galiziella puts on the clothes of the Saracen champion and defies Riccieri, hoping to bring him back as a prisoner. The battle between Riccieri and the lady dressed as a knight is fierce. When she is unhorsed, however, her helmet falls off and her beautiful hair is unveiled along with her gender. Upon this discovery, Riccieri prevents his army from attacking her, and has her taken to the castle. Seeing Galiziella in her women's clothes once again, Beltramo, Riccieri's brother, falls in love with her. The woman warrior, defeated and captured, immediately becomes available as a potential bride.

At this juncture of the story, the question of the marriage by duel becomes central to the plot. When Beltramo asks his father Rambaldo if he can have Galiziella as his wife, the king replies that her destiny depends upon Riccieri, who took her prisoner; it is Riccieri who can decide her fate. Thus, as a prisoner, Galiziella is fully deprived of any agency, and, as a woman, she is the potential object of exchange between brothers. However, Galiziella's ability to reclaim her identity as a warrior prevents the male characters from disposing of her as a mere gift among themselves. Riccieri would generously give Galiziella to his brother as a wife, but the lady has a condition to pose: she will not marry Beltramo unless he defeats her on the battlefield. She can, however, marry Riccieri, who has unhorsed her during their duel:

> Se Beltramo m'adimanda e vuole per sua donna, pigli le sue arme, e io ancora mi armerò, e a cavallo facciamo in sulla piazza colpo di lancia; e s'egli m'abatte io sono contenta d'essere sua moglie; ma se io abatto lui io non lo voglio, imperò che *io non voglio marito che non mi possa gastigare: e voi sapete che non sarebbe ragione.* Ma Riccieri che m'ha abattuto, se egli mi vuole, io sono contenta, imperò che egli

mi potrà gastigare (*Aspramonte* XXXII, 64–65, emphasis added).

[If Beltramo requests me and wants me as his wife, let him take his weapons, and I shall take mine, and let us joust in the piazza; and if he unhorses me, I shall be happy to be his wife; but if I unhorse him, I do not want him, since *I do not wish a husband who cannot chastise me: and you know that it would not be right*. On the contrary, if Riccieri, who unhorsed me, does want me, I will be happy, since he will be able to chastise me.]

The element of the "Atalanta" choice is in this passage, as in the *Historia di Bradiamonte* and in the *Furioso*, used to avoid marrying an unwanted husband. Galiziella's choice to reclaim her warrior identity leads to war. If Galiziella had acquiesced to a traditional female role as a gift exchanged between brothers, an alliance would have been formed. Instead, her decision to require a duel to legitimize her marriage makes the alliance between the two brothers impossible, and Beltramo starts hating his brother and his own lineage to the point of betrayal. The trigger for his hatred is the marriage between Riccieri and Galiziella, who soon becomes pregnant. Beltramo starts to negotiate with the Saracens, and the city of Risa is conquered through his treachery. The alliance that could have been accomplished through the circulation of women as gifts fails, and this failure destabilizes the social, political, and religious order within the poem. It is not the Saracen woman who forges an alliance, but the Christian prince who allies himself with the Saracens. Two brothers become mortal enemies, and a legitimate dynasty loses its city.

In the *Aspramonte*, Galiziella's return to her status as a warrior is presented explicitly. While Riccieri is dressing and gathering his weapons, it is the pregnant Galiziella who defends him with a sword from the invaders, and when Riccieri storms out to defend the city, Galiziella holds the castle. Her half-brother Almonte kills Riccieri by stabbing him in the back, a clear sign that cowardice has overcome him.[48] After the death of its strongest defender, the town is taken, and after Beltramo shows her the cadaver of her husband, Galiziella abandons the defense of the castle. She curses her brother-in-law, reminding him that, as a traitor, he will not receive the consideration he expects from her former family.

The last part of the *Aspramonte* featuring Galiziella is marked by the author's proclaimed indecision between different versions of the story. Andrea da Barberino claims that he does not know for certain whether she was burnt with Beltramo, or whether she was replaced by another woman, and sent to prison in Africa. According to other authors, she gave birth to two children, a boy and a girl. If the destiny of this character is suspended in the *Aspramonte*, Boiardo and Ariosto reinterpret her as the absent mother figure of their poems: Galiziella is the mother of Ruggiero and Marfisa.[49]

This genealogical element connects Galiziella to Bradamante's story, but there is another similarity between the woman warrior in the *Aspramonte* and Ariosto's Bradamante. Like Bradamante in the *Furioso*, Galiziella in the *Aspramonte* has a prophetic vision.

Galiziella foresees Beltramo's betrayal in a dream vision, which she recounts to her husband Riccieri:

E disse: "Io ho sognato che mi pareva vedere uno fuoco aparire per l'aria, ed era portato da uno grande vento, e ardeva tutta la vostra signoria; e cominciava prima a Risa, e pareva che 'l suo principio nascesse del ventre della tua madre, e ardeva tutti voi. Iddio ci guardi da tradimento". Disse Riccieri: "Sempre queste femine vano drieto a' loro vanità e a' sogni! Ora mi lascia dormire." (*Aspramonte* XXXVI, 68)[50]

[And she said: "I dreamt that I saw a fire bursting through the air, and a strong wind was carrying the fire, and all your kingdom was burning, and it seemed that the origin of the fire was born out of your mother's womb, and the fire burnt all of you. May God protect us from betrayal." Riccieri said: "These women are always prey to their idleness and their dreams! Now let me sleep."]

It is because of the nightmare that Galiziella is awake, and is among the first to act when the town is invaded. Thus, in Galiziella's case, the prophecy triggers her warrior behavior. At the same time, it is the question of generation and genealogy (while pregnant, she dreams of a fire emanating from her mother-in-law's womb) that connects war, women, and alliances.

Galiziella herself, through her son Ruggiero, is a source of continuity in this genealogy of warrior women. Ruggiero's genealogy is, in fact, dominated by warrior women. His mother, his sister, and his bride are all warriors. His mother and bride, in particular, share the same destiny of pregnancy and widowhood.[51] The description of Bradamante's fate after Ruggiero's death (*OF* XLI, 61–66) echoes very closely Galiziella's tragic story, as Ruggiero tells it to Marfisa at the Fountain of Merlino (*OF* XXXVI, 70–74). Galiziella is linked to Bradiamonte and Bradamante by the element of the "marriage by trial." Her position within the narrative, however, is more complex than that of the heroine of the *cantare*. On one hand, the tension between war and alliance by marriage, complicated by the possibility of betrayal, is present in both texts. The condition of Galiziella as a pagan, on the other hand, is central to a more elaborate political dynamic. A double movement is performed in the text: of Beltramo from Christian to pagan (through treachery), and of Galiziella from pagan to Christian (through marriage). This element will prove central to my reading of the female warriors of the *Inamoramento de Carlo Magno*, raising a set of questions that are at the core of Bradamante's predecessors: why are women always moving from the "other" to Christian normalcy, while men are either stable or traitors? Why is alliance always performed through women, and never through men?[52]

Bradiamonte was a Christian who rejected the alliance with the Saracens; Galiziella is her pagan double, through whom the alliance is partially accomplished. The *cantare di Bradiamonte* marks a change in the Bradiamonte tradition. The lady's origins, in fact, were those of a pagan princess. This tradition, in which Bradamante was a pagan, emerges through the *cantari del*

Danese, where she was the daughter of the Soldano, sister of the knight Aquilante, lover of Ulivieri, and convert to Christianity.[53] In the fourteenth-century manuscript of *Li fatti di Spagna*, she is the wife of the pagan Marsilio, and a traitor.[54] In the manuscript Riccardiano 1904 (*Castello di Teris*), she is an illegitimate daughter of Amone.[55] The *Furioso* features a substantial change in textual politics: Bradamante is the Christian, Ruggiero the (soon to-be-converted) pagan. Alterity is displaced onto the figure of Ruggiero: the "mixed" religious origin is his. Boiardo selects a pagan man and a Christian woman as founders of the Este dynasty; Ariosto reinterprets this choice from the inside, revitalizing it through a web of classical and medieval models.

One of these models is the marriage politics displayed in the *Aspramonte*: Galiziella's superiority requires that she generate heirs with the strongest warrior she can find. The character is conveniently bipolar: she can be so strong as to discern who the strongest man is, and so beautiful as to arouse desire, jealousy, and rage. She poses no threat to the "real" man: she is just the instrument that reveals who the real men are. What is most interesting, on the other hand, is her status as go-between. At Agolante's court, she immediately adopts the role of the intermediary, interceding for the Spanish king Galafro; in crossing over to the Christian side, she loses all the rights she acquired as the daughter of a Saracen king. Her condition as a bastard and her hybrid status (being the daughter of an Amazon and of a Saracen) foreshadows her future as a converted Christian queen. She is marked as a go-between throughout her whole existence: her belonging to a group is always ambiguous, never complete.

The *Aspramonte* treats the figure of the warrior heroine ambiguously. We can look at the problem from different points of view. On the one hand, Andrea da Barberino exploits the topos, undermining its explosive potential: Galiziella is a narrative device allowing the continuation of the plot without challenging its premises. On the other hand, however, it is Galiziella's choice that elicits the betrayal and makes the war more bitter and cruel. The possibility of an alliance by marriage is rejected by the text, which does not even mention this alternative. Betrayal obviates alliance: Beltramo's action is too egregious to permit any other outcome. Much more than Bradiamonte, the female figure in the *Aspramonte* is polyvalent, and closer to Ariosto's Bradamante: she is, all at once, an object of desire, a test for manly valor, a converted pagan, a faithful wife and founder of a family, a daughter once loyal, a renegade, a go-between. The contradictions are not resolved, and serve as reminders of the multiple political functions of a female character.

The same complexities that mark Galiziella as a convert are featured in the *Danese*, where they are explicitly attributed to Braidamonte, the daughter of the sultan.[56] She begins as a negotiator, sent by her father on a mission to kill Astolfo and Riccardo, who are prisoners of a pagan king (*Danese, cantare* X, 11–15). Her passion for the twelve peers, and for Ulivieri in particular, whom she loves because of the painted image of him in her rooms, moves her to free them at first, and then to offer hospitality to the other peers upon their arrival (*cantare* XIV). In exchange for Ulivieri's love, she converts, and serves as a precious ally of the peers in war, while also facilitating the conversion of her brother Aquilante. But before this conversion, Aquilante and the king of Taccia see Braidamonte kissing Ulivieri, and they react in a way similar to the response of the the relatives of Galiziella:

Allora disse Guliasso ad Aquilante,
ch'era fratello di quella giovinetta:
"Vedi la sirocchia tua, putta gaudante,
ch'à baciato il Cristiano alla distretta?
Giuroti per Macone e Trevigante
ch'è degna che nel fuoco tu la metta!"
Diss'Aquilante: "I' giuro ad Appollino
che ardere la farò per tale latino!" (*Cantari del Danese*, XV, 28)[57]

[Then Guliasso told Aquilante, who was the young lady's brother: "Look at your sister, how she likes to have fun: she just kissed that Christian! I swear, by Mahomet and Termaga[u]nt,[58] she deserves to be burnt at the stake!" And

Aquilante: "I swear, by Apollo, that because of this I will have her burnt!"]

Like Galiziella, the Braidamonte of the *Danese* is a traitor. In this strand of the tradition, she is not a warrior; but clearly, by the end of the fifteenth century, at least two types by the name of Bradiamonte or Braidamonte circulated in *cantari* and *poemi*: the Christian female warrior and the pagan princess. Boiardo and, a few years after him, Ariosto had this rich and sometimes contradictory tradition at their disposal.

VARIATIONS ON A THEME: BOIARDO, CIECO DA FERRARA, AND MARCO POLO

The narrative structure that we have called marriage by duel is, then, a marker of the Christian female warrior Bradiamonte and of the pagan convert Galiziella. Boiardo's Bradamante does not inherit from her forebears the marriage by duel, which is, in the *Inamoramento de Orlando*, displaced onto another character, Leodilla, another adaptation of Ovid's Atalanta. Leodilla maintains all the traits of the classical myth, including the element that the competition between the woman and her suitor is not a battle but a race. In the *Inamoramento*, Leodilla implores her father to allow her to choose her husband through a competition:

Perché fingendo la facia vermiglia
A li occhi quanto io pòte vergognosi,
Con quel parlar che a pianto se assomiglia,
Nanti al mio patre in gienochion mi posi
E disse a lui: "Signor, se io son tua figlia,
Se sempre el tuo voler al mio proposi,
Commo fato ho di certo in abandono,
Non mi negar all'ultimo un sol dono.

Questo serà che non me dia marito
Che prima meco al corso non contenda;
E sia per legie fermo e stabelito
Che il vencitor per sua moglie mi prenda.

Ma fa' che 'l vinto sapia che il partito
Sia di lassar la vita per amenda,
E sia palese per tutte le bande:
Chi non è coridor non me domande!" (*Inamoramento de
Orlando* I, xxi, 55–56)

[Making my face look very red,/ Trying to make my eyes
seem modest,/ Speaking so that I seemed to weep,/ I kneeled
before my father, and/ I said, "If I'm your daughter, sire,/ If
I have always done your will,/ Which has, of course, preceded mine,/ Then don't deny me one last gift./ Accept no
man to be my husband/ Who has not run a race with me,/
And let it be confirmed by law/ That I will wed the one who
beats me;/ But let the vanquished know that he/ Must lose
his life as penalty,/ And let this be proclaimed and clear:/
One who won't race can't ask for me.][59]

Both Leodilla and Atalanta are characterized by the combination
of "prenda" and "contenda": the female passivity of being taken as
a bride ("prenda") is transformed into a competition ("contenda").

As critics have observed, Leodilla is one of the clearest examples of Boiardo's classicism.[60] Ariosto seems to recover Ovid
beyond Boiardo, in the passage already quoted, in which Bradamante poses her conditions:

Il don ch'io bramo da l'Altezza vostra,
è che non lasci mai marito darme
(disse la damigella) se non mostra
che più di me sia valoroso in arme.
Con qualunche mi vuol, prima o con giostra
o con la spada in mano ho da provarme.
Il primo che mi vinca, mi guadagni:
chi vinto sia, con altra s'accompagni. (*OF* XLIV, 70)

["Here is the (gift) I crave, your Majesty," requested the
damsel. "Permit no husband to be bestowed upon me until
he has demonstrated greater prowess at arms than I possess.
I must make trial of whoever would have me, either with
lance or sword: let the first man to defeat me win me; let the
defeated seek other brides."]

As is the case with Ovid, two icastic lines frame the possible out-comes of the contest, setting up a sharp dichotomy ("Il primo che mi vinca, mi guadagni:/chi vinto sia, con altra s'accompagni"). In this case, as in all the other examples, the act of being given is passive ("marito darme"), but the process recovers agency for the future bride ("arme," "provarme").

As in the anonymous *Historia di Bradiamonte*, however, the *Furioso* omits the element of the law, which was at the center of the episode for both Ovid ("Ea lex certaminis est") and Boiardo ("E sia per legie fermo e stabelito"). Whereas both Ovid and Boiardo mention the establishment of a law to protect the contract between the heroine and her suitor, Ariosto does not. In the *Furioso*, the contract between the heroine and the suitors is not guaranteed by an external law but only by the speech act of Bradamante, who promises publicly to accept only a husband who can defeat her.

The omission of the element of the law might appear as a mi-nor poetic difference, but it partakes of the coherent ideological world of the *Furioso*, where all laws whose establishment is nar-rated are characterized as inflexible and cruel, and situated on the axis of political failure. This is the case with the "aspra legge di Scozia" of canto IV and with the "femine omicide" of canto XX, as well as with three of the four great additions of 1532 (the episodes of Olimpia, Marganorre, and the Rocca di Tristano). It would have been impossible to connect Bradamante, the heroine of change and flexibility, with the idea of a *coutume*, an immobile feature that triggers stasis and, ultimately, evil. Consequently, Ariosto's strategy of incorporation of intertexts and previous ver-sions of his character into the poem clearly appears as predicated on his ability to change some of the characters' features on the basis of subtle variations. Ovid's Atalanta, Boiardo's Leodilla, and Ariosto's Bradamante share the same story, but the three au-thors do not share the same idea of law, and Ariosto achieves consistency for his heroine of change by eliminating the reference to the fixity of law.

Considering how careful Ariosto was in creating subtle varia-tions of the episode of the marriage by duel, we can logically in-

fer that the theme was present in the minds of his readers. The
presence of the marriage by duel as a parodical element in Francesco Cieco's *Mambriano* provides indirect proof of the popularity of the theme. In canto XV of the *Mambriano*, the old pagan
emperor Pinamonte finally meets Bradamante, whose legendary
beauty has already him filled with ardor from head to toe ("dal
capo alle piante").[61] Naturally, her beauty can only be more striking in person, and he falls prey to foolish love.[62] Whereas her
companions would prefer to punish him for his stupidity, Bradamante takes a sympathetic approach and proposes a solution
to her decrepit lover. She presents the solution, the marriage by
duel, as a trait typical of her character, and it is not difficult to
ascribe this element to chivalric intertextuality—that is, to the
traditional arsenal of traits of the literary paladins:

> Cominciò poi la dama e disse: Amico,
> Io ti amo se tu mi ami, ma non voglio
> Lasciar per questo il mio costume antico,
> Né abbandonar il consueto orgoglio:
> Sia chi si voglia, nota quel ch'io dico,
> Che per moglie mi chieda, sempre voglio
> Giostrar con lui, e se meco non dura,
> Io gli levo il cavallo e l'armatura. (*Mambriano* XV, 21)

> [She began: "My friend, I love you if you love me, but I do
> not want either to leave my custom because of this, or to
> abandon my used pride: whoever asks me in marriage, note
> what I say, I always want to joust with him, and if he does
> not last, I take his horse and his armor."]

Bradamante invokes custom and usage, and she explicitly refers to the wedding as the prize for winning the duel, in keeping
with the textual tradition of the *Historia di Bradiamonte* and the
Aspramonte texts.

Boiardo does not characterize Bradamante through the episode of the marriage by duel, contrary to most of the other authors who feature her in their texts. Whatever the reasons may be
for Boiardo's silence, Ariosto revises the character by reinscribing

this theme of the marriage by duel, thus reconnecting the *Furioso* to the *cantari*. Consequently, we can conclude that Ariosto had a choice in his representation of Bradamante between Boiardo and the *cantari*, and chose the latter. The marriage by duel explicitly connects the warrior woman to the theme of marriage. Ariosto, narrating the story of Bradamante as a woman warrior and as the founder of the Este dynasty, was pursuing a project that connected the theme of the marriage by duel to the prowess of the Este.

The warrior woman, in refusing to marry anyone inferior to her, separates the real heroes, who are worthy of her, from those who are not. At the same time, she is the hero's perfect match, destined to give birth to the perfect offspring. Ariosto can use the character to praise both the female and the male component of the Este dynasty. Marriage, in fact, does not violate the nature of the woman warrior, but rather inheres in her literary genetic code. Marriage, by itself, represents not so much the final domestication of the woman warrior as the institutionalization of her powerful nature.

Obviously, this can lead to both the fullfilment and the frustration of the expectation of marriage and alliance, and in the complex series of intertexts from Ovid to Ariosto, the authors who have engaged this tradition have exploited this expectation to dramatic effect. This has been true since Marco Polo's *Milione* or *Devisement du monde*, probably the first literary example of a marriage by duel in the history of medieval Italy.[63] Here the element of the woman warrior is fully informed by the exoticism of mysterious Asian lands, and the monstrosity and wild nature of the woman warrior are emphasized. The episode, however, still has all the features that will constitute the material of the later narrations, and so is worth reporting at length:

> Or sachiés tout voiramant que le roi Caidu avoit une file
> que estoit apellé Aigiaruc, en tartaresche, que vaut a dire
> en françois lucent lune. Ceste dameselle estoit si fort que
> en tout le roiame ne avoit damesaus, ne valet, que la peust
> veincre, mes voç di que elle les venchoit tuit. E son pere le

roi la voloit mariere e doner les baron, mes elle ne voloit; et
disoit que elle ne prenderoit jamés baron jusque a tant qu'ele
ne treuvast aucun gentilz honmes que la vinquist de toutes
forces. E le roi son pere li avoit fait berveleis qu'ele se peust
marier a sa volunté.[64]

[You should know that King Caidu had a daughter, whose
name was Aigiaruc, which means in French "bright moon."
This lady was so strong that no one could defeat her. Her
father the king wanted her to marry and give her a husband; but she did not want to, and said that she would never
marry unless she found a knight who would defeat her. And
the king had granted her the wish to marry according to her
wishes.]

As in the case of the episode we have already analysed, there is
a correspondence between the exceptional will of the *dameselle*
and her exceptional physical strength. The woman warrior is capable of resisting the authority of a father and a king, but this resistance could still function in the service of a better marriage. In
the *Devisement,* however, such expectations are frustrated.

The narrative presents the choice of her groom as a triumph
of the warrior woman's will: "E quant la fille au roi ot eu de son
pere l'otroie e le brevelejes qu'elle se poit marier a sa volunté, elle
en ot grant joie" [And when the king's daughter received from
her father the authorization and privilege that she could marry
according to her will, she was very happy]. Yet, the many victories she achieves seem to be instrumental only to the increase of
her immaterial and material dowry. As Marco Polo narrates, "Et
en ceste mainere en avoit gaagné la dameselle plus de XM che-
vauz, car elle ne pooit treuver nulz valet ne nulz damesiaus qu'elle
ne vinquist" (619), [In this way, she had gained more than ten
thousand horses, since she could not find a knight or lord whom
she would not defeat]. The almost thousand horses that she ac-
cumulates seem commensurate with her gigantic body ("E ce ne
estoit pas mervoie, car elle estoit si bien taillés de touts menbres,
et estoit si grant e si corsue que pou s'en falloit qu'elle n'estoit
geantesse") [And it was no marvel, since she was so well built,

and so big and strong that she could well be a giantess], which is a source of wealth rather than destruction. Thus, inevitably, a young prince arrives at the court after many have been defeated, and her father tries to convince her to let herself be defeated. This acquiescence would create the space for a wedding, an alliance, and the use of the accumulated dowry. The fact that she still refuses—and, like Bradiamonte, proves to be stronger even than her strongest opponent—frustrates the expectations of all witnesses and confirms her monstrous nature. By refusing the alliance that the marriage would have produced, she becomes a figure similar to the Amazon. The location of the adventure in a mysterious land makes the theme of the marvelous and the exotic more poetically interesting than the theme of the alliance.

It is not a coincidence that the first appearance of the marriage by duel in a postclassical text occurs in a travel narrative. As with the Amazons in Strabo's *Geographica*, the stratagem devised by Aigiaruc (Agiarne in the Tuscan version) is the perfect example of the collection of fears and desires surrounding the possibility of the alliance with another state. The fighting bride, who needs to be conquered, is at the same time obstacle and incentive to conquest. In symbolizing both the land to be conquered and, even more clearly, its potential for procreation and dynastic continuity, the woman warrior embodies the alliance and is, therefore, marked by all of its threats and allurements.

The *Devisement*, with its clear reference to the fact that the princess looked like a giantess, highlights the monstrous side of the female warrior from the very inception of this theme in medieval accounts. The genealogy of texts that provide the models for the *Furioso* include both this monstrous component and the more domesticated version of the classical tradition. Thus, in considering the figure of Bradamante both lines must be considered.

The comparison between Bradamante, Bradiamonte, and Galiziella is not new to the critical work on the *Furioso*, or to the studies of the warrior heroine in Italian literature, but it has been limited to the liberating component of the figure. Pamela Benson, in her study on *The Invention of the Renaissance Woman*, con-

siders both Bradiamonte and Galiziella as stereotypical, flat figures, whereas Bradamante, in her view, allows Ariosto "explicitly
[to] analyze the social and personal implications of her independence" (1992, 126).[65] Margaret Tomalin, instead, presents the
female warriors of the *cantari* tradition as "forceful and independent women" whose aspirations are "castrated" by marriages or
deaths, imposed upon them by male authors. According to Tomalin, Ariosto unearths and fulfills these heroines' attempts at
emancipation, "quietly introduc[ing] the startlingly new phenomenon of the independent woman, a comrade to man" (1992, 113).
Consequently, she sees the empowerment of women ignited by
the warriors of the *cantari* as realized in the *Orlando furioso*.[66]

The study of the woman warrior is especially challenging because it conflates the representation of many entities at the same
time. In particular, it engages constructs of masculinity and femininity, as well as their overlapping boundaries. When a character is fixed within a category, we expect that, through it, the author will speak explicitly of the category itself. This assumption
is especially powerful with respect to representations of medieval
and early modern women, since the categorization of women has
historically been much stronger than that of men. The subject is
further complicated by the primitive delineation, precisely in the
Renaissance, of literary characters that point to the individual
subjectivity of the modern novel.[67] The *Furioso* is at a crossroads
in the development of the modern literary character.[68] As Sergio
Zatti has argued, the poem is the site of an apparent paradox:
"il paradosso, che è solo apparente, di un discorso geniale sulla
psicologia umana perfettamente compatibile con l'assenza di una
psicologia dei personaggi" (123) [the only apparent paradox of
an insightful reflection on human psychology that is perfectly
compatible with the absence of a psychology of characters].[69]

In sum, the warrior woman as a literary figure, and Bradamante in particular, is caught between shifting constructions of
both gender and the literary character. Throughout the second
half of the fifteenth century, chivalric epic characters are in flux,
and they acquire their individuated personalities through collec-

tive representations. In other words, it is through different protagonists essentially cast in the same roles, with minimal but significant variations, that literary characters in the chivalric epic
evolve and gain psychological depth.

CONVERTING PRINCESSES AND SHRINKING
GIANTESSES: THE *INAMORAMENTO DE CARLO MAGNO*

Critics have traced precise distinctions between the refined characters of the learned tradition and the more popular female giants
and warriors of the *cantari* and *poemi cavallereschi*. Pio Rajna
was careful to point out that boundaries between these sets of female characters are well defined and impossible to breach: "We
shall not confuse female warriors and female giants, since the
latter belong to *a special race*, in some ways *halfway between
humans and beasts*."[70] Rajna is here reenacting the movement
of displacement that Ariosto realizes in the *Furioso*. By carefully
constructing Bradamante as a Christian female warrior, Ariosto
obscures at least in part the aspects of "otherness" that her predecessors displayed. A careful examination of the *Inamoramento
de Carlo Magno*, a crucial intertext, will demonstrate that this
type of text works as a "political unconscious" for the *Furioso*,
where the tensions between war and alliance, legitimation and
betrayal, are represented but not resolved.

Before Boiardo's *Inamoramento de Orlando*, the *Inamoramento de Carlo Magno* (Charlemagne in Love), probably published for the first time in Venice in 1481 and again ten years
later, had enormous influence over the chivalric poems written in
Italy.[71] The seventy-seven cantos of the *Inamoramento de Carlo*
tell a complex story of travel, war, and love, triggered by the desire of an elderly Charlemagne.[72] Charlemagne's senile love is the
origin of a series of adventures, the first of which is Rinaldo's
attempt at conquering the unnamed daughter of the pagan king
Trasumeri. Desire, in its multiple variations, is the driving force
of the narrative, which amounts to an endless series of adventures, wars, and battles between Christians and pagans, loosely

organized around the figure of Rinaldo. The focus on love and
the features of the characters make the *Inamoramento de Carlo*
an ideal precedent of the *Orlando furioso*.

In line with the Italian chivalric tradition, in the *Inamoramento de Carlo* Rinaldo is reinterpreted as not only a rebel but
also a womanizer. He is surrounded by the typical male figures of
the Carolingian tradition: Roland, Charlemagne, Gano the traitor. They are the most well-defined male characters throughout
the 5,942 octaves of the *cantare*. But the interest of the *Inamoramento de Carlo* for this study lies in its female figures, an endless
procession of queens and princesses, female warriors and giants,
who animate the narrative and play a variety of roles therein.

The poem presents a succession of three pagan princesses:
Belisandra, the damsel loved by Charlemagne; Dandolia; and
Calidonia. These three figures are carefully arranged in a sequence of repetition with variation: all three make men fall in
love with them instantly, and all three fall in love with Rinaldo.
Belisandra, the first to appear, is a bidimensional character with
little more than supreme beauty, and represents the "degree zero
princess."[73] The second, Dandolia, instead, is a slightly more developed character: her role as a helper of the Christians characterizes her as a traditional go-between in a long genealogy of
characters from Medea onward. The character of Calidonia, the
third princess, includes all of the aforementioned elements but is
elaborated even more fully. Her conversion makes her a mediator,
and allows her to traverse the distance between the pagan and
the Christian world. As is often the case with female figures who
abandon their original communities, her destiny is ultimately to
be killed as a traitor to the religion of her people. As in the case
of Galiziella in the *Aspramonte*, it is the brother who carries out
revenge, following the order of the father and the community.[74]

The figure of the woman as go-between has been explored in
depth in Latina feminist studies and Chicana theory. Literary
studies of such representations have focused on appropriations of
the figure of Malintzin, a historical and legendary princess who
played a central role as Hernán Cortés's advisor during the con-

quest of México, and was stigmatized as "la Vendida," or "la Chingada" (the sell-out, the fucked one).[75] The pagan princess in the *poema* carries out a similar function: she represents an object-subject who can be captured through love and still carry with her the living prize of her cultural difference. Only the ultimate suppression of her life allows the members of her original community to suppress the threat that her power of knowing posed.[76]

In the *Inamoramento de Carlo*, a parade of warrior heroines (Rovenza, Trafata, Fanarda, and Anfrosina) balances the presence and the role of the three princesses (Belisandra, Calidonia, and Dandolia). Every time the poem introduces a scene of love and conquest whose protagonist is one of the princesses, a war scene immediately follows, featuring one of the warrior women. The opposition between love and war is reflected directly in the opposition of these characters. As I have repeatedly shown in the course of this chapter, however, the theme of the marriage by duel serves as a check on the critical temptation to overemphasize such an opposition.[77]

Like Marco Polo's Aigiaruc, the warrior women in the *Inamoramento de Carlo*, with the exception of Bradimonte, the textual predecessor of Ariosto's Bradamante, are giants.[78] To the three princesses, positioned in the text in a sequence of increasing psychological depth and efficacy, corresponds a triad of giants, depicted in precisely the same sequence. As Belisandra was a "degree zero princess," so Rovenza is a "degree zero warrior." Thus the giantesses and the princesses could be described as partial refractions of the unitary character of the woman warrior in the episode of the marriage by duel. Even though it is not necessary to posit unity as the original and separation as the derivation, or vice versa, the theme of the marriage by duel is what allows some of these poems to constitute these characters singly, and others to keep them separate.

The first female giant to make an appearance is Rovenza (canto VIII), who induces wonder in the Christian army: who could have possibly given birth to her?[79] Her deeds are later described as exceptional, and her strength as superhuman. As in the case of Belisandra, Rovenza's role is exhausted by her marvelous appearance: exceptional size and pure monstrosity correspond to perfectly proportioned features and exceptional beauty. Her immediate defeat seals her role as a purely monstrous enemy.

The second position of the functional trajectory in the development of the warrior's character is taken by a mother-daughter duo, Trafata and Fanarda. These two giantesses and warriors terrorize the Christians from canto XIII to canto XXIII. But the two characters soon take different roads: the daughter, Fanarda, becomes a "helper" to the Christians: She converts and then marries a Christian.[80] From this moment on, her gigantic stature is not mentioned, making the reader suspect that as a result of the conversion she has shrunk in size. The conversion becomes the site of dynastic tension in the text, as it did with the princess Calidonia: "Trafata alhor parlò cotai sermoni:/ 'Figlia per madre più non mi domandi.'/ Disse: 'Tua figlia non son più niente/ se tu non te batizi primamente.'" [Trafata said: "Daughter, do not look for me as a mother." And she replied: "I am no longer daughter to you, unless you are baptized."] Thus, in the case of the second warrior giantess, the division happens within the character itself, in the figures of the mother and daughter, whose destinies diverge. As the princess Dandolia becomes a go-between, constantly caught in the mediation between the two worlds, Trafata and Fanarda together constitute a go-between because, as a couple, they become permanently split between the two worlds.

The third level in the progression is occupied by Anfrosina, whose conversion and wedding to a Christian are not only more fully elaborated from a literary point of view, but also politically important for the geography of Christianity taking shape in the text. Anfrosina's size, as in Fanarda's case, is forgotten after the wedding with Tirante. But as with the third princess, Dandolia, her role as a go-between who transgresses her original boundaries causes her death. Even when safely outside of the original community, both the woman warrior and the princess cannot escape the consequences of their betrayal, despite the fact that conversion and marriage have supposedly marked their acceptance in the new community. In this case, Gano, the figure of the traitor, is responsible for the death. When the court of Charlemagne is reunited in France, with Tirante and the pregnant Anfrosina as guests of honor, Gano poisons their wine, killing them and effacing their genealogy.

Throughout the text of the *Inamoramento de Carlo*, the female giants undergo a "civilizing process." They start out as grotesque and quasi-comical figures (Rovenza) and become objects of desire almost indistinguishable from the princesses (Fanarda, Anfrosina). The author of the *Inamoramento de Carlo* progressively erases the elements of distinction and monstrosity, to the point that any reference to their gigantic nature disappears from the text. The presence of characters with different degrees of complexity allows the reader to see the development of this civilizing process in a dynamic perspective that reveals the bifurcations of the process itself. The symmetry between princesses and giantesses also enforces the impression of the *Inamoramento de Carlo* as a cautionary tale that crosses the boundaries between nature and character.

In the Italian tradition, the grotesque features of the warrior woman are at first displaced onto the figure of the female giant, and then discarded altogether. Bradamante, in the *Orlando furioso*, is completely immune from monstrous elements; she is even domesticated as a Christian lady. The purification undergone by Bradamante's body displaces a few unsettling elements onto Ruggiero, who is a pagan. However, the cautionary tales that the female founder of the Este dynasty hears and sees throughout the poem call her back to her literary past: they are tales of violence, alliance, and marriage.

The *Inamoramento de Carlo* displays a predatory attitude: women are the connection to another world, the opportunity to conquer and expand. An emblematic moment in the text is that of the conversions, where the appropriation of the women by the world of Christianity is ritualized. The giants Fanarda and Anfrosina demonstrate that there is no difference, at least on the ideological level, between the female giants and the foreign princess. The femaleness of these figures makes them into a site for the negotiation of competing needs and desires. Battles with giants, weddings with princesses: in the *Inamoramento de Carlo*, these sorts of episodes involve both the representation of political alliance, regardless of the gender of those who contract it, and the recognition of women's crucial role within the alliance. Women ensure the stability of the alliance by introducing the reproductive element, by creating and preserving a stable genealogy.[81] The woman warrior allows the movement that transforms the political contract into a love story and war into erotic contestation, and obscures the reproductive role of women under the appearance of sameness.[82] In the person of the warrior woman, enemy becomes ally, and ally becomes bride. Women are the narrative device used to make the foreign, the other, and the different into the accessible and acceptable. They are the intermediaries that allow mixture and expansion, appropriation and conquest.

The "normalization" of the female warriors, who turn from giants into princesses, refutes Rajna's claim that the female giants are "another race." As this study of genealogy suggests, the female giant is traditionally the most grotesque version of the female warrior, not its inverse or opposition. The destabilizing aspect of the contact with the "other," mediated through the female character, was represented in the monstrosity of her appearance. But Rajna was also right, since when Ariosto constructs the character of Bradamante, he expunges the elements of "otherness" that her predecessors had embodied.[83]

The *Inamoramento de Carlo* makes clear what was already present in the *Bradiamonte* and the *Aspramonte*: the wedding is a central element in the encounter with a woman warrior or a foreign princess. In the *Furioso*, the wedding is displaced to the end of the poem: this displacement covers up its open-endedness and its disruptive potential. In favor of the stability of representation, this relocation obscures the fact that the focal point of representation is the alliance, which can become unstable, and turn into war all over again. The wedding is not, as critics have argued, the closure of an open-ended life for the woman protagonist. The "strategy of containment" is not the final marriage, but rather in the lady knight herself. Even though she has been "purged" of all elements of "otherness," her being remains the site of the foundation and of the alliance.

The study of these intertexts poses a problem of definition for the Ariostan character: namely, the position of Bradamante within the field of reference given by the traditional figures of women warriors and amazons. In the next chapter, I will try to answer precisely this question: is Bradamante an Amazon? And, perhaps more seriously: what is the reason for the success of Amazonian narratives in the culture of late medieval and early modern Italy?

CHAPTER TWO

An Amazonian Past

*Female Rule and the Threat
of Illegitimacy*

Bradamante, Marfisa, and the other female warriors that populate the Renaissance chivalric tradition, like Rovenza, Ancroia,
Trafata, and Fanarda, or Pulci's Antea, are all free agents, individual warriors that happen to be women. Like the warrior Camilla of Virgilian memory, they are members of an army, albeit
very visible ones. What is, then, the distinction between these
figures and their classical ancestors, the Amazons? Ariosto offers
a possible answer to this question with the tale of the "femine
omicide," the murderous women of cantos XIX and XX, introducing in his poem a state entirely composed of and ruled by female warriors. With this episode, a true Amazonian society enters the space of the poem and is the stage for the deeds of the
other woman warrior of the text, Marfisa. Marfisa's nature, in
turn, further puts into question the status of Bradamante as a
character.

Between the battlefield and the dynastic marriage, Bradamante
embodies the conflicting dynamics of the woman warrior, and
fulfills all the necessities of this role. What is her connection to
the structured violence of the Amazonian society? This chapter

surveys the descriptions of Amazonian societies in the Italian epic
tradition preceding Ariosto, interpreting them as necessary narrative and ideological preludes to the construction of the female
warrior in the *Furioso*. In the context of Ferrarese culture in the
age of Ercole d'Este, the revival of the Amazon imagery emerges
as the product of a society obsessed with fears of illegitimacy.
The figure of Marfisa, the most Amazonian of all the characters
in the poem, is the fulcrum of the distinction, or lack thereof, between the Amazon and the warrior woman.

The Amazonian episode starts in canto XIX of the *Orlando
furioso*, when Marfisa and her companions are forced to go
ashore in a bay shaped like a half-moon, whose dangerous nature
is immediately revealed. It is Alessandria, the land of the "femine
omicide," whose terrifying custom is the subject of canto XX.
The land of the "femine omicide" follows an ancient and cruel
custom, we are told, that represents a modified version of the
monosexual Amazonian society.[1] The men who arrive in their
land are either imprisoned or killed, and only the ones who can
kill ten men and sleep with ten women are integrated with honor
in this society. This, in a nutshell, is the custom of the "femine
omicide," recounted to Marfisa and her companions by Guidone
Selvaggio. Guidone, who is the winner up to that point, must
fight the newcomers in order to save his privilege and, more seriously, his life. He also explains the etiology of this custom, which
is divided into a number of phases. Not only does the foundation
of the society have a double history (first with the adventures of
Phalanthos and then with those of the Cretan women), but also
the custom itself undergoes changes and modifications throughout the years.

Ariosto plays on the traits of classical Amazonian societies by
inserting new elements: the basic Amazonian custom of excluding males from the state, for instance, acquires the added challenge in knightly and sexual prowess. Moreover, Ariosto achieves
a number of effects (some comical, others more serious) by placing Marfisa, the woman warrior par exellence of his poem,
within the specific context of a female-ruled society. The cen-

trality of Marfisa to this episode is part of a conscious narrative
strategy, as confirmed by the addition, in 1532, of the new, mirroring episode of the "Rocca di Tristano." At the Rocca, Bradamante is faced with a parallel gender dilemma to that of Marfisa
among the "femine omicide." Like Marfisa, who decides to enter
the Amazonian society as a man, Bradamante will choose to stay
at the Rocca on the basis of her knightly prowess and not of her
beauty. As she asserts in her debate with the lord of the castle,
two identities are possible:

> Io ch'a difender questa causa toglio,
> dico: o più bella o men ch'io sia di lei,
> non venni come donna qui, né voglio
> che sian di donna ora i progressi miei. (*OF* XXXII, 102, 1–4)

> [I, who am embracing her cause, affirm that, whether or not
> I am fairer than she, I did not gain admittance as a woman
> and I will not have my prospects determined as though I
> were one.]

Echoing Marfisa, well aware that she could succeed as a woman
in this newly found society,[2] Bradamante exploits the double nature of her persona, going beyond her future sister-in-law's inflexible binarism. Moreover, what in the case of Marfisa is evi-
dently perceived as a lack (she would not be able, "mal atta," to
take on the second part of the challenge, that is, to sleep with ten
women) in the case of Bradamante will become excess, overabundance of talents (she could stay at the Rocca both as the most
beautiful woman and as the most valiant knight).[3]

If these are all reasonable textual explanations for the episode,
Ariosto's background offers additional elements to explain the
presence of an Amazonian society in the poem. Ariosto is not
alone in representing Amazonian societies and the particular
brand of structured violence they display. At the beginning of the
sixteenth century in Italy, and particularly in the northern courts
such as Ferrara and Mantua, Amazons were a familiar presence.
Not only did they figure prominently in a variety of texts, from
epic chivalric poems to travel narratives, but also they were the

main protagonists of texts devoted entirely to them, like Andrea
Stagi's *Amazonida*. Whereas Boccaccio's *Teseida* stands as an
isolated instance in its time, the descriptions of female-only societies became a staple in the popular epic production during the
first years of its printed history, and an equally expected presence
in travel accounts of the period.[4]

From the pervasive presence in the literary milieu of these de-
cades, Amazonian societies seeped into the poetry of the *Furioso*.
If the character of the single woman warrior fulfills a clear representational need, namely, that of turning the adversary into a
bride and securing "her" reproductive potential in the most effi-
cient and comforting way, Amazonian societies respond to a different, if connected, logic. Women organized in a society of their own
clearly translate, in literary terms, the threat of female self-sufficiency, possibly a reason for anxiety in a society in which a small
minority of women was steadily acquiring more power.[5] But there
is more: a society entirely ruled by women represents on the page
the fear of complete female control over reproduction and lineage.

AMAZONIAN TIMES

Paintings realized between the fifteenth century and the beginning of the sixteenth century provide examples of the imagery
surrounding the Amazonian type. Amazons appear both in fifteenth-century fresco cycles, like that of the Castello della Manta
in Saluzzo and that on *Famous Men* by Andrea del Castagno,
and in early sixteenth-century depictions, like Vittore Carpaccio's *Theseus Receives the Queen of the Amazons*.

In the two cycles, Amazons are present as a counterpart of
male heroes. In the Saluzzo cycle, the anonymous artist portrayed, along with Godefroy de Bouillon and Charlemagne,
not only Hippolyta and Penthesilea, but also less well-known
figures, such as Sinope, Menalippe, Lampedo, and Tomyris.
All the Amazons, in fifteenth-century garb, couple the elements of military prowess (the swords and the gauntlets) with
feminine attire (see figure 1).[6] The same is true of the cycle

Figure 1.   Anonymous, *Braves and Heroines Series: Sinope and Hippolyta*. Fifteenth century, Castello della Manta (Saluzzo) Courtesy of Scala / Art Resource, N.Y.

painted by Andrea del Castagno, who portrays Queen Tomyris (figure 2).

In Carpaccio's painting (figure 3) Hippolyta, queen of the Amazons, is depicted as she approaches the court of Theseus, escorted by her army.[7] The subject of the depiction is the first book of Boccaccio's *Teseida*, an enormously influential source for representations of Amazons. The fascination with a female society seems here to be just another version of the fascination with the female

Figure 2.   Andrea del Castagno, *Queen Tomyris*
from the *Famous Men* cycle, fresco, ca. 1448. Original
detached, transferred to canvas, from the loggia of
the Villa Carducci, Legnaia, now at the Galleria degli
Uffizi, Florence. Courtesy of Scala / Art Resource, N.Y.

warrior. The fantasy of conquest, from the battlefield to the bed-
room with no change in partners, is apparently only multiplied. On
the other hand, the image of the Amazon as a strong and empowered woman took a symbolic role for some female humanists, as a
representation of their obligation to abandon feminine weakness.
The comparison of their chastity, morality, and strength with those
of the Amazons seems to be a commonplace rhetorical strategy,

Figure 3. Vittore Carpaccio, *Theseus Receives the Queen of the Amazons*, ca. 1502. Original (oil on panel, 102 X 145 cm.) at the Musée Jacquemart-André, Paris. Courtesy of Scala / Art Resource, N.Y.

used both by the female humanists themselves and by their male counterparts as a form of praise. The Amazons emerge in letters and pamphlets by women humanists, from Laura Cereta to Isotta Nogarola, providing a model of manlike valor.[8]

A related perspective on the Amazons is that of works that insert the theme within a *querelle des femmes* of sorts, from the point of view of the defense of women. This is the case, for instance, of the book published in Venice on January 18, 1503, by the otherwise unknown Andrea Stagi.[9] It is entitled *Amazonida*, and it is a poetic history of the classical Amazons in seven cantos.[10] The prologue by the author explains the reason for the book, which is to be found in the oblivion that has, so far, obscured the deeds of these female warriors:

> Et perche ve sia nota la cagione
> De li antiqui poeti e loro scusa

Perche hanno scripto de donne amazone
Si poca particella e si confusa
Chi feriti damore a lui loppone
Et chi de celebrar donne recusa
Et Saphos charia pinta ogni partita
Se scusa chel suo phaon lha impedita (*Amazonida*, c. 3v)

[And so that you may know why the ancient poets have
written so little and in such confused way about the Amazons, here are their excuses: some claim it is because they
were wounded by love; others because they did not want
to celebrate women; and Sappho, who would have painted
every achievement, puts forth the excuse that her Phaon has
prevented her from doing it.]

Stagi uses the topos of the silence that has doomed women's
deeds because of the envy of the male poets (with the twist of
Sappho's culpable complicity), a topos that Ariosto himself will
adopt in canto XXXVII, 23–24.[11] Time has obscured its fame,
but in its day the *Amazonida* was a popular text. What is even
more relevant is that a copy of this book is found in the inventory of the Ferrarese bookshop of Domenico Sivieri.[12] The *Amazonida* attests to an interest in Amazons, in Ferrara, in Ariosto's
days.

Further exploration of the inventory of the Sivieri bookstore and
in the libraries of the time reveals that the interest in Amazons that
prompted Stagi to devote his work to them is in tune with a real passion for the deeds of warrior women of sorts, the legions of cruel
warriors, half giantesses, half women, like Rovenza and Ancroia.
The *Dama Rovenza* is one of the books a young Isabella d'Este asks
her bookfinder in Venice, Giorgio Brognolo, to acquire for her.[13]
The *Ancroia* is present in the inventory, along with the *Aspromonte*,
which narrated the deeds of Galiziella.[14] One of the most important
chivalric poems of the fifteenth century, the *Libro della regina Ancroia*, marks an explicit connection between the chivalric world and
the Amazonian theme.[15] The rather long and discursive *explicit* of
the book (in the 1479 edition) underlines its connections with the
Amazonian tradition, boasting it as a selling point:

Il libro di lanchroia qui finisse impresso ne la magnifica
cita de vinesia ne glanni dil signore 1479/ ali giorni .28.
di setembre per magistro philipo de piero miser johanne
mozenico felicissimo du ce im/perante et non vi para lectore
maraviglia di combatere terribile di questa donna. Anchora
in/ molte altre istorie si legge le donne havere combatuto
come panchasilea:orthia:lampedo;con//tra de le quale fu
mandato Hercule tanto era il furore loro da la gente temuto.
Simile camilla la/ quale il poeta domanda honore de italia.
Non dubitate di acomprare questo libro peche eglie/ cor-
recto con ogni bona et perfecta diligentia et de le lhistoria di
carlo magno cum glialtri suoi/ paladini contiene li qual fu-
rono ne gli anni del signor octocento et quindese et mori in
aquis./ grani havendo liberato italia dal furore de longobardi
si che sotto varie fictione qui parte de li/ soi gesti egregia-
mente si veghano.

[Here ends the book of Ancroia, printed in the magnificent
city of Venice in the year 1479, on the 28th of September by
master Philippus Petri, while Lord Giovanni Mocenigo was
doge. Do not wonder, reader, at the terrible fighting of this
woman, for you can read in many other stories that women
were warriors, such as Penthesilea, Orthia, and Lampedo;
Hercules was sent among them, so great was the fear they
induced in the people. Another example is Camilla, honor
of Italy according to the Poet. Do not hesitate to buy this
book, since it is corrected with every diligence, and it tells
the stories of Charlemagne and his peers in the year 815.
Charlemagne, who died in Aquisgrane, freed Italy from the
fury of the Longobards, and therefore here we see beneath
different fictions a part of his great deeds.]

The advertising strategy of the press clearly plays on the connection between the formidable queen Ancroia and the Amazons of
the past, bridging the gap between classical myth and popular
romance fiction.

In the epic-chivalric tradition of the fifteenth century, both in
prose and in verse, the staging of some of the action in the legendary kingdom of the Amazons becomes a commonplace. Such is

the case for the *Morgante*, in which Rinaldo and his companions
find themselves in the land of Saliscaglia, inhabited by ugly and
hairy women who fight and wear armor like the legendary crea-
tures of the classical myth.[16] Similarly, the long prose text *Fortunato*, devoted to the adventures of the eponymous hero, includes
an episode set in the reign of the Amazons:

> arrivarono nel regno dell'amanzone dove regniavano le
> donne, le quali erano valentissime in battaglia et era in quel
> tempo una Reina regniante chiamata Spinalia la quale era
> in sull'età d'anni XVIII e molto era bellissima e era regina
> e valentissima in arme quanto femina o homo che arme
> portasse e faceva guardare li passi fuori dalla terra suoi; né
> alcuno vi potea passare per quello regno che allei non si ap-
> presentasse e il più delle volte rubava e amazzava i viandanti
> purche avesseno avuto robba alcuna che li fusse piaciuta.
> (fol. 240r)[17]

[They reached the Kingdom of the Amazons, ruled by
women, who were very valiant in battle. At that time, the
queen was Spinalia, who was eighteen years old, very beautiful, and extremely valiant in war, as much as a woman or
a man in arms. She had her borders securely watched, and
no one could go through her kingdom without being taken
to her. Most of the times she robbed and killed those who
passed by, if they had anything she liked.]

This kingdom possesses two elements of the classical Amazonian
tale: the young and beautiful queen and the violent defense of the
borders from intruders. When Fortunato is faced with Spinalia's
army, his reaction is derision:

> con parole comincio a svillaneggiarle dicendo che fareb-
> beno il meglio dandare affilare e andare affare laltre cose
> femminili e non volere cosi vituperare e lonorate armi e
> molte altre villanie loro fortunato disse alle ditte damigielle.
> (fol. 240v)

[Fortunato started to make fun of them, saying that they
should go to spin and do other feminine activities, and they

should stop spoiling the reputation of the honored arms, and he said many other rude things to the ladies.]

Not just poets and *canterini* but also the travelers who wrote of the new worlds' discoveries had a soft spot for Amazons. The archetype of these encounters, as in the case of the woman warrior explored in the previous chapter, is Marco Polo, who, in his *Milione*, writes of the two monosexual islands of Malle e Femele:

L'isola che si chiama Malle è nell'alto mare bene .v^e. miglia verso mezzodie, partendosi da Chesmancora. Questi sono cristiani battezzati e tengon[o] legge del Vecchio Testamento, che mai non tocherebbero femina pregna e, poscia ch'à partori[t]o, a .xl. dì. E dicovi che in questa isola no stae veruna femina, ma istanno in un'altra isola che si chiama Femele, che v'è di lungi .xxx. miglia. E li uomini vanno a questa isola ove stanno queste femine, e istanno co loro .iij. mesi dell'anno, e in capo di .iij. mesi tornano a l'isola loro, e quivi si fanno loro uttulità .viij. mesi.

In questa isola nasce l'ambra molta fina e bella. Questi vivono di riso e di carne e di latte. E' sono buoni pescatori, e seccano molti pesci, sicché tutto l'anno n'ànno assai. Qui non à signore, salvo ch'ànno uno vescovo ch'è sotto l'arcivescovo di Scara. E perciò no stanno tutto l'anno colle loro donne, perché non avrebbero da vivere. Li loro figliuoli istanno co le madri .xiiij. anni, e poscia il maschio si ne va co[l] padr'e la femina sta colla madre. (*Milione* 184, p. 266)

[The island called Malle is in the high sea, five miles to the south of Chesmancora. These people are Christians, they are baptized and they follow the law of the Old Testament, so that they would never touch a woman who is pregnant and for forty days after she has given birth. And I tell you that on this island there are no women, since they live on another island, called Femele, thirty miles away. And the men go to this island where the women are, and spend there three months every year, and at the end of the three months they return home to their island, and they go about their business for eight months.

In this island one finds beautiful amber. They sustain
themselves with rice, meat and milk. They are good fish-
ermen, and they dry out the fish, so that they can enjoy it
all year long. There is no lord here, except for the bishop,
who is under the archbishop of Scara. And because of that
they do not spend all the year with their women, since they
would have no sustenance. Their children spend fourteen
years with their mothers, and then the boys go with their fathers and the girls stay with their mothers.]

The passage lists a number of reasons for these divided societies, reasons that appear to be contradicting each other. At first, it
seems that the cause of the segregation is religious (it is the Old
Testament law that prevents them from spending the year with
the women, since they are supposedly pregnant during the re-
maining months). Then, the explanation becomes practical and
tied to survival (they would have no food if they did not spend
part of the year fishing and drying the fish). The two explanations are conflicting, and they are linked by the remark on the
bishop's rule, which seems to connect the custom, once again, to
a religious aspect of life. Nonetheless, there seems to be a need for
various explanations, and the weakest is the practical one (there
would be no reason why the women cannot spend the rest of the
year with the men as they fish). Ultimately, the passage in the *Milione* calls attention to the issue of pregnancy and reproduction,
which is crucial to the Amazonian society. On the one hand, we
have two societies, segregated along gender lines; on the other
hand, there must be a moment of exception to the rule that allows
reproduction and perpetuation of both societies.

The archetypal narration of the Amazonian societies encoun-
tered by the explorer repeats itself over and over again in the
travel accounts of the fifteenth and sixteenth centuries, where it
is part of the topsy-turvy world of the Other, where order is in-
verted and women perform the deeds normally reserved to men.
From Leo Africanus's *Descrittione dell'Africa*, where there is a
city (Tesset) where women teach and learn (Ramusio I [1978],
349), to the "Book of Odoardo Barbosa," where women are seen

in an army (Ramusio II [1979], 547), to the "Travels to Ethiopia" of Francisco Álvares, in which queens take center stage (Ramusio II [1979], 316), the encounter with a female population of unprecedented strength and courage is an integral part of the process of discovery and conquest.[18]

In this cultural atmosphere, Boccaccio's *Teseida* played an important role as a model for Amazonian stories. In particular the first book, with the wedding of Hyppolita and Theseus, provided a standard reference for the construction of Amazonian figures in the Italian Renaissance.[19] In Ferrara, the Commentary to the *Teseida* authored by Pier Andrea de' Bassi was dedicated to Niccolò III, and it opens with a genealogy culminating with the Este ruler, an element that further demonstrates the strong connections between Amazonian themes and genealogical concerns.[20]

In the genealogy of the main characters of the *Orlando furioso*, the Amazonian past is strongly present. In particular, Ruggiero and Marfisa are of Amazonian descent, since their mother Galiziella is portrayed as an Amazon in the tradition. The same is true, even though in a different genealogical sphere—purely literary—for Bradamante, who, as we have seen, is modeled for some traits on Galaciella, the protagonist of the Aspromonte texts analyzed in the previous chapter. Galiziella's Amazonian status is clear in the Laurentian manuscript that preserves the prose account conventionally titled *Aquilante e Formosa*:[21]

> ein questa andata deste Agholante arrivo cholui una sua
> figluola detta ghaliziella danni sedici chera molto bella e
> avea inmodo imparato affare fatti darme chela sera allenata
> cholle donne damazone neregno feminoro e nel suo tempo
> non trovo chavaliere che labatesse da chavallo senno ricieri i
> quale innunabattaglia labatte e lei sarende a lui e batezossi e
> fu suo donna e ingravido di ricieri i duo figluoli. (fol. 2v)[22]

> [In this expedition, Agolante brought along his daughter,
> called Galiziella, who was sixteen years old and was very
> beautiful, and she had learned to fight since she had trained
> with the Amazons in the kingdom of Feminoro; and in her
> time, she did not find a knight who unhorsed her except for

Ricieri, who defeated her in a duel. She surrendered to him, she baptized, became his wife and bore him two children.]

In this succinct account, all the traits of Galiziella's life are highlighted. In both the *Cantari d'Aspramonte* and in Andrea da Barberino's *Aspromonte*, Galaciella is a bastard daughter of Agolante, and she comes from the kingdom of Feminoro, realm of the Amazons.[23] Not only is the presence of Amazonian societies pervasive, but also the theme of bastardy seems inextricably linked with the figure of the Amazon. In the epic-chivalric tradition, the rule of the Amazons is clearly connected with fears of loss of control over reproduction and threats of illegitimacy.

These same perceived threats and the anxiety they induce seem to be the reason behind the popularity of Amazons in the unexpected context of weddings. Wedding chests, the Renaissance artifacts that accompanied new couples of a certain social standing in the beginning of their married lives, have a number of set themes, including violent ones. It is not uncommon for the wedding chest, or *cassone*, to display conflictual moments of male/female relations, to the point of extreme violence: the classical Rape of the Sabines, and the Boccaccian stories of Griselda and Nastagio degli Onesti are examples of this tendency. Experts generally explain the violent subjects as cautionary tales for the new brides.[24] The common presence of Amazons in these artifacts, however, seems to complicate this explanation, and has warranted further elaborations. Cristelle Baskins, in particular, has suggested that the Amazonian imagery "provided models for filial transitions from natal to conjugal families, whether voluntary or coerced."[25] Indeed, Amazons did not just provide a cautionary tale but also fostered a reflection on the passage of the woman from one lineage to the other. The pervasive presence of Amazons in the decorations of wedding chests is further evidence of the connection between the Amazonian theme and the anxiety over generation and succession in the late medieval and early modern period.

WAYWARD MEN AND FEARSOME WOMEN:
THE FOUNDATION OF ALESSANDRIA
IN THE *ORLANDO FURIOSO*

The foundation of Alessandria in the *Furioso* explicitly connects
the theme of female rule with an uncontrollable anxiety over legitimacy, embodied by the errant youths that frame the narrative of Amazonian foundation. The identity of the narrator of the
birth of this state is a premonition of the theme to come. He is, in
fact, none other than Guidone Selvaggio, who, in the popular chivalric tradition preceding Boiardo and Ariosto, is the illegitimate
son of Rinaldo. Amone's most famous son is, in fact, the protagonist of a number of poems that feature his wanderings and his
adventures far from Charlemagne's court, where he seduced princesses and ladies and generated a few bastard sons.[26] Guidone's
feats are the subject of a poem we have already had occasion
to mention, the *Ancroia*, devoted to the deeds of the formidable
eponymous queen. In the first canto of the poem Rinaldo, out of
the usual hostility against Charlemagne, travels to the Holy Land.
There he falls in love with Solizano's wife, Costanza, and, as he
leaves, he asks the lady to send him his daughter or son, once he
or she grows up. After the death of Solizano, a son is born, Guidone, who will reach puberty, discover the truth, and embark on
a trip to find his father, with the veiled aim of converting him to
Islam.[27] During the same years of publication and early fame of
the *Furioso*, other poems feature the adventures of Guidone, this
time giving the character the honor of the title: in 1523, in Padua,
Giovanni Antonio Remondini publishes Giovan Battista Dra-
goncino's poem *Innamoramento di Guidon Selvaggio*, and only
a few years later, in 1535, Antonio Legname's *Guidon Selvaggio*
sees the light.[28] In all these texts, both preceding and contemporary to the *Furioso*, Guidone is an illegitimate son who travels to
the West in search of his father, not only eager for recognition but
also bearing the knowledge of an alternate lineage.

In the *Furioso*, the obsessive attention to blood and lineage
is the first element of Guidone's self-presentation. As he intro-

duces himself to Marfisa and her companions, he withdraws his name for almost three octaves,[29] and draws attention instead to his important lineage; "Io credo che ciascun di vui/ abbia de la mia stirpe il nome in pronto" [I think that my lineage will be well known to each one of you.] (*OF* XX, 5, 3–4).[30] Guidone uses the language of generation to proclaim his noble birth, arguing that his mother "made him" out of the "noble blood" of the House of Chiaramonte:

> Di questo sangue, dove ne l'Eusino
> l'Istro ne vien con otto corna o diece,
> al duca Amone, il qual già peregrino
> vi capitò, la madre mia mi fece. (*OF* XX 6, 3–6)

> [From this blood my mother made me, where the Danube flows by eight or ten channels into the Black Sea, for my father, Duke Amon, who had wandered there during his travels.][31]

In an imitative game that combines the classical myth and the more recent popular chivalric tradition, the beginning of the story Guidone tells to Marfisa and her companions on the foundation of Alessandria echoes his own. Illegitimate youths are the first root of the social and dynastic disorder that will bring about the foundation of the Amazonian state. Once the duel between Marfisa and Guidone has come to a standstill, Marfisa asks the reason for the scarcity of men in the land, and Guidone proceeds to explain the reason ("la cagione") of the peculiar situation of Alessandria. The story he tells is a carefully woven foundational account that combines classical sources and medieval rewritings, in particular Boccaccio's *De claris mulieribus*.

The foundational tale has four steps: the Greeks marginalize the bastard sons they find upon their return after the Trojan War; the wayward youths, guided by Phalanthos, pillage and rob the coasts until they arrive in Crete, where they are hired as military; after the war, they decide to leave and are followed by the Cretan women, whom they abandon on the shores of the future Alessandria; the abandoned women, following Oronthea's lead, decide to stay and create a female society that takes its vengeance on any men who comes near the shore.

Critics have interpreted this narrative as an original combination of episodes from Apollonius Rhodius's *Argonautica* and Strabo's *Geographica*. In the *Argonautica*, the Lemnian women, betrayed by their husbands, murder them.[32] The Latin rewriting by Valerius Flaccus slightly modifies the story, blaming Fame for having made the women jealous.[33] Apollonius Rhodius's text circulated widely in Italy in the late fifteenth century, albeit probably only in Greek. Yet its diffusion is attested by the presence of an *incunabulum* printed in Florence by the Venetian Laurentius de Alopa (1496), and it is not surprising to find precisely this text in the Ferrarese library of Domenico Sivieri.[34] Ariosto refers directly to the episode of the women from Lemnos in canto XXX-VII, while describing Ruggiero's fears as he enters the kingdom of evil Marganorre.[35] Strabo's account includes the generation of the bastard sons of the Lacedemons during the Trojan War, called the Parthenie, and the name of their leader, Phalanthos. It also accounts for an attempted revolt of the Parthenie, and for the decision to send them off to colonize a new territory (hence the foundation of Tarentum). The text also establishes a connection with the Cretans, who would be the population already settled in Sicily, welcoming the newcomers.

Boccaccio's *De claris mulieribus* provides a much stronger model for the episode, one that already combines some of the elements of the different classical sources. It tells a slightly different story: the wayward youths are the Minyans (Menie), "fine young men of no little nobility [who] figured among the companions of Jason and the Argonauts."[36] After the end of the expedition, they settled in Sparta, where they were welcomed and integrated, achieving visibility and marrying the finest Spartan women. Their greed for power induced them to stage a coup, after which they were imprisoned and sentenced to death. At this point, the tale of missed integration of a group of wayward youths acquired the element of the loyal wives that will be adopted by Ariosto. The wives of the Minyans substitute them-

selves to their husbands with a stratagem and save them from
death.

Three basic plots are conflated in Ariosto's story: the tale of the
wayward youths who threaten a state and are sent away to found
a new one (Phalanthos, who founds Tarentum with his group,
according to Strabo's *Geographica*); Boccaccio's tale of the Min-
yan women, who show loyalty to their husbands while rebelling
against their fathers, translated by Ariosto into the decision of the
Cretan women to leave with the youths; and finally, the tale of
the women from Lemnos, who, in the *Argonautica* tradition also
present in Boccaccio,[37] kill all their men except for one and found
a female-only society. An added element is that of the seduction
and abandonment of a group of women, which may or may not
be attached to either of the two plots (both Phalanthos and the
Lemnos husbands can be depicted as traitors). What these three
narratives have in common is the foundation of a new state.

The pre-text of Alessandria's foundation provides a new element as the root of the Amazonian society: the threat of a herd
of illegitimate offspring. The two elements (wayward men and
Amazonian society) could be connected because of their proximity in the narrations of Boccaccio's *De claris mulieribus*. The
deeds of queen Penthesilea, the founder of the Amazonian state,
are preceded by the tale of the anonymous wives of the Minyans,
which is clearly a precedent for the narration of Phalanthos's adventures. Moreover, the two elements are already connected in
one of the Amazonian narratives of the *De claris mulieribus*,
none other than the sections on Marpesia and Lampedo, the two
Amazonian queens who are the subject of chapters XI and XII.

Ariosto seems to be using the model of the *De claris mulieribus* in a pervasive way: on the one hand, he reetymologizes
Marfisa as a descendant of Marpesia, making her the protagonist of the Amazonian episode told by Boccaccio in the chapter
devoted to her; he takes the connection between the wayward
men and the Amazonian society present in the Marpesia chapter and revitalizes them through the narrative of the wives of the
Minyans. The intertext seems to be globally present in the text,

and the sequences derived from it are linked. In other words, the model is so powerfully present in the destination text (and to the author's mind), that it "sticks" to it, leaving textual particles, as it were, that echo each other throughout.[38]

The genesis of this etiological narrative is fairly clear, thanks to the discovery of Boccaccio's *De claris mulieribus* as a comprehensive model for the episode. What remains to be explained is the relevance of such a complex story for Ariosto's poem and its intended audience. This causal nexus between the wayward bastards and the Amazonian foundation creates in the canto a particular sense of circularity and forced repetition. In this obsessive repetition of exclusions and failed integrations, the focus of the canto seems to be on the issue of the control of legitimacy.

The Amazonian state of Alessandria presents both the threat (total loss of control of the males over their offspring and generative power) and the solution (violent control over generative power).[39] This double movement of fear and desire seems particularly relevant to the self-representation and propaganda of a ruling dynasty, which bases on legitimacy the right to succession. The Este, in particular, had a vexed relationship with legitimacy. Since the twelfth century, as we have seen, they had acquired and maintained power despite a tainted fame of bastardy. The ruler who had played the most important role in the steady acquisition of power on the family's part, Niccolò III, is the emblematic example of this dynastic negligence. Not one, but two of his many bastard children succeeded their natural father into power. Leonello and Borso, both children of Stella de' Tolomei, ruled over Ferrara and Modena from 1441 to 1471, despite their less than proper place in the family line. This imperfect status is one of the causes for concern and outright anxiety over purity of blood and family trees the writers and historiographers of the family display in their texts.[40]

Ariosto writes in a time of restored legitimacy, under the rules of Ercole (the legitimate son of Niccolò III, duke from 1471 to 1505) and Alfonso (r. 1505–1534). These times were marked by a heightened sense of dynastic propriety achieved through the control of the paternal bloodline.[41] The myth of Phaeton itself, so central to the courtly culture of Ferrara, may be the emblem of a perceived anxiety over legitimate succession and paternity.[42] Many texts of the time, including the *Furioso*, may provide insight into this deep-seated social fear. It is the case, however, that the clearest forms of this representation are not to be found in the openly dynastic accounts, but rather in the veiled ones.[43] The *Furioso*'s Amazonian state is such an episode, with its repeated preoccupation with generative powers and the necessity of controlling them.

EXCEPTIONS TO THE STATE: AMAZONS AND THE LAW

We have just seen how Ariosto constructs the foundation of the Amazonian state of the "femine omicide," using strands from different traditions. The successive moments that make up the foundation of this state, both from the intertextual and from the narrative point of view, mark the developments of this society, which, one may argue, exists in a permanent state of exception to the law.[44]

Most important, a monosexual state is by itself an exception, since every state is based on and aimed at its own perpetuation. Because of this, the first step in all narratives about Amazonian societies, like the ones we have seen in the *Milione* and in the *Fortunato*, is to make an exception to the rule of the absence of men in order to permit reproduction. This is also the case in Stagi's *Amazonida*:

> E perché nostro numero non pera
> Al procreare è forza dare effetto.
> Fingem la pace e mostram lieta ciera
> Tenendo l'arme in mano e più nel petto,
> Andaremo in lor terra e lor riviera,
> Che'l seme acquistarem per lor dispetto,
> E ritornate a casa cresceremo
> Il nostro regno e così il manterremo. (*Amazonida*, c. 5v)

> [It is necessary to procreate in order for our people to survive. Let us pretend we come in peace, with pleasant faces,

holding our weapons in our hands, but more in our hearts, and let us go to their lands and arbors, and to their detriment (or: despite them) we shall gain the seed, and once we return home we shall make our kingdom grow and thrive].

Alessandria is no exception: after a few years of solitude, the women see that they would cause their own demise ("il proprio danno," *OF* XX 29, 3). They therefore decide to select ten of the knights that happen to land on their territory over the course of four years, the bravest and most valiant, and keep them as collective husbands.[45]

This modification to the law is necessary to survival, but the women think of it as a singular occurrence. That is, it is not meant to become repeatable. It has, however, consequences, in the form of sons who are born, and who threaten, with their number, the superiority of the women. Another practice is then introduced to save the law that constitutes the foundation of the monosexual society. The women decide to keep only one son and kill or send away all others. The foreigners who arrive are sentenced to death, and the only innovation in this sense is that there is no more than one killing each day (*OF* XX 33–35). Once again, wayward men are a group to be managed and controlled, as in the beginning of the story.

The monosexual law of the "femine omicide," then, needs a first adjustment, or exception, and then a second adjustment, or recodification of the law itself. Men are allowed back in and then their presence is limited. Once they are back in, though, the space opens up for a new exception, represented by the story of Alessandra and Elbanio. Orontea's daughter, Alessandra, falls in love with the brave and handsome Elbanio and, upon his request, asks her mother to modify the law, allowing the newly arrived a chance to survival by defeating ten men. As in the case of the first modification to the law, the council debates this proposal. The strongest opposition comes from Artemia, one of the original settlers. In her speech, she uncovers the two opposed forces of the Amazonian logic, self-sufficiency and paragon of strength. Her

argument is simple: originally, the founders of Alessandria did
not decide to integrate men for protection, but for the only purpose of generation.[46] To attract a very strong man, one who can
beat ten others, would defeat the whole purpose of getting rid of
them, by undermining the proposed self-sufficiency.[47] This argument represents very well the double nature of the Amazon. On
the one hand, the Amazon represents the threat of female rule
and self-sufficiency; on the other, as we have seen in chapter 1,
she becomes the object of a fantasy of generative superiority: the
man who can subjugate the Amazon and make her his bride is
clearly superior to the other men. These two elements are conflicting, and in the debate over the future of Alessandria, the latter wins. The exception to the law results, once again, in a new
law.

The nature of the Amazon as an instrument to find the best
possible man is uncovered in Orontea's words:

> La regina Orontea fece raccorre
> il suo consiglio, e disse: "A noi conviene
> sempre il miglior che ritroviamo, porre
> a guardar nostri porti e nostre arene;
> e per saper chi ben lasciar, chi torre,
> prova è sempre da far, quando gli avviene;
> per non patir con nostro danno a torto,
> che regni il vile, e chi ha valor sia morto." (*OF* XX, 47)

> [Queen Orontea summoned her council and told them:
> "Our constant need is to discover the best men available
> to guard our harbors and beaches. Now to know whom to
> spare, whom to do away with, it is necessary to make trial
> of them as the occasion arises, so that we should not to our
> detriment suffer the cowards to rule while the valiant are
> put to death."]

The Amazon is the tool the community can use in order to better
itself, and in this case, the Amazon and the community constitute
the same entity. Stagi's *Amazonida* had already presented this
clear investment of the community in its own generative power,

connecting the lack of control over generation with the threat of
bastardy. When queen Pantesilea establishes the rules of her kingdom in the beginning of canto I, she expresses the need to select
partners in what we could call a eugenetics project:

> Ma fà bisogno usare arte maggiore,
> Prendere il seme di uomin virtuosi
> Nell'arme esperti con gloria e onore
> di ingegni acuti pronti e animosi;
> E nulla fie se impacci con vil cuore,
> Ma prima resti usar gli atti amorosi
> Che voglia imbastardire il nostro regno,
> Ma di potente seme farlo degno. (*Amazonida*, c. 5v)

> [It is necessary to use greater skill, and obtain the seed of
> virtuous men, able warriors who have honor and glory,
> brave and valiant, and of sharp intellects; and there should
> be no one who involves herself with a vile heart, but we
> should rather refrain from the love act than bastardizing our
> kingdom, and try to make it worthy of powerful seed].

The octaves of Stagi's *Amazonida*, which Ariosto may or may
have not had in mind, prepare the selective law of Orontea and
her people. Like the story of Phalanthos and the wayward youths,
so the law of the Amazons of Alessandria is a narrative of controlled exclusion and admission. The state, in order to survive,
needs new energies (in both cases male energies aimed at reproduction), but these new energies must be controlled. This is indeed a political narrative on the foundation and maintenance of
a state, but its focus is on reproduction. It is not a coincidence
that the root of this monstrous state, its first beginning, resides in
the group of bastard men who wander across the Mediterranean.
It is their disruptive presence, the first cause of the imbalance
of sexes, that generates the conditions for the monosexual state
and its extreme, albeit regulated, violence. It is rather predictable, then, that the obsessive focus of the new state be, literally,
on birth control. This anxiety over lineage control affects Bradamante as a character, since her destiny, foretold in the *Furioso*, is

that of founding the Este dynasty by herself, pregnant widow of Ruggiero.

MARFISA'S RULE AND BRADAMANTE'S EXCEPTION: AMAZONS AND FEMALE WARRIORS BETWEEN BOIARDO AND ARIOSTO

Bradamante's Amazonian past, in the form of her literary genesis (her filiation from the Galiziella type), puts into question her present in the text of the *Furioso*. In Ariosto's poem, a frontier territory between the modern subjective character and the typified, functional character, the term *Amazon* has been hinted at, played with, alluded to in the case of Bradamante. Yet it has always been rejected: what do Bradiamonte, Galiziella, and Bradamante have in common with the Amazon? Galiziella is the product of the union between an Amazon and a king: her bastardy, her supernatural prowess in battle, mark the otherness of her femininity.[48] The Amazon is a figure generally linked to the realm of the "other," and generally interpreted as disruptive. Critics have read her barbaric and violent nature as a form of female empowerment or, at least, as a reflection on gender categories.[49] In this sense, the fact that the *Furioso* depicts an Amazonian society from its foundation through the changes in its laws is a crucial element, which allows us to draw a connection between the individual representation of the woman warrior and the collective representation of the Amazons.[50] In the *Furioso* as in its predecessors, Amazonian kingdoms offer the representation of an alternative form or government, from which men are excluded. If we read Bradamante through the Amazonian society of cantos XIX and XX, it is clear that the discussion of her role in the text could say more about political structures than it does about gender definitions. Rather, even more important, it says something about the management of gender within the political structure.

The nature of Bradamante as a character is strictly tied to that of Marfisa. If it is true that the chivalric characters are still, in Ariosto's world, both multitextual and part of a collective psychology, then the status of Bradamante as a warrior woman and as a potential Amazon is made visible by its comparison with Marfisa. The two elements we have individuated as constitutive, yet at odds, within the Amazonian society of Alessandria are called back into question by the dialectics of these two singular characters. If Marfisa is, in the *Furioso*, self-sufficient and Bradamante the destined bride, the two components of the Amazonian paradox are safely divided between the two characters, losing their disruptive potential in the sociopolitical sphere. But the story of these characters is multitextual and more complicated: in building the warrior women duo, Ariosto and Boiardo before him make a series of choices that not only differentiate the two characters but also speak to their different ideological functions.

The traits with which Ariosto identifies Marfisa are fairly stable throughout the poem, from her first appearance:

> La vergine Marfisa si nomava,
> di tal valor, che con la spada in mano
> fece più volte al gran signor di Brava
> sudar la fronte e a quel di Montalbano;
> e 'l dì e la notte armata sempre andava
> di qua di là cercando in monte e in piano
> con cavalieri erranti riscontrarsi,
> et immortale e gloriosa farsi. (*OF* XVIII, 99)

> [She was the virgin Marfisa, a swordsman of such prowess that on several occasions she had brought the perspiration to the brow of Orlando, lord of Brava, and to that of Rinaldo of Montauban. Day and night she was always armed, always on the prowl, up hill and down dale, alert to measure herself against knights errant and foster her immortal fame.]

It is Marfisa's stability, almost her inflexibility, that identify her throughout the poem, as her main features are her virginity and her consistency in wearing her armor, always ready for battle and never for love. The warrior herself addresses her potential belonging to the Amazon society, when she is faced with the dilemma of what persona to adopt in the land of the "femine omicide":

Sio ci fossi per donna conosciuta,
so ch'avrei da le donne onore e pregio;
e volentieri io ci sarei tenuta,
e tra le prime forse del collegio:
ma con costoro essendoci venuta,
non ci vo' d'essi aver più privilegio.
Troppo error fora ch'io mi stessi o andassi
libera, e gli altri in servitù lasciassi. (*OF* XX, 78)

[If I were recognized for a woman, I know that the women
would honor and respect me; they would give me a ready
welcome and perhaps a position of eminence in the tribe.
But as I came here with these others, I do not want to enjoy greater privilege than they; it would never do for me
to be free to stay or go while I abandoned these others to
servitude.]

Marfisa makes her first appearance in the *Inamoramento de
Orlando*, arguably as Boiardo's own creation. Marfisa's genealogy is directly Amazonian, as her name, likely a translitera-
tion of Marpesia, betrays.[51] In terms of character construction,
however, Boiardo had used the model of the *Historia di Bradiamonte* not for Bradamante, as Ariosto would do, but precisely
for Marfisa. Marphisa in Boiardo takes her entering description
from Bradiamonte:

La seconda conduce una Regina,
Che non ha cavalier tutto il Levante
Che la contrasti sopra de la sella,
Tanto è gagliarda, e ancor non è men bela.

Marphisa la dongiella è nominata
(Questa che io dico) e fo cotanto fiera
Che ben cinque anni sempre stete armata,
Da il sol nasciente al tramontar di sera,
Perché al suo dio Macon si era avotata
Con sacramento, la persona altera,
Mai non spogliarsi sbergo e piastre e maglia
Sin che tre re non prende per bataglia. (*Inamoramento de
Orlando* I, xvi, 28–29)

[The second rank is commanded by a queen, and not a
knight in all the East could match her in the saddle. She is
bold, as bold as she is lovely. The woman I've been telling of
is named Marfisa, one so fierce that she remained in arms
five years from dawn until the dark of night. The overreach-
ing maid had sworn a promise to her god Macone to wear
her hauberk, plate and mail till she subdued three kings in
battle.]

Marphisa, here still a pagan, and most likely not Ruggiero's sister, takes on the rhyme-words "sella/bella" and the trait of "gagliardia" that had been the defining features of Bradiamonte, already quoted above:

> El quinto figliolo fu una donzella
> che fu chiamata per nome bradiamonte
> che fu honesta costumata e bella
> e porto larme indosso e lelmo in fronte
> ne homo non curo sopra la sella
> de gagliardia hera fiume e fonte
> e mai nel mondo non volse marito
> se non chilabbateva sopra el sito. (*Bradiamonte* c. IV)

[And the fifth son was a maiden, called Bradiamonte, who
was honest, virtuous, and fair; and she wore arms and a
helmet on her head, and she did not fear any man in battle;
she was the beginning and the end of courage, and she never
wanted a husband, apart from the one who could defeat her
(on the spot).]

Ariosto's Bradamante connects the dots between Boiardo's
Marphisa and the Bradiamonte of the *cantari*. The passage keeps
the rhyme-words "donzella/bella/sella" of the anonymous poem,
as well as the "gagliardia":

> Ed egli a lui: – Di quel che tu mi chiedi
> io ti satisfarò senza dimora:
> tu dei saper che ti levò di sella
> l'alto valor d'una gentil donzella.

Ella è gagliarda ed è più bella molto;
né il suo famoso nome anco t'ascondo:
fu Bradamante quella che t'ha tolto
quanto onor mai tu guadagnasti al mondo. (*OF* I, 69–70)

[The envoy said: "In my capacity I will inform you without
more ado: You have been felled from horseback by a foeman
who is a valiant and courageous woman." She is as beautiful
as she is brave; nor will I hide her celebrated name: she at
whose hands just now you suffered have such ignominy and
undying shame is Bradamante.]

At the same time, Ariosto takes the defining line of his character, the one that puts the two constitutive qualities of the warrior
woman at odds, directly from Boiardo. Ariosto echoes the sentence
"Tanto è gagliarda, e ancor non è men bela" applied to Marphisa
with his "Ella è gagliarda ed è più bella molto." Ariosto reads
Marphisa for what she is, and returns to Bradamante her original
identity. This operation is not without consequences: it strongly
links the future founder of the Este dynasty with the mixed figures
of the tradition, halfway between the Amazon and the lady.

Possibly, Boiardo wanted to keep a straight distinction between the warrior woman (Marfisa) and the destined bride
(Bradiamonte-Bradamante), in opposition to the confusion of
the *cantari* and *poemi*. In the *Inamoramento*, Bradamante's
cross-dressing is transitional, a momentary tool to reach a goal,
whereas Marfisa takes on the role of the warrior woman/Ama-
zon. This distinction appears blurred in the popular chivalric
tradition, as we have seen in the previous chapter. Ariosto seems
to be consciously using this blurring in order to expose contradictions and violences of the dynastic make-up. This hypothesis
is confirmed by one of the programmatic distinctions between
Ariosto and Boiardo in the formulation of their poetics. At the
beginning of book II, canto xxii, after the dynastic prophecy is
told, Boiardo complains about his poetic destiny, clearly establishing a dichotomy between the classics and the romance chivalric epic:[52]

Fama, sequace degl'imperatori,
Nympha ch'e gesti en dolci versi canti,
Che dopo morte ancor gli homini honori
E fai coloro eterni che tu vanti,
Ove sei gionta? a dir gli antichi amori
Et a narar bataglie di giganti,
Mercié del mondo ch'al tuo tempo è tale
Che più di fama o di vertù non cale. *Inamoramento de Orlando* II, xxii, 2

[Fame, follower of emperors!/ Nymph! Who sings deeds and lovely verse!/ You praise men even after death;/ You make eternal those you honor./ What is your station now? To tell/ The giants' wars, the ancient loves—/ Such was the world in your day, but/ Virtue and fame are—now—not sought.]

The interpretation of this passage, in which Boiardo adopts overtly polemical tones, is controversial: Tissoni Benvenuti hypothesizes a rupture between the Este and the poet, and in any case an interrupted circulation of the poem after book II, xxii.[53] The "antichi amori" that Boiardo seems to disparage in the apostrophe to Fame are what Ariosto brings back in the *first line* of the first and second edition: "di donne e cavalier *gli antiqui amori*." Considering Ariosto's writing practices and the importance of the first stanza, it could be that "antiqui amori" acquired for him almost a technical meaning, a reference to the chivalric material Boiardo had disdained. Ariosto, in 1516 and again in 1521, is reclaiming (be it for serious or ironic purposes) the material scorned (be it seriously or ironically) by his great predecessor.

In Ariosto's treatment, Bradamante is not a pure character. She brings to the poem the baggage of a popular tradition and an Amazonian past. The threat of female self-sufficiency and control over reproduction casts a shadow over the other side of her persona, that of the ideal match for a superior warrior. In an age that sought in narratives about Amazons both the thrill of their menace and the comfort of their subjugation, the presence of the woman warrior as a founder at the center of the poem creates a sounding board for political concerns over the foundation of the state. The "femine omicide" are just an experiment, a state that collapses under its inability to create a law that does not mandate continuous exceptions. Bradamante will learn from this failed state and become the paladin of negotiation, but the problematic nature of dynastic power will not fade. After discussing Ariosto's representation of a genealogy of gender in the political sphere, in the following chapter I shall analyze one of his cautionary tales on the violence embedded in alliance through marriage.

CHAPTER THREE

The Paradox of Helen

*Genealogies and Textual Hierarchies
in* Orlando furioso, *Canto XXXIV*

Under the rule of patriarchy the girl is separated from her mother
and from her family in general. She is transplanted into the genealogy of her husband; she must live with him, carry his name, bear his
children, etc. The first time that this takes place, the move is recorded
as the abduction of a man-lover. A war breaks out among men to
recapture the stolen woman and bring her back to her community of
origin.
—LUCE IRIGARAY, *Sexes and Genealogies*, 2.

Historians of the Renaissance in Italy have observed a consistent
process of crystallization of male roles within the familial and
social structures, paralleled by a multiplication of female roles:

> The social interventionism of the early fifteenth-century
> state produced official definitions of the roles of men and
> women in society, fashioning a prescriptive gender structure
> that hardened the differences between husbands and fathers
> (and by silent exclusion highlighted the otherness of unmar-
> ried male adults), and gave official standing to the variations
> and nuances of womanhood by vocation, age, marital status
> and social class.[1]

The popular epic tradition, with its overabundance of converted
pagan princesses, fighting queens, wives, and daughters, mirrors
this multiplication of roles for women in all its threatening instability, as well as highlighting the "hardening" of behavioral
sets for the male figures. In the previous chapters, I have shown
how the Italian *cantari* and chivalric texts of the fourteenth and

fifteenth centuries represent genealogies of women and locate women within genealogy. In so doing, I have underlined the marginal, grotesque features of such representations, but also their disruptive potential within the texts. These texts indicate that women are perceived as elements of instability within a genealogical structure, yet they are also the most necessary agents for the perpetuation of that structure. The role they play as the means of alliance makes them indispensable and threatening at the same time. As a quintessential example of this type of ambiguous portrayal, I have considered one of the central figures of *Orlando furioso*, Bradamante, as she has come down to Ariosto through a successful career in the preceding French and Italian traditions.

This chapter analyzes the poem's presentation of the violence implied in the dynastic foundational moment.[2] The study of the genealogical formation of Ariosto's text, realized through the combination of medieval and classical intertexts, points in the direction of the establishment, on the author's part, of a mixed intertextual and genealogical structure. On one hand, the application of a "medieval" reading onto classical models challenges the stability of a fixed, only apparently nonproblematic tale of hate and love.[3] On the other hand, in this elaboration Ariosto suggests that the classical representation of alliance through marriage and the medieval topos of the cruel woman both contain blind spots. In other words, both tales silence the voice of the woman protagonist; only by mixing them and making them collide within his new text can Ariosto show their inherent contradictions.

Ariosto seems to offer a version of what we could call the "paradox of Helen."[4] Helen, the "cause" of the Trojan War, had been traditionally accused and defended by assigning or denying her freedom of choice. According to some, she followed Paris of her own will, and is thus guilty of a serious fault. According to the defenders of Helen, on the other hand, she was kidnapped against her will.[5] Some versions of the legend, meant to free her from all charges, claimed that only her image was taken, not her real self. One of the central questions within this debate is the choice, for the woman, between her homeland and love. Ariosto divests his protagonist of the possibility of choosing, and in doing so he seems to unmask the fiction of the "choice." Being the object of an exchange in a situation of political violence, the woman has no choice. Her choice is pre-determined by the conditions created for her.

The focus, ultimately, is on the issue of female agency within the genealogical structure, in an attempt to explore the connections between Ariosto's intertextual strategies and his narrative and thematics of genealogy. The episode of Lidia in canto XXXIV of the *Furioso* clearly exemplifies how the poem at once marks its filiation with multiple textual models and generates an "offspring" which is strictly identifiable with none of them. As regards literary genealogy, Ariosto does not aim at establishing textual hierarchies,[6] but reinterprets each precursor text in light of the others.[7] Moreover, the "genealogies of texts" he establishes are based on conflict rather than derivation. Almost counterintuitively, it is the absence of hierarchy that allows and actually fosters the conflict. In a neatly divided cosmos of sources, where the romance sources provide the matter and the classical sources the form, there is no possibility for these sources to compete to orient the reader's interpretation. When the models are not as clearly ordered, however, different (and to our modern eyes less important) texts can force (or revive, for that matter) the interpretation of canonical or soon-to-be canonical texts. This is why I see in Ariosto's intertextual strategy the construction of a horizontal constellation of references rather than a vertical line of textual descent.

Similarly, in his symbolic representations of familial lineage, Ariosto focuses more on women rather than on men, and thus inscribes a genealogy that is once again more horizontal than vertical, more fragmentary than unified. Whereas the male lineage is vertically constructed on the father/son axis, female lineages are more complicated and structured, one could say, as webs. If we look at the history of a family from the perspective of its women, we find a wide variety of provenances and lineages. The female side of a family tree branches out toward fathers, husbands, and sons; each woman in it is connected to multiple other actors that define and situate her.[8] The genealogy of women implies, as a consequence, the constant tension between loyalty to the family of the father and loyalty to the family of the husband.

This tension is palpable in the Ariostan tale of the damned Lidia, which she narrates to Astolfo during his descent into hell at the beginning of canto XXXIV. The story of Lidia unveils a crucial problem in Ariosto's poem: what is the responsibility of women in the wars and alliances between dynasties? As we shall see, Ariosto questions the possibility of female agency in the context of the contemporary political system. This new facet of the poem's political reflection is visible only if we invert the usual hierarchy of literary models in our reading. We have to abandon the reading habit that makes us look for the classical texts (Virgil, Ovid, etc.) as the leading guide to the *Furioso*. The pessimistic consideration of female agency becomes apparent only if we accept the medieval texts as the primary models for this episode. This does not mean, naturally, to affirm that the classical texts were not among Ariosto's primary models. But we have to make space for the fact that the corpus of romance and epic texts, virtually unknown to the modern reader, exist in the *Furioso* as a necessary textual precondition.

ASTOLFO *PEREGRINUS*

Readers of this episode may overlook the first signal that marks it as a dynastic narrative: the presence of Astolfo, which is important for two main reasons. From the thematic point of view, Astolfo is Bradamante's textual counterpart in the *Furioso*, and this element immediately links the episode to the dynastic narrative surrounding the heroine. From the point of view of textual strategies, Astolfo's adventure prepares the reader for the subtle and counterintuitive combination of canonical and noncanonical texts that will be the main feature of the episode centered on Lidia.

In the *Furioso*, characters often work as refractions of each other. Following a tradition that is typical of thirteenth-century

romance, apparent in the *Tristan* and *Lancelot* cycles, Ariosto creates characters that serve as examples and cautionary tales to others, within the poem itself.[9] Astolfo, in this sense, is Bradamante's
counterpart because, like her, he has a privileged relation with the
spheres of knowledge and perception. The other knights are constantly in search of their objects of desire, whether they be human beings, famous weapons, or adventures, and they generally
find something or someone else, which (or who) interrupts their
search.[10] Astolfo, on the contrary, *is found* by objects and adventures that stimulate and enhance sensorial perceptions: often these
same objects bear a meaning that needs to be revealed or interpreted. When we first read about Astolfo in the poem, he is pure
voice, turned into a myrtle tree by Alcina's magical powers (VI,
26–56; VII, 17, 27, 77). He soon gains access to a magic book and
to the deafening horn (XV, 9–37); he is the one destined to visit the
underworld, and to recover Orlando's wit (which will be inhaled
by its rightful owner, in canto XXXIX, 45–50). Bradamante, as
we have seen in the previous chapters, is the character who sees the
majority of prophetical representations in the poem, the one whose
perception is crucial to the dynastic development of the plot.[11]

At the intertextual level, Astolfo's descent into hell shows the
conflicted blend of a canonical authority, Dante's *Commedia*,
and of the tradition of the chivalric poem. Canto XXXIV of the
Furioso opens with the image of the Harpies. Astolfo has just
chased them away from the banquet of the Senapo, with the aid
of the magic horn. As often happens in the *Furioso*, Ariosto shifts
from an image—a fantastic one, in this case—to a concrete historical referent:[12] the "harpies," in this prologue, quickly turn
out to be the foreigners who invade and subjugate Italy. The political invective, echoing Dante, turns the fantastic element—the
cave where the Harpies flee and are buried—into a metaphor for
contemporary issues: the Italians' error was their failure to keep
that cave closed, that boundary safe.[13] The narration then turns
back to Astolfo and provides a quick summary of his victory over
the Harpies, the theme on which the preceding canto concluded.
The British knight wants to make sure that the Harpies have dis-

appeared into the cave. In doing so, he makes a discovery, which is presented to the reader as the most natural thing in the world:

> L'orecchie attente allo spiraglio tenne,
> e l'aria ne sentì percossa e rotta
> da pianti e d'urli e da lamento eterno:
> segno evidente quivi esser lo 'nferno. (*OF* XXXIV, 4, 7 8)

[He listened carefully at the entrance and heard the air rent with shrieks and reverberating with sobs and endless wailing—a clear sign that this must be hell.]

As a number of critics have observed, in this part of the poem Ariosto engages directly with the model of the *Commedia*.[14] The playful and careless attitude that Astolfo displays in entering the infernal adventure directs our interpretation of Ariosto's rereading of the *Commedia*.

Astolfo's demeanor as he begins his underworld adventure is calm and relaxed. He has the attitude of someone who has already read everything in a book: not the book given to him by Logistilla, one could argue, but the *Commedia* itself. Astolfo, as on other occasions, has a disenchanting effect upon the literary *topoi* to which he is linked. Only a few octaves earlier, he had repeated, step-by-step, the trip which had cost the Senapo his sight and his nourishment.[15] Now he plans to visit the world of the dead, using the *Commedia* as a tourist guidebook, indicating favorite activities to pursue and dangers to avoid:

> Astolfo si pensò d'entrarvi dentro,
> e veder quei c'hanno perduto il giorno,
> e penetrar la terra fin al centro,
> e le bolgie infernal cercare intorno.
> —Di che debbo temer (dicea) s'io v'entro,
> che mi posso aiutar sempre col corno?
> Farò fuggir Plutone e Satanasso,
> e 'l can trifauce leverò dal passo.— (*OF* XXXIV, 5)[16]

[He decided to go in and look at those who have lost the light of the day, and penetrate to the heart of the place and

inspect the ravines of hell. "What should I fear if I enter?"
he asked himself. "I can always use my horn to help me. I
shall rout Pluto and Satan; and the three-headed dog?—I
shall shift him out of my path."]

Two forms of textual authority are contrasted here: to the established *auctoritas* on the underworld, the *Commedia*, Astolfo
opposes the magical tradition of the chivalric poems.[17] The least
deserving of Charlemagne's knights approaches the voyage as a
pleasure trip; unlike his predecessors, he has no goal except for
the satisfaction of his own curiosity.

LIDIA

Ariosto's intertextual strategies and their connections to Bradamante and the dynastic theme emerge even more clearly in
the episode immediately following Astolfo's entrance into the
cave (*OF* XXXIV, 6, 1–4): the encounter with the damned
Lidia (*OF* XXXIV, 7–44). A cloud of smoke marks the beginning and end of this episode, which is worth recounting in
detail. In the cave, a "fumo oscuro e fello" prevents Astolfo
from advancing; but when he decides to turn around, something catches his attention. It is the movement of a body, which
reminds him of the swaying of a hung corpse; the knight, "per
notizia averne," hits it with his sword. But it feels to him as if
he had hit fog, and he realizes that it is a damned spirit, who
begs him to stop. Astolfo answers with a formulaic expression, which once again echoes Dante: he expresses the wish
that the smoke tormenting the spirit would disappear by God's
will, and offers to bring news of the spirit back to the world
of the living.[18] The spirit replies that her desire to gain eternity
through fame is so strong that she will overcome the pain of
speaking. She introduces herself as Lidia, daughter of the king
of Lidia; she has been condemned to eternal smoke because she
has been "spiacevole et ingrata" toward her lover. Her fate is
shared by, among many others, the Ovidian characters Anax-

arete and Daphne.[19] Ungrateful men, on the other hand, are punished in an even worse section of hell, where they are burnt by fire as well as blinded by smoke. Among them, Lidia names Theseus, Aeneas, Jason, and Ammon, and she explains that their punishment is worse because women "più facili e prone/ a creder son" [are more gullible].

The difference between the forms of punishment meted out to men and to women deserves further consideration. The male damned are, strictly speaking, not only ungrateful like Lidia but also guilty of betrayal; Lidia herself seems to be aware of this distinction when, at the end of the list of ungrateful men, she adds "et altri et altre: che sono infiniti,/ che lasciato han chi moglie e chi mariti" [and yet others, men and women—there is no end to those who have deserted wife or husband.] (OF XXXIV, 14, 7–8). With this remark, she contradicts the notion formulated in the preceding octave, in which she explained that men are punished differently because their sin is worse. But if they are guilty of a different sin, why should they be presented under the same definition of "ingratitude?"[20]

Let us keep the issue of ingratitude in mind and resume the preliminary account of the episode. Lidia narrates her story and describes her "error": because of her extraordinary beauty, a knight called Alceste fell in love with her from afar, without knowing her. Alceste was at the time "estimato il miglior del mondo in arme" [was held to be the foremost champion in the world] (OF XXXIV, 16, 2). Once he arrives at the court of Lidia's father, Alceste falls even more deeply in love, and performs exceptional deeds, conquering new territories for the crown. The hero, convinced that he deserves to marry Lidia by virtue of his deeds, asks her father for her hand. The king refuses abruptly:

Fu repulso dal re, ch'in grande stato
maritar disegnava la figliuola,
non a costui che cavallier privato
altro non tien che la virtude sola:
e 'l padre mio troppo al guadagno dato,

e all'avarizia d'ogni vizio scuola,
tanto apprezza costumi, o virtù ammira,
quanto l'asino fa il suon de la lira. (*OF* XXXIV, 19)

[The king rejected him; he entertained more grandiose plans
for his daughter's marriage—a soldier of fortune possesses
nothing but his valour. My father was all too devoted to
gain and avarice, the seed-bed of all vice; he had as much
use for grace and courage as a donkey has for a harp.]

This textual moment is an internal model for the episode in which
Amone and Beatrice oppose the wedding between Ruggiero and
Bradamante at the end of the poem.[21] With this decision, Lidia's
father anticipates the attitude of Bradamante's parents, who want
her to marry the son of the emperor rather than Ruggiero:

Ode Amone il figliuol con qualche sdegno,
che, senza conferirlo seco, gli osa
la figlia maritar, ch'esso ha disegno
che del figliuol di Costantin sia sposa,
non di Ruggier, il qual non ch'abbi regno,
ma non può al mondo dir: questa è mia cosa;
né sa che nobiltà poco si prezza,
e men virtù, se non v'è ancor ricchezza. (*OF* XLIV, 36)

[Aymon listened to his own son with indignation that he
should dare to marry off his daughter without consulting
him: he proposed to make her the bride of Constantine's
son, not of Ruggiero who, far from possessing a realm, had
nothing on earth which he could call his own. Ruggiero did
not realize that nobility was worth little, and valour less,
unless allied to wealth.]

The vocabulary of the two passages is very consistent: the two men
design ("disegnano") to marry their daughters; the aspiring suitors
are endowed with virtue ("virtude") as their only possession; wealth
is the only value recognized by avarice. Avarice, in particular, is one
of the connecting themes between Lidia and Bradamante, a thread
that links the two characters both across the models that make up
their development and within the Ariostan text itself.

The plot takes a turn toward its violent and tragic conclusion. Alceste, full of scorn, leaves the kingdom and offers his services to the Armenian king, whom he convinces to wage war on the ungrateful king of Lidia. In less than a year the Armenian army, led by Alceste, prevails on the enemy and takes over his kingdom, except for the castle, which is put under siege. During the siege, the king of Lidia decides to send his daughter, "che d'ogni male era cagione" [the cause of all the trouble] (*OF* XXXIV, 24, 3), to beg for peace. In exchange for an armistice, she is to offer her person and any part of the kingdom Alceste might want. Once she faces Alceste, though, Lidia realizes that he is in her power: "mi viene incontra pallido e tremante:/ di vinto e di prigione, a riguardarlo,/ più che di vincitore, have sembiante" [he came to meet me. He was pale and trembling—to look at him, he might have been a vanquished prisoner, not a conqueror] (*OF* XXXIV, 25, 2–4). Taking advantage of the situation, Lidia assumes the offensive and accuses Alceste of having been fickle and faithless, of not having pursued his love. She excoriates him for not having persisted after her father's first refusal. Lidia herself, she claims, would have convinced her father to accept him as a son-in-law. But now, after the knight has chosen violence and war, she is resolute that she will never love him again.[22] Rather than be with him, she will commit suicide.[23]

Alceste begs Lidia to take her vengeance upon him by killing him with his own sword; the woman, triumphant, decides to consummate her victory and orders the knight to return the kingdom to her father and thus erase his "error." In this episode, the theme of pacts kept and broken takes center stage: to preserve his faith to Lidia, Alceste must break his alliance with the Armenian king, who refuses to return conquered territories (*OF* XXXIV, 33–34).[24] Alceste kills his erstwhile patron, and quickly recovers the lost kingdom, even enriching it with new land. When he arrives at the castle, Lidia and her relatives want to kill him, but are constrained by his popularity. The woman pretends to love him, and leads him to believe that she will marry him; at the same time, she imposes a series of life-threatening trials upon him, and

alienates all his allies and friends. Once the kingdom of Lidia is
made strong again, and once Alceste is alone and isolated, Lidia
reveals her true feelings: "che grave e capitale odio gli porto,/ e
pur tuttavia cerco che sia morto" [that I cordially detested him
and was seeking every way to have him killed] (*OF* XXXIV, 41,
7–8). She cannot kill him, because she would be considered too
cruel, but she deprives him of all contact with her. Alceste dies of
desperation, deprived of her presence. Lidia's ungratefulness, the
cause of her lover's death, is the sin that put her in hell, with no
hope of salvation. Once she has told her story, the woman disappears, and Astolfo, who would like to talk to other souls, is com-
pelled by the unbearable smoke to depart. This natural element
closes the episode symmetrically, as we have observed.

THE UNGRATEFUL WOMAN IN THE
CANTARI DI FEBUS IL FORTE

Critics have traditionally associated the story of Lidia with
three narratives: the *novella* of Nastagio degli Onesti (*Decameron* V.8), the episode of Anaxarete in the *Metamorphoses*,
populated by cruel women, and a passage from the *Palamedès*.
I will focus my analysis on the least studied of them: the *Palamedès* or, rather, the Italian tradition of the *Palamedès*. The
Roman de Palamedès or *Guron le Cortois*, as it is often entitled in the manuscripts, is a long prose romance, composed
later than the *Lancelot* and the *Tristan*, upon which it is modeled.[25] Its main distinguishing feature is its temporal setting: the
adventures recounted in the *Palamedès* chronologically precede
the era of Arthurian chivalry. The text attempts to reconstruct
a glorious past, a golden age of chivalric power and courtesy.
Composed in the first half of the thirteenth century, the poem
circulated widely in Italy during the following centuries. Italian translations as well as manuscripts in the original language
demonstrate its ample diffusion in the peninsula. In Ferrara,
inventories of the Estense library attest to the presence of several manuscripts on the deeds of Palamedès, Tristan's most fa-

mous rival knight.[26] Like the *Lancelot* and the *Tristan*, this romance is an enormous collection of adventures, chronologically and spatially intertwined through the method of *entrelacement*. The most important episode in relation to the *Furioso* is the adventure of Brehus in the sepulcher of the knight Febus.[27] The extant Italian versions of this episode differ by genre: a thirteenth-century *volgarizzamento*, composed around Pisa, and a fourteenth-century rewrite in six *cantari*.[28] The manuscript containing the *volgarizzamento* is a sort of anthology of excerpts from the *Tristan* and the *Palamedès*. The compiler translated only this episode, and kept the others in the original language.[29] The six *cantari*, on the other hand, are preserved in a Florentine manuscript from the second half of the fourteenth century.[30]

While the number of French and Italian versions of the episode centered on Febus and Brehus speaks to its diffusion, the close similarity between them attests to the stability of this particular adventure.[31] We do not know which version Ariosto knew, but we can safely venture the hypothesis that it was not very different from one of the texts still extant today. This consideration is supported by the comparative analysis of the Ariostan text and of the *cantari*. The protagonist of the adventure is Brehus (Breus or Breusso in the Italian versions), known to the readers of the *Palamedès* as the merciless knight, particularly cruel toward women. The knight finds himself in a cave, which has the appearance of an underground palace.[32] Passing from one richly decorated room to another, Breus finds five corpses, all lavishly ornamented. Three of them are famous knights of the past, while the fourth is the corpse of the strongest knight of the old age, Febus, and the fifth corpse is his beloved. Each of them holds a "breve," a short written document containing the reasons and circumstances of their deaths. Thanks to these "texts within the text," and to the narration of an old knight who lives in the cave, Breus comes to know the story of Febus. The knight, "de' cavalieri onore e lume" [honor and glory of chivalry] (*Febus*, I, 26, 7), had excelled in his times by virtue of his strength, courage, and authority. His only mistake was to fall in love:

una sola viltà mi partì el core
e del mio grande ardir passò le porte:
ciò fu amore, per cui mi diei a servire
una pulzella che mi fé morire. (*Febus*, I, 27, 5–8)

[Only one weakness broke my heart, and was superior to my
great courage: that was love, for whom I became the servant
of a maiden who caused my death.][33]

Febus's epitaph concludes with the introduction of the virgin
who caused his death: she is the daughter of the king of Norbelanda, who lies in the adjacent room, in a bed decorated with
golden birds. The "breve" in her purse recounts her story in a few
words: just as Adam, the father of all men, was ruined by Eve's
evil counsel ("consiglio"), Febus, the father of all knights, took
her as a "dolorosa consiglieri" (counselor of sorrow, I, 40–41).
She brought him to death, and she repented only when it was too
late (I, 42). The following octave compresses the three central elements of the narrative:

Socorso no li diei, o tapinella!
perché m'ucise el mio fratello e zio.
Mio padre disse: "Figlia, fatti bella,
e 'l tuo amore dona al nemico mio,
e usciremo di questa briga fella,
se mi ubidissi, figlia, in fé di Dio!"
Venendo qui [a lui] trova'lo a tal partito,
com'io l'abraciai cadde tramortito. (*Febus*, I, 43)

[I did not help him, alas, because he had killed my brother
and my uncle. My father told me: "Daughter, make yourself beautiful, and give your love to my enemy, and we shall
get out of this horrible trouble, if you would listen to me, oh
daughter, for the love of God!" When I arrived here I found
him in such a state, that when I embraced him he fell as if he
were dead.]

After the knight's death, the woman chose to let herself die in the
cave. The old knight whom Breus meets shortly thereafter elaborates on the clues provided by the "brevi."

A few central elements may have sparked Ariosto's interest in the story told by the *cantari*. First of all, the "brevi" held by the knight and by the lady allow an introduction of their lives and, in the woman's case, of the sin committed in the voice of the first person. In the *Furioso*, this self-introduction corresponds to Lidia's admission of her sin (*OF* XXXIV, 11). Ariosto, however, adapted the model selectively, and, retaining the female protagonist as the sole narrator, he developed the first-person narrative. Moreover, he completely erased the male protagonist, who figures only as a victim in the soul's account. In this discourse, and arguably in the *cantari* as well, two elements coexist:[34] the Dantesque formula of self-presentation,[35] and the romance tradition of the funereal epitaph, of the "speaking" grave.[36]

Ariosto has thus drastically changed the perspective of the narrative, making Lidia, the woman, the narrator of the story. Another element seems to be consistent with the shift of the narrator's position, and that is the name of the woman. In the *Febus* it was the male protagonist who first mentioned the woman, and he called her by a patronymic, not by her given name: she was the daughter of the king of Norbelanda (I, 28), and this periphrasis defined her until the end of the text. Only at her death was her name mentioned, and only once, as Albiera (VI, 51, 8). The *Furioso*'s protagonist, on the contrary, immediately announces her name: "Signor, Lidia son io" (*OF* XXXIV, 11, 1). It would seem to make sense, then, to link Lidia to Anaxarete, the Ovidian heroine who refuses the love of Iphis to the point that he hangs himself. She is in fact named, unlike the British protagonist of the *Febus*.

The name of the woman in the *Furioso*, however, seems to be something more—or something less—than a first name. Why is Lidia called Lidia? If we keep reading past the line just quoted, a crucial element is added to the picture: "E cominciò:—Signor, Lidia sono io,/ dal re di Lidia in grande altezza nata." ["I am Lydia, she began, daughter of the king of Lydia and born to eminence"] (*OF* XXXIV, 11, 1). Lidia is not simply a name but also a nominalized adjective, "the Lydian," indicating the region and its inhabitants.[37] Even if Ariosto calls his protagonist Lidia on another occasion (when she disappears), and seems to use it as a given name, the correspondence between the name and the country, between the name and the territory, does not seem to be coincidental. To say the least, the narrator thus establishes a strong bond of identity between the woman and the region. Lidia is, in the end, a patronymic as well, one that defines the woman as a function of the kingdom and of the king.[38] This element in the *Furioso* is clarified only in connection with the intertext of the *cantari*. The father, as the defining element of identity for the daughter, marks the *cantari* as a profoundly genealogical text.

FATHERS, DAUGHTERS, KINGDOMS

The *Cantari di Febus* are dominated by an obsession with father figures.[39] The second *cantare* is almost entirely devoted to the genealogy of Febus, from whom the old knight descends, as do all the other inhabitants of the cave where Breus finds himself. The three dead knights in the cave are Febus's sons.[40] Sons succeed fathers, fathers leave their kingdoms to their sons: such is the basic structure of genealogical narration, as it is presented to Breus in the cave. The genealogical frame is set up as a context for Febus's entrance into the narrative. The knight's first deeds consist of leaving his rightfully inherited kingdom to his brother and waging war against three princes who are brothers: the kings of Norgalès, Norbelanda, and Longrès. In the few words that accompany the daughter of the king on her deathbed (the "breve") there is an immediate, although not referential, use of the term *father*: Febus is compared to Adam as "primo padre dei cavalieri" [first father of knighthood].[41] Within the "breve" itself, the central episode is that of the father sending off his daughter to beg for peace.

The peace mission performed by the daughter was considered a pivotal moment of the narration, as is suggested by the many illuminations describing the subject. The manuscript of the *cantari* itself displays an image of this episode, including both the dialogue between father and daughter and the daughter's mis-

sion. Ariosto decided to use this part of the narration, and made
it central to the story of Lidia. He omitted other details of the
story: the king of Norbelanda has two brothers in the *cantari*,
the kings of Norgalès and Longrès, both of whom are killed by
Febus. Febus first sees the king of Norgalès' daughter, and falls in
love with her (III, 4–11). Only when someone praises the beauty
of the daughter of the king of Norbelanda over her cousin does
the knight fall in love with her (III, 12–14).[42]

The daughter's mission on behalf of the father is, as we have
seen, the central element of the lady's self-introduction in the *cantari*. In the account related by the old knight, in *cantare* III, the
defeated king, besieged in his castle, dispatches his daughter with
the hope that her beauty will induce pity in the enemy:

> E l'altro giorno fu terza passata,
> lo re apellò sua figlia gioconda,
> dicendo: "Sappi che nostra ambasciata
> diliberato so che tu risponda,
> sì che or*a* t'adorna come se' usata:
> forse per la beltà che in te abonda,
> quando ti vederà, in veritade,
> per te e per noi si moverà a piatade." (*Febus*, III, 31)

> [And the other day, in the evening, the king called his beau-
> tiful daughter, and said: "You should know that I have de-
> cided that you should be the messenger and take our answer
> (to the enemy); therefore, you should now make yourself
> beautiful, like you are used to: maybe when he sees you,
> because of the beauty that blesses you, he will be moved to
> compassion toward you and toward us.]

The perspective is slightly different from that offered in the first
cantare: there, in the "breve," it was written that the father asked
her not merely to induce pity but also to give her love ("donare il
proprio amore"). Once again, the concise "breve" seems to have
directed Ariosto's interpretation and rewriting of the episode. In
the *Furioso*, Lidia goes to turn herself over to the enemy, as a
prize. The real function of the woman in this episode, veiled by

her supposed role as a mediator, is unmasked. The woman is an object of exchange:

> Tentar, prima ch'accada, si dispone
> ogni rimedio che possibil sia;
> e me, *che d'ogni male era cagione,*
> fuor de la rocca, ov'era Alceste invia.
> Io vo ad Alceste con intenzïone
> di dargli in preda la persona mia,
> e pregar che la parte che vuol tolga
> del regno nostro, e l'ira in pace volga. (*OF* XXXIV, 24)

> [He was disposed to try every possible remedy before it came to that; so he sent me, as the cause of all the trouble, out to Alcestes. I went to him intending to surrender myself as his prey and to beg him to take what share he wanted of our realm and abate his wrath.]

From a direct comparison, an important difference emerges: whereas the protagonist of the *cantari* had initially refused to act as a mediator, because Febus had killed her relatives ("ma io amerei inanzi di morire/ che d'avisarmi con lui in presenza," III, 32, 3–4), Lidia, on the contrary, seems to acknowledge her "responsibility." But what is her responsibility? In the *cantari*, the notion of responsibility is absent. The daughter of the king of Norbelanda plays the role of a mediator, or—more plausibly—of an object of exchange between her father and Febus. In the *Furioso*, Lidia is *the* object. Her position is completely neutral, until the central "mission scene": the father refuses to grant her hand to Alceste, Alceste takes his revenge on the father by attacking his kingdom. Lidia is the middle term in this power struggle, and therein lies the foundation of her ambiguous responsibility: she is the *cause* of all evil, but only insofar as she is the disputed object. Lidia *is* the territory, she is the possession, objectively the cause of the war but subjectively not responsible. From this perspective, there is another text we should consider as a fundamental model in the construction of the character: the *Aeneid*.

In book VII of the *Aeneid*, Virgil describes the arrival of the Trojans on the Tiber along with the events that take place in the kingdom of the Latini. A series of prophecies convinces king Latinus that his daughter, Lavinia, is destined to marry a man from a different region—in particular, her fate is to marry Aeneas, the Trojan leader. The goddess Juno, the Trojans' fiercest enemy, calls upon a Fury to intervene and keep the wedding from happening. Latinus's wife Amata, possessed by Aletto, convinces her husband to pick Turnus, and not Aeneas, as a husband for Lavinia. Similarly driven by Aletto, Turnus himself decides to wage war against the Trojans. This is the beginning of the war between the Latini and the Rutuli on one side, and the Trojans and their allies on the other. Lavinia will not appear on the scene until book XI, when a victorious Aeneas is marching on the town of the Latini. King Latinus blames himself for having chosen Turnus over Aeneas, while the noble women of the kingdom climb to the temple overlooking the town:

> Nec non ad templum summasque ad Palladis arces
> Subvehitur magna matrum regina caterva,
> Dona ferens iuxtaque comes Lavinia virgo,
> *causa mali tanti*, oculos deiecta decoros. (*Aeneid*, XI, 477–80)[43]

> [Meanwhile a large group of women accompanies the queen to the temple, and to the palace of Athena, to bring gifts to the goddess; and with her goes the virgin Lavinia, the cause of so great an evil, with beautiful downcast eyes.][44]

Virgil uses the same expression in canto VI, when the Sybil prophesizes to Aeneas his future role of founder: "Causa mali tanti coniunx iterum hospita Teucris/ externique iterum thalami" [The cause of such evil for the Trojans will be, once again, a foreign bride, once again foreign nuptials].[45] The cause of the war is the foreign bride. Lavinia is the cause "of so great an evil," Lidia "the reason of all evil": the lexicon confirms that one of the textual models for the *Furioso* episode is the *Aeneid*.[46] In this episode, Ariosto takes up the theme of the woman

as a nonresponsible cause of war. Ariosto's skillful transfiguration has so far hidden the correspondence between the poem
and the Virgilian treatment of the theme. Rereading the *Aeneid*
through the medieval text, and adding to this constellation of
meaning the related models of Dante and Boccaccio, Ariosto almost succeeds in effacing his originary model and his originary
object of discussion. In other words, the figure of Lidia needs
to be analyzed reading the various, superimposed memories of
different textual models: if we look only for Dante's damned
soul, or for Boccaccio's cruel woman, and similarly, if we focus
on either the medieval model or the classical, we lose the political complexity of the Ariostan character, the ways in which it
shows that the foreign bride is, in fact, the transfiguration of
and the solution to the war.[47]

We have seen that Lavinia, in canto XXXIV of the *Furioso*,
is the emblem of the woman as an element of exchange in relations between states. Her presence as a model for Lidia, moreover, plays into the representation of the most ambiguous and
darkest aspect of dynastic politics. As suggested earlier, one of
the characters mentioned by Lidia as a damned soul in hell is
none other than Aeneas ("chi turbò a Latin l'antiquo regno," *OF*
XXXIV, 14, 4). Aeneas, often represented as guilty of betrayal
toward Dido,[48] is here identified differently, through a periphrasis describing, once again, a *territory*, the kingdom of Lavinia's
father. There is an ideological clash between the two figures who
share damnation in *Furioso*, canto XXXIV: Aeneas, the man
who traditionally submits to his destiny and is bound to crush
those he loves, and Lidia, who, like Lavinia, is presented as the
"cause" of the war.[49] To explain this apparent short circuit, we
can advance the hypothesis that Ariosto's text, from as early as
1516, is reflecting on the ethical implications of the dynastic marriage. This consideration acquires more weight, of course, when
we consider that the *Furioso* is a dynastic poem, and that the dynastic wedding is the aim and the end of the poem itself.[50]

In his modification of the narrative of the medieval *cantari*
through the interpretive lens of the *Aeneid*, Ariosto chooses to

focus on the figure of the father. In the French romance and in the *cantari*, Febus has never seen the woman in question, and arrives as a conqueror in the father's kingdom. The father's function, in these instances, is only to use the beauty of his daughter as an instrument, completely ignorant of the fact that Febus is already in love with her. In the *Furioso*, on the contrary, the father causes Alceste's attack on the kingdom by refusing him his daughter's hand, out of greed. Lidia's father acts out of economic considerations, as well as greed, and he changes his mind in accordance with changes in his situation. When he is faced with the possibility of dying a slave, bereft of his kingdom, he reconsiders his former attitude: "per buon patto avria mio padre tolto/ che moglie e serva ancor me gli lasciasse/ con la metà del regno, s'indi assolto/ restar d'ogni altro danno si sperasse" [He would have been more than content had he been able, by handing me over as wife, nay, servant, with half his kingdom thrown in, to ward off all further inroads] (XXXIV, 23, 3–6). The central position the king assumes in canto XXXIV, in contrast to the medieval *cantare*, leads us to consider Ariosto's own narrative as an internal "source" for the episode in which Bradamante's parents attempt to prevent her from marrying Ruggiero.

As we have already observed, both the king of Lidia and Amone, Bradamante's father, reject the marriage proposals of their daughters' suitors out of greed. Greed is a central theme in the poem, and a web of references to greed can be found in prologues and episodes strictly connected to ours. Canto XXXIV opens with an invective against the "Harpies," or foreigners who invade Italy with their greed and lust for power. Greed is described here in political terms, as eagerness to conquer a territory: the prologue is well tuned to the tale of war and conquest told by Lidia in the following octaves. In addition, the prologue to canto XLIV—in which Rinaldo is the guest of the Mantuan nobleman—execrates greed. The vocabulary of the passage is consistent with that used in the prologue to canto XXXIV, and the themes of hunger and filth, here exploited, bring us back to their personifications, the Harpies:

O esecrabile avarizia, o *ingorda*
fame d'avere, io non mi maraviglio
ch'ad alma vile e d'altre macchie *lorda*,
sì facilmente dar possi di piglio. (*OF* XLIII, 1, 1–4)

[O detestable avarice! O greed for gain! If you so easily en-
trap base souls, already filthy from other stains, that comes
as no surprise.]

The prologue is strictly linked to the body of the canto, in which
the Mantuan host tells his story to Rinaldo: out of greed and jealousy, he has lost his wife. The tale transfers the theme of greed
from the public to the private field; in particular, it opens a reflection on the control imposed by men on women. The subsequent,
added episode in which Amone and Beatrice oppose the marriage
between Ruggiero and Bradamante seems to address the theme
of greed by recomposing the two aspects, public (or political) and
private (or within the family). Such a combination of the two
sides of greed was already suggested in the Lidia episode, used as
an intratext by Ariosto in composing the 1532 version.[51]

Now that we have assessed the presence of "logical" conjunc-
tions between the *cantari* and canto XXXIV of the *Furioso*, such
as the self-introduction of the female protagonist and the scene
of the mission to the besieging lover, centered on the father, it is
worth taking a step back to compare the structures of the two
narratives. The *cantari* have a frame, divided into three parts:

I.   Breus' fall into the cave;
II. Reading of the "brevi";
III. Tale of the old knight (preceded by the description of the
     lineage of Gurone)

The third macro-sequence contains the narration itself, which
can be divided in sequences as follows:

1.   Febus conquers territories; his *innamoramento* from afar
     (through a first, vicarious love for the woman's cousin);
2.   Mission of the lady and surrender of Febus;

3. Task imposed by the lady on the knight (against the king of Organia);

4. Battles fought by Febus (against a giant near a sepulcher, against two giants at the banquet in Norbelanda);

5. Febus's demands on the lady; her refusal; Febus's threats; the lady's pretense of promising that she will ask her father for permission to marry;

6. Task imposed by the lady on the knight (Febus conquers the cave, formerly occupied by four knights);

7. Febus's victory, and his vain wait for the lady;

8. Illness and arrival of the lady; death of Febus;

9. Decision of the lady to be buried alive in the cave. End of the old knight's tale.

Let us now consider the structure of the Lidia episode, which can be analyzed as follows:

a. Alceste's request for Lidia's hand; rejection on the father's part;

b. Alceste's war against Lidia's reign;

c. Mission of the lady and surrender of Alceste;

d. Tasks imposed by the lady on the knight;

e. Alceste's victory, and vain wait for the lady; death of Alceste;

f. Lidia's damnation. End of her tale.

To the overall structure of his narrative model, Ariosto makes two major changes, concentrated at the beginning and at the end. In the *Furioso*, the story begins at the king's court, where the lady and the knight meet. The sequence we have termed 1 in the *cantari* is moved to the second position (b in the *Furioso*), and connected to the previous episode by a nexus of cause and effect (Alceste attacks the kingdom *because* he has been rejected). This change entails serious consequences from the point of view of the characters' interaction: it introduces the element of choice. Both the Lidian king and Alceste choose a particular course of action: the king rejects Alceste, Alceste reacts by waging war.[52] If the b sequence in the *Furioso* corresponds to sequence 1 in the *Febus*, sequences c and 2 show even greater overlap. From this moment on, we notice a tendency on Ariosto's part to bring together episodes that were multiplied and repeated with variations in the *cantari*. To take but one example, which I will analyze further below, Ariosto adds elements from sequence 5 to the sequence of the mission. Similarly, the short episode of the *Furioso* in which Alceste performs chivalric deeds at Lidia's request is built by combining sequences 3, 4, and 5.

The end of the tale contains the second element of radical innovation. In the *cantare*, the lady repents and joins the knight before his death (and follows him in death, since she decides to be buried alive with him). Lidia, on the contrary, does not seem to feel any guilt, and her punishment appears to be inflicted upon her by a superior power, rather than by herself. Rajna has interpreted this detail as a demonstration of Lidia's derivation from Anaxarete, the Ovidian character, who does not feel any pity for the dead Ifi.[53] The difference between the two punishments, however, does not seem to be particularly relevant, unless we want to impose on Ariosto's hell the same moral and religious superstructure that we attribute to Dante's *Inferno*. The privileged intertext of the *Furioso* is, from this point of view, the *Febus*. In particular, Ariosto is establishing a dialogue with the text that allows him to discuss the problem entailed by the choice of a course of action on the woman's part.[54] This is a case in which a deeper analysis of the combined inter- and intratextual strategies can yield useful interpretive clues.

THE VICTIM OF WAR AND THE VICTIM OF LOVE

The intertwining of the Virgilian model with the *cantare* dynamically continues throughout the development of the "mission" scene. When Lidia sees that her aggressor is completely at her mercy, an extraordinary psychological change takes place in her:

Io che conosco ch'arde, non gli parlo
sì come avea già disegnato inante:

vista l'occasïon, fo penser nuovo
convenïente al grado in ch'io lo trovo. (*OF* XXXIV, 25, 5–8)

[Realizing how he burned for me, I did not speak to him the
way I had originally intended; seeing the opportunity, I hit
upon a new idea in keeping with the condition in which I
found him.]

Lidia's "new thought," her new tactic, is to complain about Alceste's behavior and to lead him to a complete reversal of his position: the aggressor becomes the victim, and is ready to accept
any condition imposed. Since her strategy works ("poi che potere
in lui mi vidi tanto," *OF* XXXIV, 30, 2), she decides to take her
requests to an extreme: she forces Alceste to take upon himself a
series of deeds that will expose him to the risk of death, and demands that he return the kingdom to her father. In the *cantare*
model, the words of the lady against Febus are much less threatening, but when she returns to the castle, her description of what
just happened could very well apply to Lidia: "Tanto ho saputo
fare e tanto dire/ che in Organia lo mando a morire" [So much
I did, and so much I said, that I have sent him to die in Organia]
(*Febus*, III, 42, 7–8).[55]

In this scene, Ariosto draws upon another part of the *cantari*,
in which Febus asks to the lady to marry him (*Febus*, V, 5–14).
In response to the lady's refusal, Febus threatens to destroy the
kingdom. She then decides to feign love, and begins plotting his
death.[56] Ariosto apparently used this episode to build the central core of his narrative. The daughter of the king of Norbelanda promises to talk to her father about a possible wedding,
and claims to be able to convince him: "mio padre d'[i qu]este
cose pregarò/ e 'l priego mio li fia comandamento,/ sì che faranne
el vostro cor contento" (*Febus*, V, 13, 6–8) [I shall supplicate my
father to grant me these things, and my prayer will be an order
for him, so that your heart will rejoice]. In a kaleidoscopic textual
game, Lidia claims that precisely that possibility (convincing the
father and fulfilling the lover's dream) could have been realized,
if only Alceste had been patient:

E quando anche mio padre a lui ritroso
stato fosse, io l'avrei tanto pregato,
ch'avria l'amante mio fatto mio sposo.
Pur, se veduto io l'avessi ostinato,
avrei fatto tal opra di nascoso,
che di me Alceste si saria lodato.
Ma poi che a lui tentar parve altro modo,
io di mai non l'amar fisso avea il chiodo. (*OF* XXXIV, 28)

[And even if my father had persisted in his refusal, I should
so have entreated him that he would have made my suitor
my husband. But supposing I had found him obstinate?
I should so have worked on him on the sly that Alcestes
would have been no little pleased with me. But as he chose
to try this other approach, I had made up my mind that I
should never love him.]

The woman loved by Febus plots his death while promising to
convince her father to consent to the wedding: she acts in this way
in order to protect herself from violence. Lidia, on the contrary,
claims that, if Alceste had not resorted to violence, she would
have convinced her father. In both cases, the elements at play are
violence, betrayal, and the impossibility to love; but the chrono-
logical shift Ariosto has imposed on the original narrative creates an extremely complex game of intertextuality. In the *cantare*,
the impossibility to love follows logically from Febus's violence,
and becomes cruelty or vengeance. In the *Furioso*, the sequence
is much less linear.

The central question in the interpretation of this episode is
thus the following: we do not know, when reading Lidia's claim,
whether she is sincere or not. There are no textual clues in either
direction, and we have no way of knowing if the character is innocent when she recounts the alternatives that would have been
possible if only Alceste had not resorted to violence, and which
Alceste's violent act has nullified. I think it is possible to conclude
that it is precisely the violent act that has erased even the possibility of verifying Lidia's true inclinations. This may well have been
Ariosto's interpretation of the story of the nameless British lady

as recounted in the *Febus*: violence (as the realization of an all-male will) has divested the woman of any possibility of expression (with the exception of destruction or manipulation). Moreover, violence has denied the reader the ability to safely interpret the text, assigning blames and praise to different characters.[57]

THE WOMAN AS "NONRESPONSIBLE CAUSE" AND DYNASTIC FOUNDATION: LIDIA AND BRADAMANTE

The situation I have just described is the one Ariosto proposes to his readers in the 1516 and the 1521 texts. In these versions of the poem, Lidia's story already casts a shadowy, ambiguous light on Bradamante's wedding, and the poem's end. In the 1532 additions, the link between the two female figures is clearly established by a striking consistency in vocabulary. When Lidia vows never to love Alceste, she swears: "Ma poi ch'a lui tentar parve altro modo,/ io di mai non l'amar *fisso avea il chiodo*" [But as he chose to try this other approach, I had made up my mind that I should never love him] (XXXIV, 28, 7–8). Bradamante, in cantos XLIV and XLV (in the 1532 version), proclaims her faithfulness to Ruggiero twice, while her parents plot to foil her wedding. The vocabulary she uses, as Albert Ascoli has demonstrated, links these additions to canto XXI, where the theme of faith is discussed at length, starting with the *incipit* of the prologue:

> Né fune intorto crederò che stringa
> soma così, né così legno chiodo,
> come la fé ch'una bell'alma cinga
> del suo tenace indissolubil nodo. (*OF* XXI, 1, 1–4)

> [No cord, I verily believe, will ever truss a package, nor will a nail fasten a piece of wood as securely as a promise will bind a virtuous man with a tenacious, insoluble knot.]

Lidia's words challenge the classical conception of faith as a monolithic concept: faith becomes more complex and dangerous if one of its aspects is obstinacy. Faith, taken to the extremes of stubbornness, comes to border on cruelty. In 1532 Ariosto recovers the theme of faith and attempts a more convincing interpretation of it through the figure of Bradamante.

Through the combination of the two main intertexts for Lidia's story (the *cantari* and the *Aeneid*), Ariosto comments upon the eternal tale of Helen of Troy, as well as upon the principle of marriage as a foundational moment for a lineage.[58] Let us consider how this implicit commentary is articulated. The political-dynastic tale is told, in the 1532 text, in two different versions: Lidia and Bradamante. The figure of Lavinia, the "nonresponsible" cause of war, is refracted through and then crystallized in the two characters; that is, her story is retold in two versions. The element of the forbidden wedding that causes war is reworked in the story of Lidia; the aspect of the dynastic necessity of Lavinia's and Aeneas's marriage is mirrored in the adventures of Ruggiero and Bradamante. Both weddings are obstructed by the parents of the woman, and Beatrice, Bradamante's mother, may well have been modeled upon the figure of Amata from the *Aeneid*.[59] Establishing Lidia's story as an "internal model" for the wedding between Ariosto's heroes, however, adds an element of complication and questioning: Lidia fully reveals to the readers of the *Furioso* the violent side of the dynastic imperative, of the power of the father, and of the necessity/possibility for women to choose between competing loyalties. As we have seen, the transfiguration of the daughter of Norbelanda's king into Lidia creates a short circuit: it demonstrates the impossibility of solving the "Helen paradox." Ariosto unmasks the ideological nature of the debate on Helen's guilt, revealing that Lidia, Helen's alter ego, not only is damned because she has not done what Helen is accused of having done (leaving her homeland to follow her love) but also never had a real choice.

Ariosto takes the theme of choice from the medieval text. The story of the *cantari*, modified in order to show how destruction is born out of the impossibility to choose, is a model: Bradamante, the founder of the Este dynasty, must look at this *exemplum* from within the text. The '32 addition of the contrasted wedding has a twofold end: on one hand, the woman must choose between different loyalties, that to her lover (a new lineage) and that to her parents (the old lineage):

> —Ahimé! vorrò quel che non vuol chi deve
> poter del voler mio più che poss'io?
> Il voler di mia madre avrò in sì lieve
> stima, ch'io lo posponga al voler mio?
> Deh! qual peccato puote esser sì grieve
> a una donzella, qual biasmo sì rio,
> come questo sarà, se, non volendo
> chi sempre ho da ubbidir, marito prendo? (*OF* XLIV, 41)

> [Shall I pit my desires against those of one who ought to
> have greater command over my will than I have? Shall I
> make so light of my mother's wishes as to defer them to my
> own? Ah, what sin can be so grave for a damsel, what fault
> so heinous? How should it be if I were to take a husband
> against the wishes of one whom I must always obey?]

On the other hand, Bradamante's choice, which leads her to unfaithfulness in other realms, is not only a choice for love; Bradamante is also choosing to found a new dynasty, to fulfill the end of the poem. The poem strives to erase the obstacles that the narrator himself has posed to the fulfillment of this end (such as the exchange between Ruggiero and Leone, or the necessity of Bradamante marrying the latter); and in this light we could read Ariosto's attempt to make the choice of the end believable to himself through the "distant dialogue" between Lidia and Bradamante.

CHAPTER FOUR

The Poem as a Prophecy

Gendered Gifts in the Orlando furioso

In the Western canon, genealogical prophecies are given to men, by men, and are about men. Dynastic knowledge is transmitted from fathers to sons, in a replication of the patrilineal nature of family trees. In the *Aeneid*, when Aeneas descends to the Underworld and receives prophetic knowledge of his future lineage, a female intermediary, the ancient Sybil, guides him to his destination. Yet it is his father Anchises who conjures the images of the souls in front of his son's eyes and interprets them for him. Book VI of the *Aeneid*, which contains this foundational episode, is punctuated by references to the patrilineal nature of Aeneas's genealogy. *Pater* (father) and *natus* (son) are the most common words in the dialogue between Aeneas and his father, and the vocabulary of male generation and paternity predictably dominates the description of the future lineage of the Trojan hero. In another foundational text of European literature, the *Commedia*, Dante traces another, poetic and theological but still patrilineal, genealogy when he claims that he is not worthy of his mission: "I am not Aeneas, I am not Paul." Beatrice and the various saints, as well as the Virgin Mary herself, are intermediaries who intercede for Dante. Not dissimilarly, the Sybil is a medium, literally and technically a voice without a body. When Ariosto writes the *Orlando furioso*, however, he deals with the theme in a completely new fashion. By making Bradamante the recipient of the predictions of the future Este dynasty, Ariosto shatters this foundational principle of prophetic knowledge in such a profound way that the consequences of this operation, after centuries of analysis and critical work, are still unclear. The gender shift is accompanied by the introduction of another female figure, the sorceress Melissa, who imparts the prophetic knowledge to Bradamante. Neither narrative element is a simple, innocent variation on the tired old theme of the dynastic vision. Rather, they are part of a complex textual strategy that builds an alternative, potentially liberating mode of knowledge transmission.

Ariosto, scattering dynastic visions throughout the poem, constructs a revolutionary pattern of prophecy giving that operates as gift giving and, at least in principle, resists the court's logic of exchange. On one hand, Ariosto elaborates on the traditional portrait of Bradamante as an interpreter; on the other hand, he associates her with the figure of Melissa, coded as a gift giver throughout the poem, from the prophetic gifts of cantos III and XIII to the more conventional gifts of canto XLIII. By gendering the gift of prophecy and its reception as female, the poem reflects on the logic of the gift as an alternative to the logic of commerce, coded as male. Furthermore, the final vision of the poem is the work of a never-believed prophetess, Cassandra, a foil for the poet himself.[1] Presenting Cassandra as the last of the poet/prophet figures of the *Furioso*, Ariosto identifies with a true seer who was never believed, ambiguously pointing to the misinterpreted truthfulness of his poetry. In this instance, Ariosto seems to connect his poetry with the losing side of history and storytelling: the *Furioso* is a gift, freely given like Cassandra's tapestry, and like it potentially undervalued.[2] This model of gift circulation and knowledge transmission, which ties Bradamante, Melissa, Cassandra, and the poet himself, however, is not immune from contradictions and is predestined to failure within the poem itself.

The centrality of the gift to the exchange system of the *Furioso* and its oppositional connection to the concept of betrayal will become clearer as we probe the figure of Melissa in her double incarnation of good prophetess and evil sorceress. It is important, however, to introduce the model of gift circulation I am proposing for the *Furioso*.[3] The explicit presentation of the gift in the poem is connected with the poetic activity itself and with the tales told by the Mantuan host and the *nocchiero* to Rinaldo during his journey over the Po River (canto XLIII). In this episode, as Ronald Martinez has shown, the gift is framed in opposition to the commerce of tyranny.[4] The element of gender, however, comes powerfully into play in these episodes and changes our perspective on the gift. The gender of the gift givers and receivers affects the nature of the gift itself, and modifies the exchange process already at play in the act of giving.[5] If, as gift theory explains, no gift is immune from the expectation of reciprocity, the shift in gender eliminates at least the traditional use of female subjects as currency, which, as I have shown, is at play in narratives such as the story of Galiziella and the episode of Lidia.[6] Gifts given to women by women, like the prophetic knowledge Melissa gives to Bradamante, open a freer space than do exchanges between their male-dominated counterparts.

The second central element of the economy of the gift in the *Furioso* is *lack*. Ariosto implies that a true gift is, in reality, a demonstration of trust and therefore of vulnerability. As I will show, the poem is punctuated by references to the vulnerability of giving, from the motto that accompanies the *Furioso* from its first edition, *pro bono malum*, "evil in return for good," to the gift of prophecy given by Cassandra and repaid with evil. Furthermore, the equation between generosity and vulnerability emerges clearly from the stories of Rinaldo's Po journey, predicated on the combined oppositions jealousy/trust and commerce/gift. This interpretation of the gift is illuminated by Roberto Esposito's exploration of the gift as *donum* and *munus*.[7] Esposito sees the *munus* as the etymological root of the key term *communitas*, community, and explains it as a more specific version of the gift, *donum*. The *munus* is the gift that necessitates its due (*onus*) in exchange. At the root of the community, the *munus* signifies not the common good traditionally associated with the term "community"; rather, it founds it on lack and loss. This same lack, I argue, is at the core of Ariosto's theory of the gift, and what ultimately makes it vulnerable to betrayal. Betrayal is the opposite of the gift in Ariosto because, by putting trust in a constructed community, the poet and his characters (Bradamante more than anyone) become vulnerable to the violent act of those who refuse the logic of the community. I will now consider the strategies of reconfiguration of the prophetic moments in the *Furioso*, starting from the shift in gender, analyzing the figure of Bradamante as a privileged reader in the chivalric tradition, moving on to the homologies between poetic and prophetic modes, and finally exploring the construction of Melissa in relation to the economy of the gift in the poem.

THE GENDER SHIFT: BRADAMANTE AND THE DYNASTIC PROPHECY

The patrilineal transmission of prophetic knowledge is a central element of not just the classical tradition or the Dantean model. As we have seen in the previous chapter, the chivalric tradition of French import is firmly rooted in the same genealogical principle. In the *Cantari di Febus il forte*, the cruel knight Breus listened to the dynastic tale regarding the great knight of the past Febus, whose sad love story was one of the intertexts used by Ariosto to construct the story of Lidia. The opposite happens in canto III of the *Furioso*, where it is the lady-knight Bradamante who, after falling into the cave, becomes the addressee of the dynastic prophecies formulated by Merlino and by the sorceress Melissa.[8] The first gender reversal, then, concerns the betrayal: it is a man, Pinabello, who betrays a woman, Bradamante, and tries to kill her.[9] Once in the cave, the reversal continues at a different level: Bradamante finds herself in the position held by none other than the pious Aeneas in book VI of the *Aeneid*, whose genealogical vision is clearly a model for canto III.[10] Throughout the dynastic

narrative, Ariosto explicitly upholds the choice of Bradamante as
the preferred receiver of predictive discourse in the poem, and the
gender of Bradamante as addressee plays a pivotal role in shaping
the *Furioso* as a dynastic epic.

Bradamante's privileged relation to the prophetic discourse on
the future Este dynasty clearly emerges from the many textual occasions in which she is the sole receiver of predictions on the future
of her progeny. In canto III, Merlino and Melissa explain her destiny and introduce her to her descendants; in canto XIII, she asks
Melissa to add a description of her female progeny to the prophecy she has already received on her male offspring; at the Rocca di
Tristano, in canto XXXIII, she sees the Este depicted on the walls,
among other protagonists of fifteenth-century history. Finally, she
sees and understands the deeds of Cardinal Ippolito d'Este on her
wedding pavilion, in canto XLVI. If we compare these revelations
to those experienced by Ruggiero, we find that the poet gave Bradamante a more complete image of the Este lineage, destined to derive from her. Ruggiero sees the sculptures of the Fonte di Merlino
in canto XXVI, which illustrate the allegorical fight of European
princes against avarice; he then receives the prediction of the hermit, who had a vision of the destiny of the couple (canto XLI). A
few cantos earlier, Ruggiero and Bradamante together, along with
Marfisa, had listened to Atlante's prophetic voice revealing that the
knight and Marfisa are twins (canto XXXVI).[11]

In opposition to the events in the *Inamoramento de Orlando*,
where Ruggiero is not only aware of his destiny but also the primary bearer of prophetic dynastic wisdom,[12] the *Furioso* presents
the male character as shielded from knowledge. Bradamante is
completely involved in the prophetic discourse, to the point that
it becomes a defining element of her identity. After her victorious
fight with Atlante, the magician who tries to protect Ruggiero
from his fatal destiny, she mocks what she considers to be the
false prophecy of the old sorcerer:

Tu di' che Ruggier tieni per vietarli
il male influsso di sue stelle fisse.

O che non puoi saperlo, o non schivarli,
sappiendol, ciò che 'l ciel di lui prescrisse:
ma se 'l mal tuo, c'hai sì vicin, non vedi,
peggio l'altrui c'ha da venir prevedi. (*OF* IV, 35, 3–8)[13]

[You tell me that you are holding Ruggiero to ward off from
him the evil influence of his fixed stars. Either you cannot
know what the Heavens prescribed for him or, if you do
know, you have no remedy. But if you are blind to the evil
which immediately threatens you, must you not be blinder
still to the evil in store for another?]

Bradamante proclaims herself the bearer of truth, and of the true
prophecy regarding Ruggiero. Undermining Atlante's authority
as a seer and as a protector of Ruggiero's future, Bradamante
endorses a superior destiny, which she embodies and represents.
During a moment of despair, when she fears that Ruggiero might
not be returning to her, she curses her destiny and the prophecy
she has believed. The violence of her momentary refusal attests to
the strength of her conviction:

Di Merlin posso e di Melissa insieme
dolermi, e mi dorrò d'essi in eterno,
che dimostrare i frutti del mio seme
mi fêro dagli spirti de lo 'nferno,
per pormi sol con questa falsa speme
in servitù; né la cagion discerno,
se non ch'erano forse invidïosi
dei miei dolci, sicuri, almi riposi. (*OF* XXXII, 25)

[Merlin I can blame, and Melissa too, and so I shall for all
time: they used infernal spirits to show me the fruit of my
seed[14] so as to enslave me with this false hope alone. I cannot see why they did it, unless perhaps they envied me my
sweet, safe, blessed tranquillity.]

It is worth noting that Bradamante appropriates a vocabulary
and a semantic field—that of the seed, *il seme*—which is generally connected only to the male ancestor of a dynasty. The generative principle, the seed, is here associated with the female founder

of the genealogy. Renaissance culture seems consistently to treat this principle as male, at least when it comes to literary texts such as the *Furioso*.[15] Medieval and Renaissance treatises on medicine and natural philosophy discussed the problem of the existence of female "semen," or seed, and put its generative power into question.[16] Thomas Laqueur has argued, for instance, that the semen was not seen as male principle only, as it has become in modern culture.[17] The question of the different seeds, male and female, was heatedly debated in medical literature.[18] My point here is not to claim, anachronistically, that Ariosto transfers generative power from a male to a female character from a scientific point of view; rather, I would like to underline the fact that, from his literary standpoint, he treats the process of generation as indifferently pertaining to Ruggiero and Bradamante, and that he stages the latter more often than the former as the producer of the generative principle. This is a consequence of the gender reversal, and is bound to have consequences of its own on the representation of genders, and of dynasties.[19]

Bradamante's self-representation as the "seed bearer" is nothing more than a repetition of the invocation with which Melissa had greeted her during their first encounter in the cave:

> Favorisca Fortuna ogni tua voglia,
> o casta e nobilissima donzella,
> *del cui ventre uscirà il seme fecondo*
> che onorar deve Italia e tutto il mondo. (*OF* III, 16, 5–8)

> [May Fortune prosper your every wish, chaste and most
> noble Lady; from your womb shall spring the fruitful seed[20]
> destined to bring honour to Italy and to all mankind.]

In this second—and chronologically first—instance, the "seme fecondo" can be interpreted as the first descendant of Bradamante, her son Ruggiero, whereas the expression "i frutti del mio *seme*" seems to employ the word *seed* to refer to Bradamante's generative principle.[21] This is further demonstrated by the fact that, during the same episode of Merlin's cave, Melissa shows Bradamante her future son Ruggiero, referring to him as "dal

seme di Ruggiero in te concetto" (III, 24, 4),[22] and she uses similar words when she speaks to Ruggiero directly (VII, 60).[23] While
the Western, modern gendering of the term *seed* is completely different from its early modern connotation, it is worth noting that
the representation of Bradamante as a founder does not assume
the predictable semantic field of the maternal. It rather applies the
classical terminology used for the male founder.[24] The ambiguous
treatment of a woman's engendering potential, set in a context
that stages the woman as the receiver of a dynastic prophecy, creates an unprecedented image of female founder, which disturbs
the patrilineal narrative.

The rise of the female founder is parallel to the decreased importance of her counterpart, the male founder. Ruggiero is unaware, consistently represented as lacking knowledge about his
future and the destiny awaiting his progeny; he is exposed to direct allusions to the future Este family only once, when the hermit recounts his vision to him, trying to convince him to convert
to Christianity. Even in this instance, he has mediated access to
the prophecy, which was directed to him only through the inter-
cession of the holy hermit. Moreover, the hermit does not reveal
to him the entire content of his vision:

> Ma il santo vecchio, ch'alla lingua ha il morso,
> non di quanto egli sa però favella:
> narra a Ruggier quel che narrar conviensi;
> e quel ch'in sé de' ritener, ritiensi. (*OF* XLI, 67, 5–8)

> [He restrained his tongue, however, and divulged less than
> he knew—he told Ruggiero what it was suitable to disclose
> and suppressed what required suppressing.]

Ruggiero's knowledge is poor, in particular if compared to Bradamante's, as it clearly appears at the end of the poem, when the
court admires the nuptial tapestry woven by Cassandra:

> Le donne e i cavallier mirano fisi,
> senza trarne construtto, le figure;
> perché non hanno appresso che gli avvisi

che tutte quelle sien cose future.
Prendon piacere a riguardare i visi
belli e ben fatti, e legger le scritture.
Sol Bradamante da Melissa instrutta
gode tra sé; che sa l'istoria tutta.

Ruggiero, ancor ch'a par di Bradamante
non ne sia dotto, pur gli torna a mente
che fra i nipoti suoi gli solea Atlante
commendar questo Ippolito sovente. (OF XLVI, 98–99)

[The ladies and knights scrutinized the embroideries without understanding them, for they had no one to explain to
them that they represented what lay in the future; but they
took pleasure in admiring the beautifully wrought faces and
in reading the inscriptions. Alone Bradamante rejoiced in
secret: instructed by Melissa, she knew their full history. //
Although Ruggiero was not as well versed as Bradamant,
he still recalled how frequently Atlas had commended this
Hyppolytus among his descendants.]

Ruggiero has a vague recollection of a distant story, while Bradamante is the authorized bearer of prophetic knowledge. This
shift is prepared, both in the *Furioso* and in the late medieval
tradition that precedes it, by the construction of Bradamante as
a reader.

BRADAMANTE, THE INTERPRETER

To the reader who sees Bradamante perusing the images woven
in Cassandra's pavilion, the lady knight appears as the confident
possessor of the prophecy of her future.[25] Less visible, but potentially relevant to the reception of the *Furioso*, is the story of Bradamante's character in the popular epic tradition, where she is
often portrayed as an interpreter, an uncommon feature for a heroine, and even more so given her status as a female warrior, who
should be tied to active, rather than contemplative, behaviors.[26]

In the Bradamante (or rather, Bradiamonte) tradition that precedes the *Orlando furioso*, the heroine is already an interpreter of

texts and artifacts. In particular, in the *Cantari del Danese*, she falls in love with Ulivieri when she sees him in a fresco:

> Signor, sappiate che quella donzella
> avea inn una loggia figurato
> tutt'i dodici per*i*, per tale appella
> ciascuno istava in sul cavallo armato.
> E veggendo Ulivier*i* quella donzella,
> di bellezze gli parve più ornato:
> innamorossi della sua figura
> senza vederlo, la donzella pura. (*Cantari del Danese*, X 10)[27]

[And know, sires, that a fresco in a loggia of the damsel depicted the twelve peers, each of them in arms on his horse. And seeing Ulivieri in it, she found him most handsome, and she fell in love with his image without seeing him in person, the pure damsel.]

What seems to be the classic case of *amor de lonh*, the "love sight unseen" of the troubadours, is further complicated by the ambiguity of the text regarding the authorship of the fresco. The agency is unclear, but the letter of the text allows for the possibility that the painter of the fresco is Braidamonte herself. This hypothesis seems plausible in the light of another ambiguous passage in the *Danese*. Once Bradiamonte and her beloved Ulivieri finally meet, she compares him to her fresco:

> Mirandolo la donzella nel suo ciglio,
> nella mente gliel parve affigurare:
> al suo dipinto rendeva somiglio.
> Fra suo cuore disse: "Quest'è assai più bello
> che quello ch'i'ò dipinto, a ttale appello."
>
> Com'ïo dissi, questa dama avea
> in Babillonia, inn un suo palagio,
> tutti i dodici per*i* di gran nomea
> dipinti a sesta, con Gano malvagio
> e con altri baron*i* ch'ella volea.
> Affigurando Ulivier*i* molto ad agio
> a vegendolo dipinto così isnello,

innamorònne, sì lle parve bello. (*Cantari del Danese* XV,
19–20)

[Seeing his face, the lady seemed to remember him: he re-
sembled her painting. She thought to herself: "This one
is much more handsome than the one I have depicted, in
truth."// As I said, this lady had in a palace of hers in Baby-
lon all the famous twelve peers, along with the evil Gano
and other knights she wanted. Having painted Ulivieri at
ease and seeing him so pleasant, she fell in love with him, so
handsome was he.]

The ambiguous meaning of the auxiliary verb "to have" could
account for multiple meanings: Bradiamonte could have had the
peers painted for her, as she wanted, or she could have painted
them herself. In either case, she is an interpreter of the painted
text, and she uses it as a clue to foresee her future. In the *Mambriano*, Bradamante's authorial persona is unambiguous. She is
none other than the author of a chronicle, in which she described
the death of Galeano, king of Crete, literally crushed by a giant:

Pensa, lettor, come andò Galeano
Ruinandoli addosso una tal massa,
Ch'un monte si sarebbe fatto piano,
e ogni alta tor saria tornata bassa;
La cronica fu scritta in Montalbano
E puolla ancor veder chi di là passa,
E di sua man la scrisse Bradamante
Che vide ruinar quel gran gigante. (*Mambriano*, VIII, 34)

[Think, reader, what happened to Galeano when such a
load collapsed over him that would have flattened a moun-
tain and shortened every tall tower; the chronicle of this
event was written in Montalbano and is still visible today to
visitors. Bradamante, who saw the fall of that great giant,
wrote it in her own hand.]

Naturally the *Mambriano*, published posthumously in 1509, already builds on the figure of Bradamante as Boiardo had constructed it. It is nonetheless relevant that the heroine, who is now

completely Christianized, still bears the traits of the interpreter
she had in previous incarnations. Cieco places her as an author at
the center of a debate over "historical" verisimilitude:

> Riferisce costei, che nel cadere
> che fe' il gigante sopra il re di Creta,
> Tutto in terra il ficcò lui e 'l destriere . . .
>
> Tutti gli autori si accordano insieme
> Che Galeano fu morto e sepulto
> Da tal sciagura: e qui è alcun che freme
> Contra color che il voglion far sì occulto,
> Che mai non si trovasse, e per sì estreme
> Cose nacque in Parigi gran tumulto;
> Turpin, volendo poi tal question solvere,
> Scrisse che colui s'era fatto polvere.
>
> Ma poi che 'l non è articolo di fede,
> Tenete quella parte che vi piace,
> Che l'autor libramente vel concede.
> (*Mambriano*, VIII 35, 1–3, 36, 37, 1–3)

[She reports that, in falling over the king of Crete, the giant pushed both him and his horse deep in the ground . . . //
Every author agrees that Galeano was killed and buried by
this disaster: and some here are enraged against those who
want to obscure this so much, since he was never found, and
because of such extreme facts Paris was all a rage; and Tur-
pin, to solve this issue, wrote that Galeano had been pulver-
ized.// But since it is not an article of faith, believe, readers,
what you wish, for the author freely grants you this.]

Beneath Cieco's irony on the struggle for authority of the com-
pilers of medieval epics and chronicles, Bradamante keeps her
pseudo-authorial role in the tradition. In the *Furioso*, she writes
only letters, but is established as a privileged reader.[28] Her centrality to the prophetic moments of the *Furioso* begs for further
scrutiny. What are the stakes for Ariosto in choosing a female
character as the preferred audience for his central predictive sequences,[29] and what are the consequences of this choice for the

prophetic mode of the poem?[30] From these considerations we can
gain access to an alternative prophetic-poetic discourse, toward
which Ariosto gestures, in an attempt to construct a female genealogy. The impact of this gesture is visible only if we examine the
poem's self-representation and interpretation as a prophetic text.

THE POEM AS A PROPHECY

The dynastic theme has paid the price of an open scholarly opposition since the nineteenth century. Rajna, for instance, does not
hide his uneasiness about, or rather his utter disapproval of, the
prophetic sections of the poem. He briskly dismisses Bradamante's vision of her progeny with this observation: "Pur troppo qui
si passa ad una parte, di cui il poema farebbe a meno con molto
vantaggio" [Unfortunately, the part that follows could be omitted to the poem's greater advantage] (1990, 133). He completely
omits discussion of the catalog of Este ladies in canto XIII, ob-
serving that it is very boring (236). Finally, he groups together
the ekphrastic scenes of the poem, all of which contain premoni-
tions and predictions: the sculptures of Merlin's fountain (XXVI,
29), the frescoes in the Rocca di Tristano (XXXIII, 1), the stat-
ues seen by Rinaldo in the Lombard palace (XLII, 73), and finally Cassandra's pavilion, whose description is one of the last
scenes of the poem (XLVI, 77).[31] The encomiastic theme is for
the scholar insincere, artificial, and poetically disastrous. In an
ideological atmosphere that prized the autonomy of the artistic
endeavor as one of its finest qualities, together with originality,
Rajna saw the prophetic, dynastic scenes as the heavy burden imposed on poetry by its slavery to power.

The renewed interest in the *Furioso*'s prophetic mode stems
precisely from the grouping of prophetic visions as ekphrases, one
of the many underdeveloped insights of *Le fonti*. Ascoli has demonstrated that there is a textual link between the prophetic inspiration leading to divining objects like the prophetic tomb and the
sculptures, and the inspiration of the poet himself. While he further pursued the connection between the poetic and the prophetic

furor, Eric MacPhail has studied the prophetic scenes of the *Furioso* from a historical perspective, arguing that Ariosto writes at a "prophetic moment" in Italian history. The instability created by wars, invasions, and disorders created a need for a form of expression that would give at least a presumption of knowledge of the future.[32] Ariosto's response to this particular moment is, according to MacPhail, a movement that represents and at the same time undermines prophecy. Neither approach, while casting light on the nexus between the prophetic and the poetic, accounts for an important ideological premise of the poem: the position of women within a dynasty and their role in its foundation.

"DI CHE MERITO SON IO?" PROPHECY AND FEMALE GENEALOGY

The choice of Bradamante as the bearer of prophetic knowledge in the *Furioso* is part of a strategy aimed at undermining a form of knowledge and praise transmitted from men to men. The gender shift from the traditional pattern of prophetic transmission has a series of consequences for the text. When Melissa receives Bradamante in Merlin's cave, and she communicates to her that her visit had been expected for a long time, according to Merlin's prophecy, Bradamante modestly withdraws, inquiring as to her role:

> Stassi d'Amon la sbigottita figlia
> tacita e fissa al ragionar di questa;
> et ha sì pieno il cor di maraviglia,
> che non sa s'ella dorme o s'ella è desta:
> e con rimesse e vergognose ciglia
> (come quella che tutta era modesta)
> rispose: —Di che merito son io,
> ch'antiveggian profeti il venir mio?— (*OF* III, 13)

> [In bewildered silence (the daughter of Amone) listened to her words; such was her amazement, she was not sure whether she were awake or dreaming. And, modest by nature, "What is my worth," she asked with humble mien, "that prophets should be foretelling my arrival?"]

Bradamante's demeanor provides a successful hybrid of the modest lady ("vergognose ciglia") and of the humble pilgrim ("Di che merito son io?"). The most famous pilgrim of Italian literature, Dante, had questioned whether he was worthy of the supernatural journey prepared for him: "Ma io, perché venirvi? o chi 'l concede?/ Io non Enea, io non Paulo sono;—/ me degno a ciò né io né altri 'l crede."[33] Dante the pilgrim recoils from, and in so doing fully participates in, a literary tradition. He situates himself within the genealogical sequence of descents to the Otherworld, which Aeneas epitomizes. It is typical of this ambiguous and contested relationship to prophetic authority that Bradamante does not adopt a male persona—rather, she wonders what her worth, her "merito," might be.[34]

The arrival of such an unlikely pilgrim assumes even more significance if inserted in the poem's ambiguous treatment of the figure of Aeneas. When Astolfo visits hell and encounters the damned Lidia, he is told that Aeneas is suffering punishment for betraying a woman. It is unclear, in that episode, whether he is damned for the betrayal of Dido, or for reasons connected to the periphrasis that describe him ("chi turbò a Latin l'antiquo regno," OF XXXIV, 14, 4). As we have seen in chapter 3, however, his "piety" is challenged in relation to his disregard for the role of women in dynastic foundation. The destabilization of Aeneas as a founding father continues, even more openly, in the scene of Astolfo on the moon. After seeing the Parche who weave the threads of future lives, and admiring Time who destroys the memory of past lives, Astolfo listens to St. John the apostle, who delivers a famous speech on the power of literature to maintain forever the memory of few lives. As many critics have noted, St. John's discourse is a powerful critique of literature as encomium, one that almost nullifies the existence of the Furioso as a dynastic poem itself.[35] And once again Aeneas, the founder of the dynasty, is unmasked as a fraud:

> Non sì pietoso Enea, né forte Achille
> fu, come è fama, né sì fiero Ettorre;
> e ne son stati e mille e mille e mille

che lor si puon con verità anteporre:
ma i donati palazzi e le gran ville
dai descendenti lor, gli ha fatto porre
in questi senza fin sublimi onori
da l'onorate man degli scrittori. (*OF* XXXV, 25)

[Aeneas was not as devoted, nor Achilles as strong, nor Hector as ferocious as their reputations suggest. There have
existed men in their thousands who could claim preference
over them. What has brought them their sublime renown
have been the writers honoured with gifts of palaces and
great estates donated by these heroes' descendants.]

St. John exposes the deceiving power of poetry, and reveals its
political role.

A theme at least in part connected to this revelation is the fame
of women, and their relation to poetry: immediately after the
mention of Aeneas, the Apostle challenges the fame that derives
from victory, and that poets have sanctified as truth:

Omero Agamennon vittorioso,
e fe' i Troian parer vili ed inerti;
e che Penelopea fida al suo sposo
dai Prochi mille oltraggi avea sofferti.
E se tu vuoi che 'l ver non ti sia ascoso,
tutta al contrario l'istoria converti:
che i Greci rotti, e che Troia vittrice,
e che Penelopea fu meretrice. (*OF* XXXV, 27)

[Homer made Agamemnon appear the victor and the Trojans
mere poltroons; he made Penelope faithful to her husband,
and victim of a thousand slights from her suitors. But if you
want to know what really happened, invert the story: Greece
was vanquished, Troy triumphant, and Penelope a whore.]

Paradoxically, Ariosto suggests, the opposite of the story is closer
to the truth. In this vision, both famous men and famous women
celebrated by poets are undeserving, or less deserving than others
who never attained glory. Women, however, bear the burden of
an additional disadvantage: their stories have been told by men,

who have distorted reality and represented them unfairly. This is
the case that the narrating voice makes in the *proemio* to canto
XXXVII, in which he argues that, if women wrote poetry, they
would have the power to make their deeds eternal, and to defend
themselves from the accusations of male poets. This argument
puzzlingly turns into a praise of male poets who honor women in
their work, and ends in the tribute to the poet Vittoria Colonna,
a woman who celebrated her husband, not herself.[36]

Ariosto establishes the existence of two concurrent phenomena, which affect the making of human history by way of the
erasing agency of power: poetry sings the praise of the powerful,
men and women both, obliterating or condemning the weaker;
on the other hand, an essentially male poetry has silenced women
and unjustly blamed them. These two "systems of oppression"
coexist, and the poet does not seem to solve their possible contradictions. An example of the parallel, irreconcilable existence of
the two systems is to be found in the treatment Ariosto reserves
for his patrons.[37]

St. John's unveiling of the real value of poetry destabilizes Ariosto's praise of his patrons. If we reread one of the first mentions
the poet makes of Ippolito d'Este, we immediately perceive the
link between his glory and the (false?) praise granted by poets
like Ariosto himself: ". . . Ippolito, ch'a prose, a versi, a rime/
darà materia eterna in ogni idioma;/ la cui fiorita età vuol il ciel
giusto/ ch'abbia un Maron, come un altro ebbe Augusto" [Hip-
polytus . . . ; in every tongue many enduring works shall be written for him in prose and verse: and the just heavens have seen fit
that his own flowering era should have its Virgil, as Augustus
had before him]. (*OF* III, 56, 5–8).[38] Ariosto, in canto XXXV,
will criticize the power of poetry to give eternal life to unworthy
beings, using precisely the example of Virgil (who was unfair to
Dido, and praised Aeneas unjustly). The mechanism of dynastic
encomium seems to be broken: every word of praise the poem
contains seems to be inherently undermined and devoid of meaning. Ariosto's conception of the "systems of oppression," how-

ever, allows him the space to gesture toward sincere and reformed praise.

This limited movement against the insincerity of praise is even more visible in the treatment of another patron of Ariosto, Isabella d'Este.[39] Being the sister of Ariosto's two patrons, Ippolito and Alfonso, Isabella plays in the poem the role of the female patron, completing the image of the Este family in the poet's days. The longest and most elaborate description of Isabella is set in the context of the second prophetical discourse received by Bradamante: in canto XIII, Melissa mentions her among the female progeny of the future Este dynasty. Readers have been mystified by the fact that Isabella is presented as a defender of Penelope, who, as we have seen, is unmasked as a whore by St. John. While her husband Francesco Gonzaga can boast his military deeds, Isabella endorses the cause of the wife par excellence, Penelope:

> S'un narrerà ch'al Taro e nel Reame
> fu a liberar da' Galli Italia forte;
> l'altra dirà: —Sol perché casta visse,
> Penelope non fu minor d'Ulisse. (*OF* XIII, 60, 5–8)

> [If (Francesco) speak of the might he displayed on the Taro and in the Kingdom of Naples when he drove the French out of Italy, (Isabella will say)]: "Just by virtue of her chastity Penelope was no lesser mortal than Ulysses."]

Reading retrospectively the principles uttered by the Evangelist in canto XXXV, some critics have seen the words in Isabella's mouth as another hidden instance of denigration of the poet's patrons.[40] It is true that the lady, putting herself in the position of Penelope, identifies with her. It is also true, however, that Isabella assumes in this passage the role of defender of women, carving out for herself a position outside of poetry, and outside of the praise-blame dichotomy. But Ariosto is unable—or unwilling—to resolve the contradictions between the two "systems of oppression": he plays one against the other. The voice of silenced women rises against dominant men, and the unspecified voice of those who are forgotten by history reveals the falsehood of poetic praise.[41]

On one hand, as we have seen so far, Ariosto enacts a series of strategies that undermine the prophetic praise of the Este dynasty and challenge from within the concept of prophetic text.[42] On the other hand, Ariosto simultaneously tries to construct a prophetic, dynastic, and textual space endowed with different values, and concurrent with the first one. The second space, constructed around Bradamante, is not totally exposed to the threat of falsification because it performs a revolutionary act: it rebels against the "system of oppression" of male poets over female subjects. I do not wish to argue that this second form of prophetic circulation is immune from ambiguity. The construction of the prophetic sequences, however, proves the willingness on the poet's part to represent an alternative form of dynastic prophecy. This strategy is enacted in three principal ways, to which I will now turn: metatextual remarks, the character of Melissa, and finally the construction of a system of prophetic circulation that excludes men, favoring gift giving over commerce.

In canto XXXVII, the poet concludes his observations about the exclusion of women from poetry (and their consequent humiliation within it) with two octaves that provide a connection with the adventures of Bradamante and Marfisa, which he is going to narrate:

Donne, io conchiudo in somma, ch'ogni etate
molte ha di voi degne d'istoria avute;
ma per invidia di scrittori state
non sete dopo morte conosciute:
il che più non sarà, poi che voi fate
per voi stesse immortal vostra virtute.
Se far le due cognate sapean questo,
si sapria meglio ogni lor degno gesto.

Di Bradamante e di Marfisa dico,
le cui vittoriose inclite prove
di ritornare in luce m'affatico;
ma de le diece mancanmi le nove.

Queste ch'io so, ben volentieri esplico;
sì perché ogni bell'opra si de', dove
occulta sia, scoprir, sì perché bramo
a voi, donne, aggradir, ch'onoro et amo.
(*OF* XXXVII, 23–24)

[To conclude, ladies, every age has produced many a woman
meriting a legend, but the envy of writers has deprived you
of posthumous renown. This will no longer be true now that
you see to assuring your own immortality. Had the two sis-
ters-in-law been capable of this, their excellent deeds would
all be better known:// I mean Bradamante and Marfisa,
whose eminent victories I attempt to restore to the light,
though nine out of ten of them have slipped me by; those
that I do know I most willingly describe, for every good
action that lies hidden ought to be revealed, and besides, I
crave to please you, ladies, whom I love and respect.]

A discourse about truth has become impossible in the realm of
praise of the (male) patrons, too contaminated by the powerful
falsifications of poetry; Ariosto, however, presents it as still possible when the subjects are women. In two octaves, the poet concentrates the creation of a need for the world (that the deeds of his
protagonists be told) and the fulfillment of this need. The fiction
of recovering the feats of Marfisa and Bradamante is the reality
of poetic invention. Ariosto has chosen to prophesy the advent of
the Este dynasty from a female perspective, because it is the only
one allowing him to gesture toward the truth. He has created for
himself a space of freedom, immune from the rules and limitations he himself has established for encomiastic poetry in canto
XXXV. In this space, the character of Melissa takes center stage.

MERLIN REVISED: MELISSA FROM BETRAYAL TO GIFT

The new space for prophecy is realized, in the first place, through
the "gender reversal" mentioned earlier. In the next chapter, we
will discuss the prophecy regarding the Este women, another episode that is engaged in the construction of a female genealogy.

These strategies work both side by side with and in opposition to the patriarchal narrative that is at the center of the dynastic dynamics. Let us now go back to consider the first prophetic episode, the visit of Bradamante to the cave of Merlin, and concentrate on the figure of Melissa as it interacts with the traditional magical space. After a short introduction, the most important part of the prophecy—the conjuring of Bradamante's descendents—is not performed by Merlin, but by Melissa. She is the one who takes over the role that in the *Aeneid* was played by Anchises, Aeneas's father. In the Latin poem, dynastic knowledge was passed from father to son, establishing that genealogical continuity against which women represented a necessary accident, an unpleasant interference. In the *Cantari di Febus il forte*, a descendent of Febus recounted his ancestor's deeds to Breus, and a dynasty of knights, fathers and sons, was buried in the cave.[43] In the *Furioso*, the linear relation father/son is still strongly present: we have seen the importance of the father figure in the story of Lidia; the same passage quoted above, in which Bradamante asks why she is the object of predictions, introduces her as "d'Amon la sbigottita figlia." [Amon's daughter, bewildered] The relation Bradamante/Melissa, however, configures a different kind of communication. As opposed to the passing of knowledge as property from father to son in the Rocca di Tristano episode, the predictions made by Melissa are pure gifts, freely given by the prophetess to the listener.[44]

This focus on the gift is a consequence of the shift operated by Ariosto on the prophetic scene of canto III. The setting of the first prophecy, the cave of Merlin, is an original reelaboration of the cave in the *Febus*. In choosing Merlin, Ariosto followed a rich Italian tradition deriving from the French texts on the *Prophecies Merlin*. In Italy, the figure of Merlin was extremely popular, and it was very common to see him represented as a prophet as well as a magician.[45] The *Historia di Merlino* (also known as *Vita di Merlino*) was a very popular prose text printed for the first time in Venice in 1480 and possibly owned by Isabella d'Este.[46] It gave a succinct account of how the magician, madly in love with the Lady of the Lake, was entombed alive by her. His body decomposed, but his prophetic spirit remained alive, and continued prophesizing the future: "Madonna, disse Merlino, la carne mia sarà marza infino ad uno mese, et il spirito mio non fenirà di parlare a tutti quelli che venirano quivi" [My lady, said Merlin, my flesh will be rotten in a month, and my spirit will never stop speaking to those who will come around.][47]

Merlin's aim in preparing the sacred cave had been to provide an eternal shelter for himself and his beloved, in order to preserve their bodies in the interval of time before the Universal Judgment. The betrayal perpetrated by the Lady of the Lake epitomized the refusal of this gift. Entering Merlin's sacred cave, which is also the place of his death by betrayal, we are introduced to the double-edged nature of the economy of the gift in the *Furioso*. The contrary of the gift is betrayal: an act as free as gift giving, but opposite in nature. Both Merlin and Bradamante enter the cave as victims of betrayal; for both of them, betrayal turns into the gift of eternity. Merlin, even though his body is dead, maintains his spirit and his ability to predict the future; Bradamante gains access to the future of her lineage.

A discordant element disrupts the vision: the ghost of betrayal at the heart of the future dynasty strikes Bradamante:

e domandò: —Chi son li dua sì tristi,
che tra Ippolito e Alfonso abbiamo visti?

Veniano sospirando, e gli occhi bassi
parean tener d'ogni baldanza privi;
e gir lontan da lor io vedea i passi
dei frati sì, che ne pareano schivi. (*OF* III, 60, 7–8; 61, 1–4)

[(Bradamante) parted her lips to ask: "Who were those two we saw so abject between Hippolytus and Alfonso?// They sighed as they came, listless and sad was the look in their downcast eyes, and their brothers, I saw, walked at a distance from them, as though seeking to avoid them."]

The already mentioned episode of the treachery of Giulio and Ferrante d'Este, a dark and unclear mixture of love rivalry and political fight, ends the pacific vision of the future, echoing the words devoted by Virgil to the prematurely departed Marcellus, Augustus's nephew.[48] Melissa, whose face changes when she hears Bradamante's words, veils the truth and ends the vision. The sorceress is trying to shield the heroine from the foreshadowing of violent betrayal that seeps through the prophecy.

The sweetness of the gift always opens the way for the potentiality of bitter betrayal, as it almost contains betrayal in itself. A freely given gift, excluding commerce and exchange, may be soiled by betrayal, its constitutive opposite. In the episode in Merlin's cave, Melissa and Bradamante are at the center of a reversal of the betrayal that had brought both the magician of the Arthurian legend and the woman warrior of the poem into that space. Canto III is the poetic moment in which the prophecy is established as a gift, passed by female hands. The constitutive link between gift and betrayal seems to shed light on the long-discussed image that closes the *Furioso*, the emblem of the bees (see figure 4). The bees forced to flee their hive by the fire of the farmer, and the motto *pro bono malum* seem to represent precisely this concept. The bees' generosity in freely giving honey is repaid by the farmer's betrayal and his violence to the hive. The motto icastically represents the response to this free gift. Together, motto and emblem convey the message of the unstable, contradictory, yet courageous ideology of the gift.[49]

The connection between the emblem and this alternative model of prophetic circulation, embodied in the pair Melissa/Bradamante, has the advantage of anchoring the emblem itself to a specific aspect of the poem, rather than leaving it as a reflection on the truths of life in general or connecting it to an unlikely retort, on Ariosto's part, against his patrons.[50] The hypothesis seems particularly evocative if we consider the fact that in ancient Greek the name of the bee is precisely *melissa*. As I will further illustrate after an analysis of the features of Melissa as a literary character, it seems particularly apt that the name Ariosto chooses for the prophetess of his poem is not only that of a priestess who had nurtured Jove on Mount Ida during his

Figure 4. Emblem present in the first two authorized editions of the *Orlando furioso* (1516, 1521). Ferrara: Giovanni Mazzocchi, 1516. Courtesy of the Pierpont Morgan Library, New York. Purchased as the gift of Julia P. Wightman, 1972. PML 62432, fol. 2v

infancy, but also that of the honey bee, the protagonist of his emblem.[51]

STATTI COL DOLCIE IN BOCCA: MELISSA AND THE GENDERING OF THE PROPHECY

The sweetness of Melissa, the honeybee, is also the sweetness of the censorship she effects on the figures of the two traitors of the House of Este, Giulio and Ferrante, in canto III: "statti col dolcie in bocca," "keep the sweetness in your mouth." If the centrality of Bradamante as the recipient of prophecies is a revolutionary innovation of the *Furioso*, Bradamante's counterpart, Melissa, equally renews the prophetic moments of the poem. Melissa's character is so complicated and, at times, apparently contradictory, as to escape the finest analyses. Through her multifaceted persona, Ariosto establishes a new centrality of the dynastic prophecy and openly genders it female. Melissa is the principal "helper" or "donor" of the poem:[52] she magically summons the souls of the future Estes in canto III; she helps Ruggiero to free himself from Alcina's captivity in canto VII, and requests Logistilla's help for Ruggiero (X, 65); in canto XIII, she consoles Bradamante, instructs her on how to defeat Atlante and describes to her the most prominent women of the future Este dynasty; she comforts Bradamante again in canto XXXVIII, and interrupts a duel between Ruggiero and Rinaldo by assuming Rodomonte's features (XXXIX); she is the protagonist of the tale on jealousy and greed told by the Mantuan host to Rinaldo (XLIII); finally, she saves Ruggiero from death, and provides the nuptial pavilion woven by Cassandra for the wedding of Ruggiero and Bradamante (XLVI).

As Fredric Jameson has argued, the most useful element of Propp's model of interpretation is the *donor*, the *actant* who helps the protagonist to reach his goal.[53] The centrality of the donor, which depends on the figure's multifunctionality, becomes even greater in cases where it also embodies the functions of other actants, such as the protagonist.[54] This donor-cum-protagonist is a character that propels the action in a specific direction, by opening new paths in the interlaced narrative of the poem; moreover, the donor qualifies the action through his or her persona. In other words, the fact that a donor acts as a protagonist in other strands of the action adds meaning to the narrative moment of the helping or, in our case, of the prophetic gift.

Melissa is an exceptional example of such a multifunctional donor: her construction as a character is based on a constellation of functions, and the multiplicity of her roles is crucial to our understanding of the prophetical discourse of the *Furioso*. The elusive quality of Melissa could not find better representation

than in a painting by Dosso Dossi, an artist contemporaneous to
Ariosto, who worked at the Este court in Ferrara. The subject of
the painting, conserved at the Galleria Borghese in Rome (figure
5), is not even positively identified with Melissa.[55] The figure has
been interpreted as Circe after the transformation of the knights
into animals (hence the presence of the dog and the birds), or possibly Alcina. When the figure is identified with the Ariostan Melissa—Dosso is the author of a few paintings with Ariostan subjects—the episode critics see as the subject of the painting is still
a metamorphic one: the image could represent Melissa turning
the enchanted knights back into human shape, undoing Alcina's
magic, in canto VIII.[56]

It is also possible that this painting represents Melissa, and
precisely her actions in canto III of the *Furioso*. The magical writings on the ground, and the fact that she is enclosed in a magical
circle, in addition to the object in her right hand, which has a pen-
tacle on it, seem to all point to the following lines in the poem:

> Poi la donzella a sé richiama in chiesa,
> là dove prima avea tirato un cerchio
> che la potea capir tutta distesa,
> et avea un palmo ancora di superchio.
> E perché da li spirti non sia offesa,
> le fa d'un gran pentacolo coperchio;
> e le dice che taccia e stia a mirarla:
> poi scioglie il libro, e coi demoni parla. (*OF* III, 21)

> [Then she summoned the damsel to her in the pillared
> chamber, having first traced there on the ground a circle
> wide enough to encompass her if she lay down, and a palm
> wider still. And lest she be harmed by the spirits, she made
> a great pentacle to cover her. She told Bradamant to watch
> her in silence; then she opened her book and spoke to the
> demons.]

Despite the outdoor setting (Dosso's painting shows no trace of
a *chiesa*), the elements of magical conjuring are all present. One
might even be tempted to see in the little swirling figurines at the

top, left of the enchantress, the demons who make their ritual three turns as they enter Merlin's tomb ("entravan l'ombre, poi ch'avean tre volte/ fatto d'intorno lor debite volte").[57] On the other hand, there is in canto III no explanation for the strangely human dog and the two birds, one nested on the armor and one on the ground, who flank the sorceress on the viewer's left. Ultimately, the painting responds to its own logic and escapes the confinement to one specific subject.[58] In this sense, it mirrors the essence of the figure of Melissa, the elusive sorceress of the *Furioso*.

In the painting as in the *Furioso*, Melissa is ambiguously positioned at the intersection of many figures: the Sibyl, the sorceress (a third variation of the figure already embodied in Alcina and Logistilla), the female opponent of Atlante.[59] The *Furioso* adds an additional, crucial element: Melissa is the lover-sorceress from Mantua who brings about the ruin of Rinaldo's host (canto XLIII). This last element, which positions Melissa in a medieval context, is also the one that complicates her relation to the genealogical model of the gift as opposed to the model of commodity exchange.[60] The complex tale of canto XLIII may be summarized as follows. The Mantuan host narrates to Rinaldo the story of the magic vase ("il nappo fatato"), and recounts how he tragically lost his wife. Soon after he got married, the sorceress Melissa tempted him, encouraging him to betray his faithful wife. At his refusal, based on the determination to be faithful toward someone who is faithful to him, Melissa persuades him to test his wife. The "test" is realized through metamorphosis and gifts: the husband, turned by the sorceress into a Ferrarese youth, many times rejected by the wife, tempts her and wins her over with superb presents. Melissa accompanies him, disguised as a page. The episode is based on the alternation between gift and commerce, between generosity and avarice; the false suitor promises greater gifts: "E le dico che poco è questo dono/ verso quel che sperar da me dovea" [And I told her that this gift was trifling next to what she might expect from me] (*OF* XLIII, 37, 1–2). A few minutes later, when Melissa unveils his true identity, the husband accuses his wife of selling herself, and his honor: "Me

Figure 5. Dosso Dossi, *Circe* or *Melissa*. ca. 1531. Oil on canvas. Galleria Borghese, Rome, Italy. Courtesy of Scala/Ministero per i Beni e le Attività culturali / Art Resource, N.Y.

tradiresti dunque tu, consorte,/ quando tu avessi chi 'l mio onor comprassi?" [Would you betray me, wife, with one who would purchase my honor?] (*OF* XLIII, 40, 5–6). The *exemplum* ends tragically, with the wife leaving the Mantuan host, and fulfilling Melissa's prophecy by joining the Ferrarese suitor.

This episode, if not read in the context of the gift/commerce dichotomy that marks Melissa as a character, may seem puzzling for the good sorceress of canto III, to the point that the existence of two Melissas in the *Furioso* has been regarded as a plausible hypothesis.[61] This position, I would argue, derives precisely from that multifunctionality of the donor discussed above. In this episode, Melissa unveils the ambiguous nature of the gift. The name of gift is not enough to turn a bribe into a disinterested present: the exchange of women for commodities, and their participation in this market, is stigmatized in canto XLIII. Even more blameworthy is the blindness of the husband, who agrees to impose a price on his wife. Gifts are dangerous, Melissa says; prophecies can be tragic, and they might come true.

The paired story of Adonio and Manto, which closely follows in canto XLIII, is again centered around a gift: in this case, the sorceress Manto, saved by Adonio when she was in the form of a snake, agrees to help him conquer the heart of his beloved Argia, the wife of Anselmo. The conquest is realized though the gift of a magic dog, none other than Manto herself, who produces jewels and endless riches. The wife, "da doni grandissimi corrotta," seduced by enormous gifts, becomes Adonio's lover. The two stories are strictly linked in the poem, and they echo medieval tales of love, magic, and deceit. The *ponzela gaia*, the lady-snake protagonist of fifteenth-century *cantari*, who is the daughter of the Lady of the Lake, seems to be present to Ariosto's mind in elaborating the episode of the Mantuan host in canto XLIII.[62] By proximity with Manto, Melissa's connection with the Merlinian tradition is revitalized.

Melissa's name may provide another key to understanding her character: "Melissa" was the name given to ancient priestesses,[63] and Jupiter was nurtured by a princess of that name. I would like to stress again the importance of the name itself: *melissa*, the bee. This element connects the character to a collective society, opening the way for a reflection on Melissa and Bradamante as the "reformed" actants in a new genealogical discourse.[64] Moreover, the image of the bee recalls the emblem that opened the poem in 1516, connected to the poetics of the gift and the ideology of the poem as a prophecy.

In the sixteenth century, bees were still considered a female population ruled by a king, in keeping with the Aristotelian tradition, which will be challenged only a century later.[65] This is apparent in Giovanni Rucellai's poem *Le api*, an Italian rendition of book IV of the *Georgics*.[66] What also emerges from *Le api*, however, is the picture of a female society of chaste and fecund beings, who live in perfect community and generosity, and whose primary activity is gift giving:

Mentr'era per cantare i vostri doni
Con alte rime o Virginette caste,
Vaghe angellette de le herbose rive,
Preso dal sonno, in sul spuntar del l'alba
M'apparve un choro, de la vostra gente,
E da la lingua, onde s'accoglie il mele,
Sciolsono in chiara voce este parole. (*Api*, 1–7)

[As I was about to sing your gifts with lofty verses, oh chaste virgins, fair angels of the verdant slopes, taken by sleep, in the time near dusk, a chorus of your people appeared to me, and untied these words with their tongues, where they collect honey.]

The gifts of honey ("celeste don," heavenly gift, line 27) and wax are what the bees prepare, as foreseers of the winter to come ("divinatrici de gl'horribil tempi," line 488). Their activity is annihilated in the community: "riponendo in commune i loro acquisti" (line 490). From Virgil to Rucellai's poem, the bees have consistently been the symbol of a perfect community. The qualities of this society—female chastity, prudence, generosity, a sense of belonging to the community that verges into loss of distinction from it—have become, for Ariosto, an evocative counterpoint to the attempt to create a system of circulation immune from the venality of commerce.

These same qualities appear in the prophetic version of the character of Melissa, whose additional features in the *Furioso* are her investment in the dynastic theme, her metamorphic quality, and her prophetic ability. Not only does she transform into Atlante (canto VII) and into Rodomonte (canto XXXIX), but her role of lover in canto XLIII connects her almost inextricably to Manto, the lady-snake who founded Mantua. Both women have metamorphic qualities: Melissa turns into a boy servant in order to assist the Mantuan host, Manto is both a snake and a magical dog. These qualities find a parallel in a text that, intriguingly, features a character of the same name.

Il paradiso degli Alberti, composed around 1425 and set in 1389, is a dream-vision novel, modeled on collections of *novelle* like the *Decameron*, framed by a dialogue of intellectuals.[67] In the *Paradiso*, however, the frame of the stories exceeds its role as such, and the greatest part of the text is occupied by discussion of doctrinal problems (such as whether the love of the father is stronger than that of the mother or vice versa). The story of Melissa is one of the longest *novelle* in the text, and it involves a series of elements that make it particularly interesting when compared to the character of Melissa in the *Orlando furioso*. Melissa is the daughter of Odysseus, whose mother, also named Melissa, was a Trojan; she has kinship ties with Cassandra; she has metamorphic qualities (she is turned into a hawk); found by four knights, she is saved and turned back into a beautiful lady; after a long debate between gods over which one of the loving knights should become her husband, she is allowed to choose, and with him, she becomes the founder of the new city of Pratovecchio.

We do not know whether Ariosto knew the *Paradiso*. It is striking, however, that Ariosto and Gherardi both portray a figure who, invoking a female genealogy, refuses violence as the pillar of dynastic foundation. When the knights of the *Paradiso*, all madly in love with the transformed Melissa, decide to settle their argument in battle, the woman offers a heart-breaking monologue in which she laments her destiny, fatally linked to death and destruction. She recounts the deadly fate of her mother, predicted by her relative Cassandra ("ma Appollo già mai concedette che creduta si fosse," 100), and the complete destruction of Troy, and of her entire female lineage ("distrutto e finito ogni mio sangue materno," 101). She rebels at the idea that her beauty can be the cause of further violence, and she begs the knights to kill her, rather than resorting to bloody fights. Melissa's wish for the end of foundational violence will be realized by the gods in charge of deciding the dispute: Venus and Minerva ultimately make Melissa herself responsible for choosing her husband. Whether or not Ariosto had this figure in mind when creating Melissa the sorceress, the values she embodies have a predecessor in the female genealogy of the *Paradiso degli Alberti*. This is a mixed genealogy: classical and medieval readings of a foundational marriage tale coexist, conflict, and ultimately produce a reformed reading of history.

THE TRAFFIC IN WOMEN AND THE GIFT OF PROPHECY

The system of prophecies as gifts exchanged between women, threatened by betrayal, has its apotheosis with the appearance of Cassandra's pavilion. For Ruggiero and Bradamante's wedding, Melissa prepares "il maritale albergo," the nuptial chamber (*OF* XLVI, 76, 3). The last prophecy of the poem is another artifact, the wedding tapestry woven by Cassandra, depicting Ippolito's childhood and education. The story of the tapestry, and its circulation between empires, is told in octaves 80 to 84.[68] Cassandra had given it as a gift to her brother Hector.[69] After the conquest of Troy (described as "tradimento," betrayal), the pavilion then passed to Menelao, who gave it to Proteus, king of Egypt, in exchange for Helen. The subsequent "adventures" of the tapestry follow the usual path of wars and pillage. The three most important female figures of this process are Cassandra, Helen, and Bradamante. Melissa returns the object, a prophetic gift from a woman, the prophecy on the future of a dynasty, to its true addressee: Bradamante. Melissa's gesture, recalling the object in the realm of the gift, attempts to erase the system of commodity exchange it had been subjected to. Helen, the object of exchange par exellence, had been equated with the prophetic text as an object in the violence of genealogical history.[70]

The *Furioso* rebels against the traffic in women. It does so by representing women as gift exchangers and addressees rather than gifts themselves, by challenging the idea of the circulation of women (for instance, Angelica extracts herself from circulation, by choosing to follow her own desire), and by foregrounding the representation of poem-as-prophecy and of prophecy-as-poem in female hands. Ariosto portrays two competitive forms of genealogy: one is based on commodity exchange, the other on the gift. Depicting the gift system, Ariosto gestures toward a genealogical history free of violence. The text, however, denies the realization of this dream: Bradamante fully participates in the violence of the first set of values.[71]

CHAPTER FIVE

Externi Thalami

The Orlando furioso as a Nuptial Epic

Weddings between members of the ruling classes were crucial events in the life of a Renaissance city. Carefully planned and lavishly funded processions, festive rituals, and celebrations stretched over months in palaces, churches, and streets. Every aspect of the marriage, from the bride's abandonment of the paternal house to the encounter of the newlyweds in the nuptial chamber, was represented and ritualized.[1] The centrality of these events is clear in the artistic productions that accompanied them: hundreds of epithalamia, orations, and celebratory poems took their place alongside the paintings, frescoes, and objects manufactured specifically for these occasions.[2] Along with the display of wealth and power, the weddings were often occasions for (more or less staged) acts of violence and subversion. Often ritualized, these acts provided a controlled unleashing of social tensions, in the framework of the dichotomy of violence and stability characteristic of what Bakhtin has termed the carnivalesque. In February 1491, when the young Anna Sforza entered Ferrara as the bride of Alfonso d'Este, the populace destroyed the bridal canopy as soon as she left it and started climbing the stairs of the palace.[3]

In all their glory and tension, weddings, both real and ficti-
tious, populate the Italian literature of the Renaissance—high
and low, courtly and humanistic, in Latin and in the vernacular.
The wedding is a central feature of popular chivalric literature,
as we have seen in chapters 1 and 2; Maffeo Vegio's addition to
the *Aeneid* completed the Virgilian poem with the wedding of
Aeneas and Lavinia; Leon Battista Alberti's *Books of the Family*
discussed the institution of marriage; Francesco Barbaro praised
it in his *De re uxoria*; and most humanists wrote epithalamia and
nuptial orations. Ariosto himself, whose views on marriage are
famously the topic of *Satira V*, wrote an epithalamium for Lucrezia Borgia's wedding to Alfonso d'Este. In this context, it is surprising that the element of the wedding in the *Orlando furioso*
has so far received little critical attention.

The marriage of Bradamante to Ruggiero, one of the few plot
lines that runs through the fabric of the poem from beginning
to end, is among the least studied episodes of the *Furioso*, for a
variety of reasons.[4] Traditional studies of the sources have ne-
glected the dynastic theme altogether, because of its supposed
dependence on the Este patronage, and thus its ostensible insincerity.[5] More recent studies, focused on gender, have marginal-
ized or disregarded the marriage episodes, considering them as
the "closure" of private roles imposed on the female character,
Bradamante.[6] Both approaches identify the dynastic theme with
the linear epic plot, and the wanderings of romance with a pro-
gressive narrative force, be it an open destiny for women or the
creative fantasy of the poet (as opposed to the shackles of patronage). Textual evidence suggests, instead, that the wedding at
the core of the dynastic narrative may be a site of tension in the
poem. Very much like the historical narrations of weddings in
Renaissance Ferrara, this narrative theme in the poem occasions
both celebrations of and challenges to political power. The *Furioso*'s wedding attempts to represent the foundational moment
of marriage as both the pacification and the renewal of tensions.
Set in the context of the Este marriage politics and of Ariosto's
own poetic strategy, the institution of marriage is a site of tension

(both in society and in literature), a "strategy of containment" that is always showing the signs of the containment itself.[7]

In the preceding chapters, I have examined a series of strategies that Ariosto deploys in the construction of his poem, and that demonstrate a particular tension in the treatment of gender as a component of the genealogical moment. The woman warrior that Ariosto invents bears the traces of a literary genealogy of gender, and enters the dynastic narrative as a political actor precisely because of this past, at once displaced and displayed. The violence of the dynastic marriage as a political strategy is the central theme of the infernal episode examined in chapter three. The bestowing of the dynastic prophecy in female hands, as I showed in chapter four, seems to offer a temporary way out of the economy of exchange imposed on both art and love. In this final chapter, these three themes converge in the analysis of exogamy as a crucial element of the politics of marriage, both historical and textual. After situating the *Furioso* in the context of the representation of Renaissance marriage politics, I will analyze how the poem reflects on exogamy and its implications for women. I will focus in particular on a series of additions to the 1532 edition, and on fragments of text that Ariosto did not include in the final edition—possible traces of an unrealized project of expansion of the poem.

EXOGAMY, HYPERGAMY, AND THE POLITICS OF MARRIAGE

Exogamy, the principle of marrying outside the circle of relatives and close acquaintances, was endorsed by the Church throughout the Middle Ages.[8] As Saint Augustine had claimed, exogamy was a means to limit discord and attain peace within and among communities. The alliance contracted through marriage was one of the founding principles of society, for the peasant as well as the lord.[9] Particular case studies suggest that this general assumption needs to be complicated and applied with caution to each local area. Anthony Molho, for instance, in his study of late medi-

eval Florence, argues that a restricted circle of powerful Florentine families practiced endogamous intermarriage for centuries.[10]
Owen Hughes suggests that other cities, such as Genoa, had a
very high rate of endogamous unions, while cities such as Pal-
ermo and Venice exemplified exogamous tendencies.[11] Regional
differences remain largely unstudied; a comparative study of various urban locales would provide important insights into life and
culture in Italy between the Middle Ages and the Renaissance.

Whereas there is no analysis of marriage practices in the town
under Este rule, substantial critical attention has been devoted to
the marriage politics of the Este family itself, especially during
the fifteenth century.[12] Under the influence of Duke Ercole (1471–
1505), the Este managed to build a strong net of political alliances
sealed by marriages.[13] The wedding of Ercole himself to Eleonora d'Aragona, daughter of an emperor, is but one example of
a pervasive strategy to attain control over other lineages. In this
sense, the Este lineage is based on hypergamy, inasmuch as the
family tried to build alliances through external connections, and
to extend its control over neighboring areas.[14] Weddings served
the purpose of supporting an aggressive expansionist politics.

Kinship bonds were extremely important and subject to enormous social pressure under the rule of Ercole d'Este, as demonstrated by the sustained production of genealogical works during his reign.[15] If this is true of Ercole in particular, all of the
Ferrarese dynastic texts partake of a similar strategy of self-representation and self-fashioning by the House of Este in relation
to kinship bonds and blood ties.[16] It appears clear that the most
vulnerable subject in this economy of marriage were the women
located "in between" their roles as daughters and sisters and
their roles as wives. After marriage, a wife might contend with
conflicting loyalties: to the family of origin and to the acquired
family. This would have been particularly true in the case of
the court of Ferrara, where the hypergamic tendencies put the
family in competition with the most important Italian and European lords.

EXTERNI THALAMI: THE RHETORIC OF EXOGAMY

An aggressive pursuit of marriage alliances, exogamic marriages, and a tendency toward hypergamy define the politics of marriage of the Este dynasty between the second half of the fifteenth century and the first half of the sixteenth century. These elements render marriage a site of definition and anxiety, the crucial and problematic moment of self-representation of the dynasty.[17] Ariosto participated in this cultural tension, as he shows in the little treatise on matrimony contained in his *Satira V*, where the need to marry "within one's station" recurs in Ariosto's suggestions to his friend Malaguzzi. The fear of illegitimacy, the Satire contends, sometimes makes men marry below their station, bringing about social disruption:

> Quel che acerbi non fér, maturi e mézzi
> fan poi con biasmo: truovan ne le ville
> e nelle cucine anco a chi far vezzi.
> Nascono figli e crescon le faville,
> et al fin, pusillanimi e bugiardi,
> s'inducono a sposar villane e ancille,
> perché i figli non restino bastardi.
> Quindi è falsificato di Ferrara
> in gran parte il buon sangue, se ben guardi;
> quindi la gioventù vedi sì rara
> che le virtudi e li bei studi, e molta
> che degli avi materni i stili impara. (*Satire*, V, 61–72)[18]

[What these great men abstain from when they are green they do with shame when they are ripe and rotten. They find in huts and kitchens girls to fondle. Sons are born and sparks begin to fly, and at last, faint-hearted and false, they are persuaded to marry country girls and chamber maids, so that their sons will not be bastards. And this is why, if you take a close look, a great part of the good blood of Ferrara is adulterated. This is why you see so few among the younger generation who put their minds to virtue and the beautiful studies, and so many who adopt the style of their maternal ancestors.][19]

If the corruption of the good Ferrarese blood is a danger, however, the other danger is the foolish desire for social mobility:

> Non cercar chi più dote, o chi ti porte
> titoli e fumi e più nobil parenti
> che al tuo aver si convenga e alla tua sorte;
> ché difficil sarà, se non ha venti
> donne poi dietro e staffieri e un ragazzo
> che le sciorini il cul, tu la contenti. (*Satire*, V, 118–23)

> [Do not look for the wife who will bring you the richest
> dowry, with titles and vanities, and relatives more noble
> than befits your rank; because it will be hard for you to
> please her unless you give her twenty dames in waiting to
> follow her about, and footmen, and a boy to air out her posterior (131).]

In the *Satire*, Ariosto constructs his authorial persona around direct, no-nonsense advice like that given above. This is only one of the aspects of the complex textual attitude Ariosto displays toward dynastic marriage. A different narrative voice characterizes the epithalamium Ariosto wrote for the wedding of Alfonso d'Este and Lucrezia Borgia in 1501. After two broken marriages, haunted by the notoriety of her family, Lucrezia entered Ferrara in 1501 as the bride of Alfonso, one of Ariosto's patrons.[20] Ercole I, Alfonso's father, had decided to found on this marriage his alliance with Pope Alexander VI, disregarding all the defects of the bride: besides being the daughter of a pope, she had lost both her brother Juan de Gandia and her second husband Alfonso of Aragon in mysterious and violent circumstances; additionally, the brutal politics deployed by her brother, the infamous Duke Valentino, were a source of terror across the Italian states.

Following a widespread custom of Renaissance humanism, Ariosto wrote a Latin epithalamium to commemorate the wedding, modeling the oration after a poem by Catullus, Carmen LXII, in which two choruses alternate in singing about the wedding.[21] In Catullus's text, however, the choruses comprise a group of maidens, companions to the future bride, who lament that their friend is leaving innocence and lightheartedness forever, and a group of young men, who praise the values of marriage. Ariosto's poem explicitly states its political meaning: the Ferrarese people compose the group in favor of the wedding, while the Romans sing against the ceremony, which will deprive them of Lucrezia. The theme of exogamy is treated here in its double nature: as alliance and conjunction, and as dislocation and betrayal. Throughout the poem, the Romans define the wedding as a violent mutilation of their state, perpetrated by a "foreign" agent: "Quid enim nisi triste efferre paramus,/ culmine deiecti tanto, cum te/ *externi invideant thalami*, Lucretia, nobis?" (25–27) [What song can we prepare to sing, if not a sad one, since we were thrown from such a high state, when foreign nuptials steal you from us, Lucretia?]. This is the first allusion to the foreign nuptials, the external intervention that changes the future of the Romans. Ariosto's phrase, "externi thalami," is the Virgilian expression used in the Sybil's prophecy to Aeneas: "Causa mali tanti coniunx iterum hospita Teucris/ externique iterum thalami." (*Aeneid*, VI, 93–94) [The cause of such evil for the Trojans will be, once again, a foreign bride, once again foreign nuptials]. Not coincidentally, this Virgilian passage is the source of the expression attached to the damned Lidia in canto XXXIV, "causa mali tanti." The fact that Ariosto's nuptial lexicon is Virgilian is not surprising; what is noteworthy, though, is that the wedding occasions the examination of one specific conceptual knot, that of exogamy ("externi thalami") and the associated guilt preassigned to the bride ("causa mali tanti"), as we have seen in chapter 3.

In Ariosto's epithalamium, the Roman chorus laments the loss of Lucretia in these terms two more times, on both occasions representing the marriage as a loss through the vocabulary of stealing, snatching, seizing:

O septem colles, Tiberis pater, altaque prisci
imperii monimenta, graves intendite luctus!
Nuper Atestini fratres, proceresque propinqui,
Hercules iuvenis patria quos misit ab urbe,
quod pulchri fuerat vobis impune tulere,

externoque decus vestrum iunxere marito.
Dure Hymen, Hymenaee, piis invise Latinis! (87–94)

[Oh seven hills of Rome, oh father Tiber, oh tall monuments
of the Old Empire, do watch our horrible losses! Only a little time ago the Este brothers and the noble relatives that the
Herculean youth sent from the fatherland effortlessly took
from you what you had of beauty, and united your glory to
a foreign husband. Oh cruel Hymen, god of marriage, hateful toward the pious Latins!]

In this passage, the lexicon of blood relations ("fratres," "propinqui," "urbe patria") is mixed and opposed to the vocabulary
of violence and loss ("graves luctus," "impune tulere"). The ambiguity of the marriage contract is all contained in the emblematic expression "externo marito," where the kinship tie is defined
as foreign, imposed, unfamiliar, and threatening. The apex of
drama is reached toward the end of the song, where the Romans
represent marriage as a violent act of separation:

Dure Hymen, Hymenaee, piis invise Latinis,
qui potes e lacrimis miserorum auferre parentum
ardentique viro trepidam donare puellam,
et procul a patria longinquas ducere ad oras!
Dure Hymen, Hymenaee, piis invise Latinis! (115–18)

[Oh cruel Hymen, god of marriage, hateful toward the pious
Latins, you who can seize the trembling girl from the tears
of her parents, and give her to the desiring husband, and
take her far away, to lands far from her fatherland! Oh cruel
Hymen, god of marriage, hateful toward the pious Latins!]

Suffering and distance ("lacrimis," "procul," "longinquas") characterize the realization of the wedding in the words of the Romans. The two male figures, the husband and Hymen, the Greek
god of marriage, are the only ones who act and desire; the virgin
and her parents are represented as passive objects by the Romans.
To them, the Ferrarese reply by inverting the representation:

Blande Hymen, iucunde Hymen, ades, o Hymenaee,

qui cupido iuveni cupidam sociare puellam
tendis, qui tacitos questus miseraris amantum,
qui nympham haud pateris viduo tabescere lecto,
longinquasque urbes geniali foedere iungis.
Blande Hymen, iucunde Hymen, ades, o Hymenaee.
(120–25)

[Sweet Hymen, joyful god of marriage, do come, oh Hymen, you who want to unite the desiring youth to the desiring virgin, you who have compassion for the silent lament
of lovers, you who do not allow that a virgin waste away in
a lonely bed, and who join distant towns with a marriage
pact. Sweet Hymen, joyful god of marriage, do come, oh
Hymen.]

The Ferrarese account posits desire equally on both sides ("cupido
iuveni," "cupidam puellam"). Moreover, the wedding is openly presented as an alliance ("sociare"), and the distance between the cities,
expressed with the same adjective, "longinquus," that was used by
the Romans to describe the heartbreak of loss, here reinforces the
bond between different "patriae." The chant of the Ferrarese presents the marriage as an alliance, and glosses over the Romans' allusions to violence with the affirmation of mutual desire.

Naturally, the epithalamium is a political act of praise of the
Este and Ferrara. One of the dominating themes in the poem is the
ascent of Ferrara to power, paired with Rome's descent from impe-
rial glory to decadence. The transfer of the woman, Lucrezia, from
Rome to Ferrara marks the reversal of fortune of the two towns,
both symbolically and physically. Rome, once superb and glorious, decorated by temples and palaces, is now in ruins; Ferrara the
humble, once poor and dominated by wilderness, is now splendid
with palaces and walls, streets and bridges: it thrives in the glory
of studies and new technologies.[22] The debate lingers on the beauty
of the Roman and Ferrarese women: the Romans insinuate that
Lucrezia's beauty will obscure that of the humble Lombard virgins (126–31); the Ferrarese reply that, as the light of dawn makes
beautiful things visible, adding to their beauty, so the beauty of the
Roman Lucrezia will illuminate the virgins of Ferrara, "longum

incultae tenuique in honore" (133) [uncultured for a long time, and
for long neglected]. The poem domesticates the threats of exogamy
by erasing violence and insisting on alliance, and by pointing to
civic and domestic concord as the goal and result of the union.

Ariosto attains these goals by manipulating the genre of the epithalamium. As D'Elia has shown, epithalamia were keen on exalt-
ing the political virtues of marriages. Their treatment of the violence
underlying the alliance, however, is highly ambiguous. In particular,
D'Elia quotes two examples of orations that use classical episodes of
violence as foundational moments in praise of marriage. The rape
of the Sabines, in one instance, is presented as the pretext of nuptial
alliance. Like the rape of Lucrezia is a prelude to the birth of the Roman republic, the violence against the Sabines leads to, and is obscured by, the peace between Latins and their neighbors: "Haec sane
res est quae plerumque hostes facit amicos. Hoc enim coniugali fe-
dere Romanis Sabini ob nuptas mulieries infestissimi una die hostes
amici fiunt" [Marriage is such that in most cases it turns enemies
into friends. Through the conjugal pact, by reason of the marriages
with their women, the most inimical Sabine became allies of the Romans overnight].[23] Christiane Klapisch-Zuber has already noted the
violence underlying alliance, and therefore nuptial ceremonies, in *Li
nuptiali*, the treatise on marriage written by a sixteenth-century Roman noble, Marco Antonio Altieri:[24]

> For our humanist, . . . many nuptial ceremonies have no
> other meaning than that of perpetuating the memory of the
> legendary Roman origins: the violence of the founding of
> Rome, built on a murder and on marriage by force, but also
> on the peace that ensued. References to that ancient legend
> return constantly to his pen: "Every nuptial act recalls the
> rape of the Sabines"; "the least gesture in the espousal cer-
> emonies puts us in memory of the rape of the Sabines; when
> someone takes his wife by the hand, he is showing that he is
> using violence on her." (1985, 255)

Although Altieri's insistence has a slightly obsessive quality, and
although he elides the fact that a Roman humanist might have

been more inclined than a Ferrarese toward references to the Roman past, he succeeds in capturing the way in which the violence at the core of the marriage alliance remains for Ariosto a nucleus of meaning and ambiguity—alluded to, hinted at, displaced, erased, and displayed. Ariosto, in the *Orlando furioso*, reinterprets this violence so as to reflect on exogamy and its effects on female figures.

CONFLICTING GENEALOGIES

Lineage, in the *Orlando furioso*, is not openly debated; yet it surfaces from time to time, indicating a latent concern with legitimacy. Certain figures activate an anxiety over legitimacy anxiety, such as Guidone, a knight who participates in a series of adventures side by side with Marfisa. In the medieval and early modern Italian tradition, Guidone is the bastard son par excellence, the offspring of Rinaldo and Queen Ancroia, the fierce warrior queen of a popular group of *poemi cavallereschi*.[25] In the *Furioso*, the arrival of Guidone on the scene generates narratives of illegitimacy. In canto XX, Guidone recounts the origin of the law of the island of the "femine omicide," linking it to the Trojan War and the resulting birth of many bastards.[26] These illegitimate sons, however, who ultimately cause the unnatural and cruel custom of the "femine omicide," are socially less acceptable than Guidone himself. Whereas Guidone is a bastard on his mother's side, these Greek men were maternally legitimate and paternally illegitimate.[27] Predictably, Guidone can claim brotherhood with Rinaldo and be accepted into the lineage, while the Greek bastards of canto XX are rejected and expelled.[28]

Control over generation and lineage are at the core of one of Bradamante's greatest crises in the poem, her jealousy of Ruggiero's supposed affair with Marfisa. Her predicament, in fact, originates with a communication that presents the two alleged lovers in terms of their generative power. The Gascon knight who gives Bradamante the false news about Ruggiero represents his marriage to Marfisa as a "pagan victory": their union is bound to create "una razza d'uomini da guerra/ la più gagliarda che mai fosse in terra" (*OF* XXXII, 31, 7–8) ["a race of warriors the likes of which were never known"].[29] Bradamante's despair brings her to the verge of committing suicide, but the consciousness of descending from a great lineage ("tant'alto lignaggio") prevents her from succumbing to this temptation (*OF* XXXII, 44, 7). She responds to the threat to her new lineage, the one she is supposed to found together with Ruggiero, by gathering strength from her *old* lineage, the one she belongs to before getting married. Bradamante's appeal to the lineage of her father is emblematic of the double status of many women in the *Furioso*: they belong to two different houses, and they are divided between competing loyalties.

It is not by chance that Melissa's presentation of the female members of the House of Este, in canto XIII, is similarly divided between daughters and the wives. For the lineage to function properly, the loyalty of both categories is needed:

> Da te uscir veggio le pudiche donne,
> *madri* d'imperatori e di gran regi,
> reparatrici e solide colonne
> de case illustri e di domini egregi;
> che men degne non son ne le lor gonne,
> ch'in arme i cavalier, di sommi pregi,
> di pietà, di gran cor, di gran prudenza,
> di somma e incomparabil continenza. (*OF* XIII, 57)

> [I can see among your issue chaste women, the mothers of emperors and kings, the solid pillars and restorers of illustrious houses and splendid realms. For all their feminine attire, they, no less than the knights in their armour, shall be endowed with eminent virtues—mercy, courage, prudence, matchless continence.]

Melissa then goes on to praise Isabella and Beatrice d'Este, as well as all the others, who will "rule the splendid dynasties of Italy" (*OF* XIII 65, 7). In this phase, the text points to expansion, to the spreading of Este rule through its daughters. It is imperative that

Isabella, Beatrice, and all the others maintain their identity as Este once they become mothers, the "pillars" of other lineages.[30]

No symmetrical rule can be derived from this principle for the conduct of women who marry into the Este family: for them, it is necessary to embrace the Este dynasty as their own. And the women who marry in appear to be, at least numerically, more important than those who were born Este. Melissa, in fact, describes many more wives than daughters in canto XIII.[31] She emphasizes their affiliation to the House of Este, as opposed to their dynasties of origin, by including their many sons and daughters, who belong to the Este by birth. The references to their provenance, on the other hand, are consistently downplayed. The Este need expansion abroad, but even more consolidation at home; they need blood ties to remain strong against competing family kinships and marriage ties to become stronger than blood. The enormous pressure of these priorities falls on women, and on women only, because only women possess this double identity: no description of the Ferrarese lineage includes males related by marriage only. Even in nonprophetic moments, the support of the dynasty is central to the identity and function of female characters. For example, in canto XLII, all women patrons apart from the mysterious last lady (possibly Alessandra Benucci, the poet's lover) are related to the Este dynasty, either by marriage or by descent.

The ambivalent position of women within the dynasty becomes particularly evident in one of the additions of 1532. Vittoria Colonna is an emblematic figure, placed between her lineage of descent and her marriage lineage:

Vittoria è 'l nome; e ben conviensi a nata
fra le vittorie, et a chi, o vada o stanzi,
di trofei sempre e di trionfi ornata,
la vittoria abbia seco, o dietro o innanzi.
(*OF* XXXVII, 18, 1–4)

[Victoria is her name—appropriate for one born amid victories, one who, (whether she goes or stays,) is preceded or followed by victory, her constant companion, and is ever adorned with triumphal trophies.]

In the name of Vittoria, the poet finds both her descent and her marriage: both lineages are symbolized by victory. Within the name Vittoria Colonna, Ariosto inscribes the two functions of the ideal female subject in an exogamic structure of society; we can also observe that "colonna" is the term the poet uses in canto XIII to describe the Este descendents. Her case is even more interesting than those of the Este women, because Ariosto positions her between two lineages and among women who committed suicide for their husbands while paradoxically enjoying the eternizing power of poetry (*OF* XXXVII, 19–20). After "renaming" Vittoria as a go-between, caught between two lineages, Ariosto makes her the champion of her dead husband's name: "e che per lei sì 'l nome tuo rimbombe,/ che da bramar non hai più chiare trombe" [and that (through her your name has such resonance) that you need crave no shriller trumpet]. Vittoria's invincibility is akin to that of Bradamante, who is equally torn between conflicting loyalties. Bradamante, as the founder of the family, is invested with this double duty, and forced to negotiate; in the episode of the Rocca, she puts this ability to negotiate to good use.

POSITIONAL SUBJECTS: BRADAMANTE
AT THE ROCCA DI TRISTANO

The Rocca di Tristano episode is a reflection on identity. In this episode, as well as in the related episode of the messenger Ullania, both additions of the 1532 edition, Ariosto completes his construction of Bradamante as a female founder. Throughout the poem, Bradamante has generated a series of references to medieval texts, which outfit her as a warrior woman, channel her relation to prophetic knowledge, and establish her role within the generative process, as we have seen in the previous chapters. This medieval romance fabric, connecting Bradamante to and at the same time freeing her from the savage giantesses and Amazons of the past, prepares us for the reflection on identity that we witness in the Rocca di Tristano. It is the double identity of Bradamante that is at play in this episode, as well as her ability to manage the conflicting loyalties that originate from this double identity.

The Rocca episode has not received the attention reserved for other additions, such as the Olimpia episode, or the final plot of Ruggiero and Leone.[32] Recent studies have highlighted the relevance of the episode for Renaissance gender distinctions and gender identity, and this is clearly an important point of departure for the reconsideration of this part of the poem.[33] If we take into account Bradamante's roles and position throughout the *Furioso*, we can conclude that the episode involves a reflection on the conflicted nature of female identity, in both gendered and political terms. The interpretation of identity as the layering of different strata, which marks a series of (self-)representations of Bradamante, can help us to understand her performance at the Rocca. When the heroine meets Brunello in canto III, she is careful to conceal her identity:

> La donna, già prevista, non gli cede
> in dir menzogne, e simula ugualmente
> e patria e stirpe e setta e nome e sesso;
> e gli volta alle man pur gli occhi spesso. (*OF* III, 76, 5–8)

> [The damsel, forewarned, dissimulated just as well in her account of her nation, family, religion, name, and sex. And she darted frequent glances at his hands.]

The order of elements composing her personality is not coincidental; Bradamante's first trait is her "patria," her fatherland. In the construction of what Bradamante is, name and sex are only the least important, even marginal elements.[34] Identity is social: as the Rocca di Tristano episode will confirm, sex does not matter; what matters is the position the subject assumes. When Bradamante loses her hair because of a wound, Ricciardetto argues, all signs of difference but sex and name have disappeared:

> Ma poi ch'un giorno ella ferita fu
> nel capo (lungo saria a dirvi come),
> e per sanarla un servo di Iesù

a mezza orecchia le tagliò le chiome,
alcun segno tra noi non restò più
di differenzia, fuor che 'l sesso e 'l nome.
Ricciardetto son io, Bradamante ella;
io fratel di Rinaldo, essa sorella. (*OF* XXV, 24)

[But one day she was wounded in the head (it would take
too long to tell the story) and to heal her a servant of God
cut her hair till it only half covered her ears. After that there
was nothing to distinguish us beyond our sex and name: (I
am) Richardet, (she is) Bradamant; (I am brother, and she
sister) to Rinaldo.]

The poet's words on these occasions do not explicitly define gender roles; what they do, in fact, is point to the pivotal role of lineage for self-definition. Women are political subjects: hence the
importance of negotiation for these subjects divided between two
different lineages, split between competing loyalties and senses of
belonging.

The episode of the Rocca can be divided in four sequences: the
encounter between Bradamante and Ullania, the custom of the
castle (only the most beautiful lady present and the most valiant
knight present can be guests of the castle), Bradamante's manipulation of the custom, and the prophetic paintings.[35] The plot is
linear: Bradamante decides to leave her palace because Ruggiero
has kept her waiting for long weeks, and because she has heard
that he is in love with Marfisa. Crazy with jealousy, she meets
Ullania and her companions, on a mission to deliver a shield to
Charlemagne. The shield is a gift from the queen of Iceland, to
be assigned by Charlemagne to the most valiant knight of his
court, who will be destined to marry the queen herself. The shield
thus introduces the principles of choice and competition, foreshadowing the competitive element of the custom of the castle:
this object, belonging to the most beautiful lady in the world ("di
beltà sopra beltà miranda,/ dal cielo mai, se non a lei, concessa,"
XXXII 52, 3–4), must be given to the best knight ("il miglior
cavallier"):

Ella, come si stima, e come in vero
è la più bella donna che mai fosse,
così vorria trovare un cavalliero
che sopra ogn'altro avesse ardire e posse:
perché fondato e fisso è il suo pensiero,
da non cader per cento mila scosse,
che sol chi terrà in arme il primo onore,
abbia d'esser suo amante e suo signore. (*OF* XXXII, 53)

[As she regards herself—and rightly so—as the most beautiful woman who ever lived, she wishes to find a knight who
is unsurpassed for courage and strength. She is rooted and
fixed in her intention (which is proof against a hundred
thousand shocks), that none but the man who holds the primacy of honour in arms shall be her lover and her lord.][36]

The competitive nature of the shield as a symbolic object is also
present in an episode of the *Tavola ritonda*, which is one possible intertext for the construction of Ullania's shield.[37] Twice in
the *Tavola ritonda* a damsel bearing a shield runs into a knight.
In the first instance, a messenger of Morgain meets by chance
Tristan, and tells him that she is carrying the shield, which depicts a beautiful lady and a brave knight, and which is cracked
in the middle, to King Arthur. The shield symbolizes the most
beautiful lady and the most valiant knight, and is meant to warn
Lancelot and Guinevere that they have lost their primacy. The
damsel does not explain, but the two figures represent Tristan
and Iseult:

E quando lo perfetto e lo leale amore saranno congiunti
in fra li due belli e liali amanti del mondo; ciò sarà in fra
la più bella dama, e lo più bello cavaliere e lo più cortese
del mondo e lo più pro'; questo scudo aperto sì si risalderà,
sì come mai non fosse stato rotto. E quando gli due liali
amanti verranno a morte per cagione dello amore, questo
scudo s'invecchierà tutto, sicché non vi si parràe veruna
figura. (158)

[And when perfect and loyal love will be united by the two
most beautiful and loyal lovers of the world, that is between
the most beautiful lady and the most handsome and noble
and brave knight, this cracked shield will heal, as if it had
never been broken. And when the two loyal lovers will come
to death because of their love, this shield will become old,
and no image will be visible in it.]

This episode is present in the *Tristan en prose* and in the Italian
version, called the *Tristano Riccardiano*.[38] The specificity of the
Tavola ritonda, however, is precisely the element of the excellence of the couple over every other couple.[39] Ariosto seems to
have recovered this feature, not only for Ullania's shield but also
for the custom of the Rocca. In particular, it is possible that the
character of the shield is precisely the reason for this episode's
coupling, in the poem, with the custom of the castle: repetition
with variation is a strategy of *entrelacement* that Ariosto uses
with great skill throughout the *Furioso*.

   An anticipation of the third sequence, which I have described
as Bradamante's manipulation of the custom, appears in octave
79, when the lady-knight reveals her beauty and her female identity by removing her helmet.[40] This scene, reminiscent of the episode in the *Inamoramento de Orlando* in which Ruggiero discov-
ered Bradamante's identity,[41] will be the cause of Bradamante's
defense of the right of Ullania to stay in the castle, despite the
presence of a lady more beautiful than she is. Even though this
scene clearly portrays Bradamante as a beautiful object of desire,
she does not therefore lose her active role as a warrior.[42] It is precisely her continuous negotiation between active role and passive
beauty that gives meaning to the debate over the custom. If we in-
sist too much on the operation of stable gender norms, we might
obscure the text's interest in the possibility of occupying different roles simultaneously, as in Bradamante's manipulation of the
custom of the castle.

MANIPULATING CUSTOMS

Multiple manipulations take place at the Rocca di Tristano: Ariosto interweaves this episode with elements of the Tristanian texts, changing the rule of the castle; Bradamante, on the other hand, manipulates the custom itself in order to allow Ullania to stay. Let us first consider the organization of the custom in Ariosto's text. Convention dictates that only one knight and one lady can be hosted in the Rocca; if more than one party arrives in the same night, competition ensues. The knights must joust, and the ladies' beauty must be judged. A shepherd first describes the custom to Bradamante; later, when she and Ullania are inside the castle, their host explains the origins of the convention. In the times when Fieramonte was king, the lord of the castle was a knight named Clodione, who was very jealous of his lady and always kept her locked indoors (octaves 83–84). One day, Tristano arrived at the castle, accompanied by a lady he had just rescued. Out of jealousy, Clodione refused to host Tristano and the lady; such discourtesy prompted Tristano to defy the lord and his ten guards: whoever won would have the right to sleep inside. Tristano vanquished the knights and so earned hospitality for the night. To excite Clodione's rage even more, Tristano decided to keep the lady inside with him, sending the less beautiful damsel who accompanied him outside with Clodione. Tristano's words emblematically inaugurate the custom:

> Questa sarò contento che fuor esca,
> e ch'ubbidisca a tutti i suoi comandi;
> ma la più bella mi par dritto e giusto
> che stia con quel di noi ch'è più robusto.
> (*OF* XXXII, 90, 5–8)

> [I am content for her to go out and obey him in all that he commands; but it seems to me right and proper that the fairest damsel should remain with the most stalwart among us.]

Ariosto is faithful to the basic structure of the Tristanian adventure as outlined in the *Tristan en prose* and in the *Roman de*

Palamedès (also known as *Guiron le courtois*).[43] Several important elements, however, differentiate Ariosto's text from its predecessors. The most striking is the introduction of the beauty
contest for the women, absent from the French models. Moreover, Ariosto introduces the theme of jealousy: in the creation of
the custom, the cause of conflict between Tristano and Clodione
is the latter's extreme distrust of his lady. Jealousy is one of the
pervasive elements of the poem; not only has Bradamante just left
her house possessed by jealousy, but the whole episode of Rinaldo's travels, and the stories he hears on his way, are a macro-sequence dedicated to the excesses of the jealous. The entire Rocca
sequence, in fact, could be read as a commentary on Bradamante's jealousy. This element completely changes the structure of the
episode that gives rise to the custom; in the *Palamedès* it is the
arriving knight ("le petit chevalier") who acts discourteously toward the knight who is already in the castle (Uterpendragon). In
the *Furioso*, on the contrary, Tristano reacts to an unreasonable
refusal on Clodione's part. Tristano's action assumes the quality
of a challenge to an irrational exclusion: in this respect, Bradamante's challenge of the rule that would exclude Ullania redou-
bles Tristano's founding action.

   I will return to Ariosto's insertion of female competition, and
to the challenge to the custom, while analyzing Bradamante's manipulation of the rule; the element of jealousy, however, deserves
immediate attention, because it entails multiple intertextual connections.[44] In the *Tavola ritonda*, a jealous knight hosts Tristano
and his companion Astore against his will, evincing concerns
similar to those of Clodione in the *Furioso*:

> E sappiate che Breus era cavaliere errante, nipote dello re di
> Normelanda; e dimorava in quella sua rocca, perch'era con-
> trada assai diserta, e perch'egli non era d'una compressione
> cogli altri cavalieri: ch'egli era lo più geloso e lo più crudele
> cavaliere del mondo; e avea una sua dama che, per gelosia,
> nolla lasciava vedere a niuna persona; ed era sanza niuna
> cortesia. . . . [E] no' voleva che in sua corte stesse cavaliere
> né donzello, se non fantesche e giovane damigelle; e odiava

ciascuno cavaliere che sentiva d'amore, per paura ch'avea
che none amassono sua donna; e diceva che tutte le dame
erano meretrici, e che la sua era piggiore che l'altre. (492)

[And you should know that Breus was a knight errant, and
the grandson of the king of Normelanda; and he lived in
that castle, since it was a very deserted area, and he was
different in spirit from the other knights: because he was
the most jealous and cruel knight in the world; and, out of
jealousy, he kept everyone from seeing his lady, and he was
completely deprived of any courtesy. And he did not want
any knight or young man at his court, but only female servants and young ladies, and he hated every loving knight,
out of fear that they might fall in love with his lady; and he
used to say that all ladies were whores, and that his lady
was worse than the others.]

Breus's jealousy makes him hide his lady when he offers hospitality to Tristano and Astore. Moreover, other elements point to
this episode as a model for the *Furioso*. Not only is Breus's castle
called "rocca," but on their way to reach it, the knights see a mysterious tower, "la quale era tutta dipinta e storiata" (492) [which
was covered in frescoes and illustrated], precisely in the fashion
of the Rocca di Tristano.

The link between the character of Breus in the *Tavola ritonda*
and the Rocca episode becomes even more explicit as the former
continues. Only a few pages later in the Tuscan text, we read of
Tristano and his companion that:

E cavalcando in tale maniera, sì scontrarono una donzella a cavallo, la quale andava forte piagnendo, e avea
sua roba tutta tagliata di torno alla cintura, sicchè sua
matera risembrava tutta addolorata; e vedevansi tutti i
suoi membri dalla cintola in giù iscoperti. Allora Tristano
la domanda perch'ella piangeva tanto duramente; ed ella
disse, ch'era messaggera della Dama del Lago, la quale da
sua parte portava uno scudo a messer Lancialotto: "ed
essendo io all'entrata di questo diserto, io iscontrai uno
cavaliere, lo quale dice ch'è appellato Breus senza pietà; e

com'egli mi vidde, così mi domandò che iscudo era quello
che io portava; e io gli dissi ch'io il portava a messer Lancialotto. Allora egli lo mi tolse, e tutto lo fece scalpitare
agli piedi del suo cavallo; e per più vergogna, sì mi tagliò
tutta mia roba, sì come voi vedete; e sì mi fece giurare,
ch'io no' muterei altra roba per infino a tanto ch'io non
parlerei a Lancialotto, e ch'io gli dicessi che ciò faceva egli
per suo dispetto. (497)

[And while they were riding, they ran into a damsel on a
horse, who was desperately crying; and her gown was cut
off at the waistline, so that her nature was painfully showing; and her whole body was naked from the waistline
down. Tristano then asked her why she was in such great
pain, and she replied that she was the messenger of the Lady
of the Lake, and that she was bringing a shield to Lancelot
from her lady's part: "and while I was entering this desert,
I met a knight, who called himself the merciless Breus, and
as soon as he caught sight of me, he asked me what shield it
was that I was carrying; and I answered that I was bringing
it to Sir Lancelot. Then, he seized the shield from me, and
he had his horse stomp all over it: and to make my shame
worse, he cut all my gown, as you can see; and he made me
swear that I would not change clothes until I had spoken to
Lancelot, and until I had told him that he had done that to
spite him.]

The messenger of the Lady of the Lake becomes Ullania in the
Furioso: there is no doubt that Breus has provided a suggestion
for the creation of Marganorre, the evil tyrant who shames Ullania and her damsels in canto XXXVII.[45] This observation is not
irrelevant, because the character of Breus has already emerged in
more than one occasion. It is Breus (from the *Cantari di Febus il
forte*, another text derived from the *Tristan* in Italy) who falls in
the cave, tricked by an evil lady, and is destined to see the lineage
of the famous knight Febus; Breus thus provides the model both
for Bradamante's descent into Merlin's cave in canto III and for
the story of the damned Lidia in canto XXXIV. The adventures

of the "merciless knight," ranging from cases of horrible misogyny to dynastic narrations, featuring violent humiliations and fear of betrayal, constitute a pervasive influence on the *Furioso*. The modality of imitation of this medieval narrative is characterized by what Segre calls *vischiosità*, or stickiness.[46] In the case of the *Furioso*, the sequences are linked by a specific character that functions as a catalyst: none other than Bradamante. The existence of Breus as a pre-text for all these sequences in the *Furioso* is all the more important because the Rocca di Tristano and the Marganorre episodes are among the 1532 additions. Ariosto thus seems to have maintained his interest in this text throughout his revisions. I would argue that the misogynistic theme connected to Breus became increasingly salient for Ariosto during the last revision, during which he consistently created spaces of self-assertion for female figures. These 1532 interpolations thus constitute instances of what we could call intertextual irony: the model, linked to Breus, the woman-hater, emerges in the destination text as linked to a character who undermines his legacy, the woman warrior Bradamante.

One such space of self-assertion is the Rocca episode, where Bradamante manipulates the custom. Not only does Bradamante's response to the custom constitute the affirmation of the individual against an unjust rule, but it is also a gendered response.[47] This is the case not just because she is proclaiming female empowerment, rather, it is so because of the political implications of exogamy for female subjects.[48] By imposing conflicting loyalties, exogamy pressures women to negotiate among competing demands. The effects of the exogamic model on women are at the same time threatening and empowering. In the Rocca episode, Ariosto chooses to emphasize empowerment by dwelling on women's ability to occupy different subject positions simultaneously. Bradamante proclaims her right to choose her function within society:

Io ch'a difender questa causa toglio,
dico: o più bella o men ch'io sia di lei,
non venni come donna qui, né voglio

che sian di donna ora i progressi miei.
(*OF* XXXII, 102, 1–4)

[I, who am embracing her cause, affirm that, whether or not I
am fairer than she, I did not gain admittance as a woman and I
will not have my prospects determined as though I were one.]

With this speech, Bradamante is re-etymologizing her nature as
a warrior. As we saw in the beginning of this book, the woman
warrior realizes the fantasy of possessing the enemy, and of turning the adversary into a bride. By saying that she is both a bride
and not a bride, Bradamante does not act as an empowered
woman, at least not primarily. Rather, she asserts her ability to
play multiple roles by taking advantage of the same process of
wish fulfillment that created her narrative persona.

THE PROPHETIC FRESCOES: HISTORY BECOMES NEGOTIATION

This interpretation of Bradamante's claims is further confirmed
by the pairing of this episode with the historical prophecy depicted on the walls of the Rocca. This particular prophecy, the
last to be added to the poem, modifies the political equilibrium
of the text.[49] According to the historical events he had witnessed,
the poet chose to give more or less space to historical figures in
this episode. The frescoes, which show a series of wars fought
over the Italian territory, warn against fixed and inflexible positions: if the French try to conquer Italy, they will suffer great
losses. The principle upheld in the narrative of the frescoed cycle
is once again flexibility: the politics of alliance and negotiation, if
unstable, are at least more applicable to the contradictions of history. Bradamante, the champion of negotiation, sees images that
reinforce her principle of conduct.

Bradamante's performance at the Rocca demonstrates the perfect yet precarious balance of the warrior woman figure as Ariosto constructs her. Like a dynastic wedding, the warrior bride
fulfills desires and resolves political tensions. By making her own

multifarious nature explicit, the heroine permits the participation of female subjects in historical processes. Such participation,
however—predicated as it is on multiple and conflicting subject
positions and on competing loyalties—can only be achieved as
a poetic performance. This interpretation is consistent with the
strategies of omission and correction adopted by Ariosto for the
historical part of the episode. Originally, the prophecy was probably meant to be engraved in Ullania's shield, and contained a
much more ambitious narrative. Instead of featuring a series of
cautionary tales against invasion, the shield elaborated the "history of Italy."[50] The omission of such a complex history in favor
of a more focused series of episodes points in the directions that I
have indicated: from the shield of Elissa to the paintings of Merlino at the Rocca, history becomes negotiation. The 1532 addition of the Rocca di Tristano is thus part of a singular narrative
strategy, coupling a pointed rebuttal of misogyny with the praise
of negotiation as a political tool.[51]

Mixed Genealogies

The Orlando furioso *as Hybrid Text*

In the poem entitled "A Pio Rajna," Eugenio Montale remembers his first and only meeting with the philologist (Montale 1977, 19). Rajna, "announced neither by the braying of oliphants nor by the clashing of Durendals," appears to the poet as "one who made his nest among/ the interstices of the oldest sagas,/ almost a bird without wings known only/ to the paleornithologists/ or a model of what *Homo sapiens* was/ before knowledge became sin." Rajna's nest in the trees of the old legends of the past becomes for Montale a privileged site for understanding the nonlinearity of time, its horizontal nature:

> C'è chi vive nel tempo che gli è toccato
> ignorando che il tempo è reversibile
> come un nastro di macchina da scrivere.
> Chi scava nel passato può comprendere
> che passato e futuro distano appena
> di un milionesimo di attimo tra loro.
> Per questo l'uomo era così piccolo,
> per infiltrarsi meglio tra le fenditure.

[There are some who live in the time/ allotted to them, not
knowing/ that time is reversible like/ the ribbon of a type-
writer. He/ who digs into the past would know/ that barely
a millionth of a second/ divides the past from the future./
That's why the man was so small,/ the better to fit into the
crevices.] (translation by G. Singh 1980)

The image of the greatest scholar of Ariosto's sources as a wing-
less bird who nests in the tree of intermittent textual connections,
all present at once—we can think of this figure as an emblematic
conclusion to this book, which takes the genealogical tree as its
point of departure. Rajna's trees, for Montale, are the genealogical trees of filiation, from one legend to the other, and from one
text to the next. But the study of the past, he tells us, breaks the
verticality of genealogical descent and arborial growth, showing that time is not linear but reversible, and that stories have the
power to reverse time. In this book, I set out to explore these alternative possibilities of the genealogical tree.

The trees with which I started are genealogies of fiction: they
narrate the construction of a fantastic past for a noble family,
while evoking the textual practice of emulation and imitation.
First, I investigated the construction of the *Orlando furioso* as
a work of fiction that was responsive to its historical context in
imagining a position for women within the formation of a lineage. Second, I proposed links between such genealogy and the
intertextual strategies of the *Furioso*, analyzing the construction
of a number of female characters firmly rooted in the popular tradition of *cantari* and *poemi cavallereschi*, a web of texts largely
ignored in contemporary critical practice. Finally, I reconsidered
the genealogies of gender in the *Furioso* through sustained exploration of its representation of the woman warrior. In the construction of the character Bradamante, and in the fictional genealogy
of the House of Este, I aimed to trace the interdependent literary
and gendered genealogies that make the *Furioso* a dynastic poem.

The *Furioso*, as a text founded on imitation and emulation,
suggests nearly infinite pathways to follow, and so a number of

distinct genealogies and genealogical tales have emerged in the course of this study. Some are strictly connected with the formation of the character of the woman warrior. The recurring image of the pregnant warrior who gives birth and disappears from the narrative, for instance, is in the literary genetic code of Ruggiero, whose mother Galiziella and bride Bradamante share this same destiny outside of the text; this topos is tied to the obscure figures of warriors of the chivalric tradition, such as Ancroia and Anfrosina. The evolution of the literary character from classical Amazon into Bradamante, the bride of Ruggiero, has revealed itself as a self-fulfilling prophecy, given the fact that the originary figure contained the element of biopolitical selection of the best man. Similarly, the textual genealogy of the tale of the "marriage by duel" uncovers the tensions implicit in the forging of political alliance through marriage. Marriage alliances thus emerged as the site of a textual paradox, one that attributes blame while questioning responsibility, in the case of the damned Lidia in canto XXXIV. The text's association of illegitimate offspring with the violent foundation of a new state constitutes a somber counterpart to the historical violence tied to bastardy in the House of Este itself.

Parallel to the woman warrior, other figures have appeared as significant players in Ariosto's genealogical narrative. The cruel woman, embodied in the *Furioso* by Lidia, pointed my analysis toward Ariosto's reconsideration of the *querelle des femmes*. The complex figure of the sorceress/prophetess Melissa, on the other hand, provided a final installment in the flourishing Italian tradition of representations of Merlin, while also acting as Bradamante's counterpart in the gender shift of the prophetic circulation of knowledge enacted by the poem.

There are countless genealogical threads that this book could not follow. Within the reconstruction of Bradamante's Amazonian past, for instance, Boccaccio's work might have played an integral role. Similarly, the interplay with the Dantean model in both episodes that have Astolfo as their protagonists is a textual genealogy I did not pursue. These choices derived not only from this book's interest in less authorial and authoritative sequences of texts but also from a programmatic decision to select the combinations of intertexts that would allow me to follow the thematic thread of female genealogy and foundation.

The focus of this book has been on disappearing genealogical formations. Throughout this study, we have seen female figures disappearing from texts and narratives. The countless giantesses and ruthless warriors of the *cantari* and *poemi cavallereschi* lived intense lives on the pages of the first printed books in Italy, only to be dismembered in fiction, according to the trope generally prescribed for their departure, and forgotten in the reality of critical history. Their destiny is shared by the pregnant female warriors of the tradition, like Galiziella, who simply fall off the radar of literary studies. Even Bradamante as a character in Ariosto's masterpiece, despite her central role in the genealogical plot and in its poetics, ultimately becomes the less interesting half of the dynastic pair, playing second fiddle to a character as insubstantial as Ruggiero.

The filiations and interconnections among these disappearing figures constructed an alternative genealogical pattern. The term that better describes the genealogical structures of the poem that emerge from this study is *mixed*. I have demonstrated that by revitalizing classical tales through their medieval rereadings, Ariosto elaborates a horizontal genealogy. From a textual perspective, my study emphasizes the *Furioso*'s hybridity, steeped as it is in the genre of the humble chivalric epic of the preceding century, and almost daring in its tenacious loyalty to its dynamics in the age of humanism. Ariosto's loyalties to his sources are, in a way, as conflicted as those of the women negotiating their roles as daughters and brides. Opposing the vertical lines of filiation that perpetuate traditions and transmit riches and authority from father to son, the poet organizes a web of mothers, daughters, sisters, and wives permanently caught between different worlds and different loyalties.

In the *Furioso* these figures—Bradamante and Melissa in particular—are the protagonists of a network of free circulation of prophetic knowledge, based on the model of the gift that expects nothing in return. The feminine transfer of prophetic knowledge is, in the poem, a process of free circulation, in opposition to the commerce of dynastic praise and the patriarchal handling of female bodies. Ariosto's attempt to create a literary open space, in which art and wealth circulate freely, however, is not devoid of ambiguity. In order to participate in the dynastic foundation, Bradamante's character has been "purified," rendered virtually immune from the otherness of femininity, paganism, or an existing body. Distant are her predecessors, the female giants and the warrior women of the tradition: even the character of Marfisa has lost any trace of the grotesque.

An even more serious limitation attends on this potentially liberating moment, since Ariosto, as I have shown, sees the gift as an expression of trust. The opposite of the gift in this sense is betrayal, which attacks those who have put their trust in the other or in the common good, like the bees with their honey. Betrayal looms threateningly but omnipresently over the poem. Genealogically speaking, the narrative of Ruggiero and Bradamante is based on a double foundational betrayal: that of Beltramo, the brother of Ruggiero I, against him and his wife Galiciella (*OF* XXXVI, 60, and XXXVIII, 14), and that of the Maganzesi against Ruggiero (*OF* XLI, 61, and III, 24), triggered by Bradamante herself. In the historical genealogy, betrayal is present from the first images we have of the Este, in the person of Giulio and Ferrante, the illegitimate half-brothers who plot against their own blood (*OF* III, 60–62).

Ariosto has challenged the traditional view of the foundation as violence against women. Another foundation is possible, one based on loyalty, mutual agreement, and negotiation, and woman could be the political subject who is free to realize it. Violence, however, is a threat from within this delicate balance, and betrayal is the other side of the gift. *Pro bono malum.*

INTRODUCTION

1. Quorum unius cuiusque principio arborem apponendam censeo, cuius in radice pater assit propaginis, in ramis vero iuxta degradationis seriem apponere omnem dilatatam propaginem, ut per hanc videas de quibus et quo ordine in sequenti libro perquiras. Quos libros etiam debitis comperies distinctos rubricis ampliori sermone pandentibus, quod unico tantum nomine per frondes arboris primo perlegeris. Boccaccio 1998, 60. All translations, unless otherwise noted, are my own.

2. For reproductions of both, see Wilkins 1923. The volume reproduces images from the Chicago manuscript, prepared for and owned by Coluccio Salutati. The decorative initials of the volume's chapters are copied from book initials from the 1494 Venice edition.

3. The first extant printed versions of the text omitted the trees, at first by leaving the space to draw them (Venice: Wendelin of Speier, 1472; Reggio Emilia, 1481) and then by omitting them entirely (Vicenza, 1487). See Wilkins 1923, 14–15.

4. Both texts, dating to the second half of the fifteenth century, represent the Este dynasty in a genealogical progression. For details on the *Genealogia*, see Daniele Bini, "Genealogia dei Principi d'Este," in Iotti 1997, 94–145.

5. For recent reflections on trees as forms of thought in medieval and early modern culture, see Kay 2007 and Moretti 2005. Bizzocchi (1995) has shown the importance and forms of genealogical thinking in the context of Early Modern and Modern Italian dynasties.

6. "Di qua e di là dal Po son tutti figli di Nicolò," quoted by, among others, Chiappini 2001, 110.

7. "Here is an extraordinary fact about the family: within recent memory no legitimate son has ever inherited the title; fortune has smiled so much more on the children of the mistresses than on those

of the wives. It is a circumstance contrary not only to Christian teaching but to the law of almost every nation." Pius II 2004, 358–61. This passage is also quoted by Bestor 1996, 549, who has done groundbreaking work on the Este dynasty and its literary representations. See Bestor 1992, 2000, and 2005. As she clearly states, "The House of Este stands out among the ruling dynasties of Italy on account of its unique succession. For almost one hundred fifty years, illegitimates ruled its dominions" (1996, 549).

8. Even Dante's mention of Obizzo d'Este in *Inferno* XII connects the tyrant to a troubled lineage: "Obizzo da Este, who truly was murdered by his bastard up in the world" [è Opizzo da Esti, il qual per vero/ fu spento dal figliastro su nel mondo]. Dante Alighieri, *Divine Comedy, If* XII, 111–12.

9. Chiappini 2001, 109.

10. The dynasty itself becomes the site of a threat from within, in the form of the plot organized by the illegitimate Giulio and Ferrante against their half-brothers Ippolito and Alfonso, and is suffocated in blood. Giulio and Ferrante, who are not killed, unlike their co-conspirers, are imprisoned within the Este castle itself, as a constant reminder of the internal threat. On the episode, see Bacchelli 1966, Chiappini 2001, and Gundersheimer 1973.

11. This central element of the character was first analyzed by Constance Jordan in her article "Writing beyond the *Querelle*" (1999). Jordan rightly observes that Ariosto's constructions of gender and generativity take us beyond the *querelle des femmes* and are "consistently brought into focus in episodes that illustrate a reading of history" (295). Her insights on the prophetic episodes of the *Furioso* have been very important in the conception of this book. Jane Everson also underlines this crucial aspect of the *Furioso*, "a dynastic theme based on a female protagonist," which she sees "lightly adumbrated" in Francesco Cieco's *Mambriano*; see Everson 2001, 343.

12. Irigaray is one of the pioneers of the concept of "sexual genealogies"; see *Sexes and Genealogies* (1993), 3.

13. "Preface" to *Gender Trouble* (1990), xxix.

14. On this, see canto XXXV, and my discussion of it in chapter 3.

15. There are a few important exceptions: in particular, Daniela Delcorno Branca and Marina Beer, who have studied thematic aspects; Michael Sherberg, who has focused his attention on a character in particular (Rinaldo); David Quint and Ronald Martinez, who have studied specific episodes where the intertextual strategy reveals a conscious use of medieval models. See Delcorno Branca, *L''Orlando furioso'* (1973); Beer, *Romanzi di cavalleria* (1987); Sherberg, *Rinaldo*

(1993); Quint, "The Figure of Atlante" (1979); Martinez, "De-Cephalizing Rinaldo" (1994). Marco Praloran, in his book *Tempo e azione nell'"Orlando furioso"* (1994), has explored the revitalization of the *entrelacement* technique on Ariosto's part.

16. Ascoli 2001, 488–90. For studies on *epica* and *romanzo* in the *Orlando furioso*, see Zatti 1990; Quint 1979; Bruscagli 1983.

17. Cf. Javitch 1984, in particular pages 1029–30.

18. The need for such an approach is demonstrated by the discovery by Eugenio Garin of a previously unknown work by Leon Battista Alberti, the *Intercoenales*, an important model for the journey of Astolfo on the moon. See Segre, "Leon Battista Alberti e Ludovico Ariosto," in *Esperienze ariostesche* (1966), 85–95. The study of the Ariostan poem would certainly benefit from a comparison with eclectic imitation practices such as that performed by Poliziano. See Ascoli 1987, 28n53.

19. See Javitch 1985, in particular pp. 238–39.

20. See for instance Ascoli 1987, 45: "I am attempting, in this chapter, to arrive at an understanding of the poem as 'inter-text' in the wider possible sense—a text dwelling between texts, past and future. The texts are around it, as con-texts which determine and bound its significance; but, surprisingly, they are also within it, absorbed as co-texts: cited and staged, faithfully or parodically re-presented, approvingly or polemically interpreted."

21. "Intertestualità e interdiscorsività nel romanzo e nella poesia," in Segre 1984, 103–18.

22. See all the articles by Javitch, above; Saccone 1974; Sitterson 1992; and Jossa 1996.

23. As mentioned earlier, Delcorno Branca, Beer, Martinez, and Quint have studied specific aspects of the revitalization of medieval sources in the *Furioso*. The most systematic study is Praloran's investigation of the *entrelacement* structure in Ariosto. Blasucci 1969, Johnson-Haddad 1992, Cabani 1990b, Segre 1966, and others have studied the influence of "medieval classics," such as Dante and Petrarca, on the *Furioso*. A completely different chapter should be opened here on the studies of the *Orlando innamorato* (or *Inamoramento de Orlando*) as a privileged intertext in the *Furioso*.

24. Ascoli 2001, Martinez 1994.

25. Segre introduced the conceptual tool called *vischiosità* in his study of direct relations between texts: "As verbal coincidences touch larger segments of the discourse, or, even better, as thematic coincidences increasingly correspond to punctual verbal borrowings, our observation reveals fragments of the linguistic-semiotic complexity of

the text, either imitated, quoted, or remembered." [Via via ... che le coincidenze verbali toccano più ampi segmenti discorsivi, o, meglio ancora, che le coincidenze tematiche corrispondono a riprese verbali, incomincia a rivelarsi alla nostra osservazione qualche frammento della complessità linguistico-semiotica del testo imitato o citato o comunque ricordato]; "Intertestualità," *Teatro e romanzo* (1984), 109. The first occurrence of the term is in his *Esperienze ariostesche* (1966), 57, 65–66.

26. For a useful survey of the misfortunes of this theme, see Casadei 1988, 8–13. The rejection of the encomiastic/dynastic theme is still present in contemporary criticism. Guido Waldman, the English translator of the *Furioso*, plainly states in his introduction: "But the task of Laureate did not suit his creative vein and it is clear that a part of him goes to sleep whenever he fulfils his duty of homage— the passages in praise of his patrons may be skipped without regret" (1998, xiv). Unless noted otherwise, I have used Waldman's translation throughout the book.

27. Critics such as Wiggins 1986, Fichter 1982, and Marinelli 1987 have studied the dynastic dimension of the *Furioso*. They have essentially focused on Ariosto's rewriting of the *Aeneid*, seeing the modernization of Virgil as the poet's central achievement in making an epic poem of the *Furioso*. Fichter insists on the "Christianization" of the *Aeneid* in the *Furioso*, while Marinelli concentrates on the privileged relation of the poem to Boiardo's *Inamoramento*, which Ariosto revitalizes through the classical model.

28. Marinelli 1987, Fichter 1982. Even in this case, the nonclassical models considered are essentially Boiardo and humanistic philosophers. Florence Weinberg, in her study *The Cave* (1986), mentions medieval sources along with classical ones for the episode of Merlin's cave. However, she does not further elaborate on such mixture, and her account is not completely accurate: to my knowledge, *La Spagna* does not contain any mention of Merlin.

29. This textual move echoes the strategy of the sorcerer Atlante within the text itself. On Atlante as a textual double of Ariosto's predecessor Boiardo, see Quint 1979, 1; on his connections with the figure of Ariosto himself, see Ascoli 1987, 362–64.

30. Rajna 1975 "prophetically" linked the question of the "mixed" sources of the poem to its gendered nature: he often refers to the *Furioso*'s mixed origins, with an Italian father and a Latin mother (see, for instance, p. 39). The hybridity of the text is represented through categories of genealogical formation. I would argue that the "gender of the sources" is reversed in respect to Rajna's idea: the "father"' is

classical, while the place of the "mother" is reconstructed through the medieval narrative.

31. MacPhail 2001, 30–53. MacPhail reads the prophecies in the *Furioso* as Ariosto's way of dealing with the specific historical moment, a "prophetic moment," in which prophecies are needed to overcome the anxiety due to political and social instability.

32. Constance Jordan introduced the question of a gendered reading of history in the *Furioso* in the article on "Writing beyond the *Querelle*" (1999). Organizing her analysis around the prophetic episodes of the poem, Jordan studied instances of female agency, and "the representation of ideas of a generativity that depends on female and feminine as well as male and masculine 'valor'" (299).

33. Jameson 1981.

1. MARRIAGE BY DUEL

1. See Tissoni Benvenuti 2007 and 2008.

2. On the intertextual development of psychological traits, see below. The idea that Renaissance chivalric psychology is not only collective but also multitextual is a development of the theory clearly expressed in Zatti 1990, in particular in the chapter "La psicologia nel *Furioso*," 113–25.

3. The definition of *intertestualità cavalleresca* is given by Tissoni Benvenuti 2007. For Tissoni Benvenuti, Ariosto is much less faithful to the tradition than Boiardo, "very rigorous" (57). On Boiardo's treatment of the Carolingian matter through the lens of the Arthurian tradition, see Praloran 1990 and Donnarumma 1996.

4. Tissoni 1996a makes this same point (72). For exceptions to this general rule, see her article in *Tre volte suona l'olifante* (2007). The methodology that considers the importance of this system of reference to Ariosto's poem is, in my view, complementary to the work conducted by Jane Everson in her book *The Italian Romance Epic in the Age of Humanism* (2001), which focuses on authorial works assumed to be studied in humanistic or para-humanistic fashion.

5. Tasso's *Liberata* marks the point of no return in this process: characters need to be consistent and respond more to the internal logic of the text than to the network of references of the epic-chivalric matter. See Stoppino 2001.

6. From Petrarca's dismissal of the chivalric matter in the *Triumphus Cupidinis* (III, 79–81); to Lovato Lovati's disparaging remarks (quoted in *Fiore di Leggende*, edited by Levi 1914); to Angelo Decembrio's *Politia Letteraria*, set at the Este court, where chivalric lit-

erature is branded as leisure literature, connected to the presence of
women and children: "libros . . . quos apud uxores et liberos nostros
nonnunquam hybernis noctibus exponamus" (quoted in Biondi 1982).
Boccaccio's *Decameron*, whose "last name" is, significantly, *Gale-
otto*, is dedicated to women and proudly upholds (and plays upon)
such a connection. The modern disparagement of popular chivalric literature is amply demonstrated by one of its most important scholars,
Pio Rajna, on which see my introduction.

7. On the Rinaldo cycle, see chapter 2, especially note 26.

8. The most important champion of the study of the chivalric tradition, after Pio Rajna, was Carlo Dionisotti. See in particular his *Gli
Umanisti e il volgare fra Quattro e Cinquecento* (1968) and *Boiardo e altri studi cavallereschi* (2003a). Marco Villoresi established the useful distinction between *cantari* and *poemi*, based predominantly on the length
of the texts ("La tradizione manoscritta dei testi cavallereschi in volgare.
Cantari, poemi, romanzi in prosa," in Villoresi [2003] 2005, 11–12). On
the *cantari* and *poemi cavallereschi*, in addition to the studies mentioned
in the Introduction, see *I cantari: struttura e tradizione* (1984), Delcorno
Branca, *Cantari fiabeschi arturiani* (1999), Beer 1987, Cabani 1988, Villoresi 2000 and 2005. A new flourishing of studies is demonstrated by the
publication of collections of critical essays, such as *Il cantare italiano fra
folklore e letteratura* (2007), *Boiardo, Ariosto e i libri di battaglia* (2007),
and *La letteratura cavalleresca dalla "chanson de geste" alla "Gerusalemme Liberata"* (2008). Among the most important editions of anonymous *cantari* are Balduino 1970, Barini 1905, Delcorno Branca 1999,
Fassò 1981, Levi (*Fiore di Leggende*, 1914), Melli 1973, and the recent
edition by Benucci, Manetti, and Zabagli (2002). Sara Furlati recently
edited the *Cantari del Danese* (2003). Various strands of the popular chivalric epic have been studied by Alberto Limentani and his school and by
Antonia Tissoni Benvenuti and her school, especially in the context of the
new monumental edition of Boiardo's *Inamoramento de Orlando* (Tissoni Benvenuti and Montagnani 1999). Anna Montanari has done fundamental work while compiling a new catalogue of Italian incunabula of
chivalric texts. On the specific media of the *libri de bataia* (the technical
term used by contemporaries to describe these texts), see the work of Angela Nuovo (1998, 2003, and 2007) and Neil Harris (especially 2007),
as well as the 2006 volume by historian Marina Roggero. On chivalric
culture at the Este court, see above all Alahique Pettinelli 1983 and 2004
and Bruscagli 1983 and 2003. Gloria Allaire 1997 has pioneered the redis-
covery of Andrea da Barberino, while Jane Everson (1994, 2005b, 2005c,
2006) has conducted foundational work on the *Mambriano* and the related tradition. For studies in English of the *cantari* and *poemi cavallere*

-*schi*, see Vitullo 2000 and *Firenze alla vigilia del Rinascimento* (ed. Bendinelli Predelli, 2006). On the question of oral circulation, I adopt the recent tendency, memorably championed in the volume *Epic Traditions in the Contemporary World* (edited by Beissinger, Tylus, and Wofford, 1999), to see the boundary between orality and literacy as very porous when it comes to epic texts. Circulations were mixed and intermittent, and the same audiences adapted to different media in different circumstances.

9. On the many reasons for the canonization of the *Orlando furioso*, see especially Javitch, *Proclaiming a Classic* (1991). Javitch explores the theoretical controversy over the *Furioso* and its ambiguous positioning between epic and romance, and convincingly demonstrates how this debate conferred on the poem its canonical status. It is precisely this process of canonization, I would add, that erased central elements of the conception of the *Furioso*, and in particular its belonging to the *milieu* of *poemi cavallereschi* and *cantari*.

10. Tissoni Benvenuti 1987.

11. I will not explore the other aspects of the character in the poem, which are nonetheless extremely interesting, such as Bradamante's elegiac persona or Bradamante as a simulator in canto IV. On the former, see Ferretti 2008 and 2010.

12. On the printed history of the *Bradiamonte*, see Beer 1987 (in particular her table of the *romanzi* printed in Italy between 1470 and 1600, pp. 326–69). I consulted the following incunabula of the text: *Historia di Bradiamonte sorella di Rinaldo* (Florence: Francesco di Dino, 23 maggio 1489), Rome, Biblioteca Corsiniana, Cors. 51 B 41; *Historia di Bradiamonte sorella di Rinaldo* (Brescia: Battista Farfengo, 1490), Milan, Biblioteca Nazionale Braidense, Rari Castiglioni 28; *Historia di Bradiamonte sorella di Rinaldo* (Florence: Lorenzo Morgiani & Johannes Petri, ca. 1492), Yale University, Beinecke Library, 1979 632. For a discussion of the topos of female beauty, including the *Bradiamonte*, see Alhaique Pettinelli 2004, 147–61.

13. I call an intertext "in the first degree" a text that shows a direct connection with the *Furioso*.

14. *Cantari cavallereschi*, edited by Barini (1905), 162.

15. For a detailed linguistic analysis of the element, see Stoppino 2007, 326.

16. The prophetic sequences of the poem will be the subject of chapter 4.

17. On Bradamante as the addressee of the dynastic prophecies, see the important remarks by Constance Jordan 1999. Jordan claims that Ariosto goes beyond the limits of the Renaissance *querelle des*

femmes, and, by staging Bradamante as the addressee of dynastic prophecies, represents "ideas of a generativity that depends on female and feminine as well as male and masculine 'valor'" (299).

18. Margaret Tomalin presents Bradamante as the quintessential "empowered woman" in her survey of warrior heroines in Italian literature (*The Fortunes of the Warrior Heroine in Italian Literature: An Index of Emancipation*, 1982). Tomalin's interpretation, as clearly stated in her title and subtitle, is based on a problematic assumption: that the literary representation of strong, independent female warriors simply corresponds to the recognition and intellectual acceptance of the possible existence of *real* independent women within the culture of the period (see in particular pp. 13–15). This assumption was challenged by Lillian Robinson in her book *Monstrous Regiment: The Lady Knight in Sixteenth-Century Epic* (1985), which considers the "contradiction between the actual status of real women and the significance of 'woman' as an intellectual or conceptual instrument" (ii). For Robinson, Bradamante and Marfisa are the only female characters in the poem who succeed in introducing the female principle into the public domain generally reserved to men, thus participating in the building of a new form of civilization. Robinson establishes an important connection between the study of the female warrior and the dynastic theme of chivalric literature, which has been further analyzed by Pamela Benson and Deanna Shemek, as well as by Constance Jordan, in the aforementioned article (1999). Benson 1992 sees Bradamante's strength in her choice not to be independent (155). Shemek 1998, in her chapter entitled "Gender, Duality, and the Sacrifices of History: Bradamante in the *Orlando furioso*" makes a convincing case for seeing Bradamante as the "model leader" (116).

19. Segre 1966.

20. Finucci 1992. Among the "dissenting voices" on the meaning of Bradamante's final choice, see Benson 1992, Shemek 1998, and Hairston 2000. According to Shemek, the past and the projected future of Bradamante resist the forced enclosure of the text's ending. Julia Hairston convincingly argues that Bradamante's greatest strength in the *Furioso* is her ability to negotiate between different values and demands imposed upon her.

21. See, for instance, Quint 1979, Zatti 1990, and Sitterson 1992.

22. For evidence on the intertextual construction of the episode, see Montanari 1995b.

23. Here I have substituted "gift" for "boon" in Waldman's translation. For a partial discussion of the theme of the gift as connected to the dynastic theme in the *Furioso*, see below, chapter 3.

24. Since Rajna, this has been the acknowledged source of the passage, but, as is often the case, the meaning of this particular adaptation has not been analyzed. Marsh 1981 and Casadei 1988, among others, have studied the addition to the poem without focusing on this particular condition posed by the female protagonist. Their readings both interpret the addition as an "epicization" of the poem's ending.

25. Very few copies of the poem still exist. It is quite short, only 125 octaves long. See Rajna 1900, Barini (*Cantari cavallereschi*, 1905), Beer 1987.

26 I quote the text from the 1489 edition, keeping editorial interventions to a minimum. Translations of the text are my own.

27. For the theorization of Christian-Saracen relations in the *cantari*, I am indebted to the work of Sharon Kinoshita, whose analyses of Old French epic bring together gender and genre studies as well as postcolonial readings of Orientalism. See especially Kinoshita 2002 and 2005. For a study of the Saracens in Italian epic, see Franceschetti 1987; for an excellent analysis of the Saracen in Andrea da Barberino's *Guerrino il Meschino*, see Allaire 1996.

28. The usual remark about pagans and Christians in the *Furioso*—that no real boundary separates them, as opposed to what will happen in a Counter-Reformation author like Tasso—needs to be challenged and further verified. A clear example of boundaries between Christians and pagans is the story of Zerbino and Isabella, whose love is considered impossible from the very beginning because of religious difference. For an original interpretation of Ruggiero's paganism and conversion, see Levi 1933, in particular 483–84. Levi argues that Ruggiero's identity as a pagan works to make him a double for Ercole d'Este, who "converted" from the alliance with the Aragonese to that with the Angevins (483 and n1).

29. See below, pp. 40–43.

30. I interpret Bradamante's inability to defeat her opponent as a defeat, even though the battle is fought to a standstill.

31. Translated by Mary M. Innes, *Metamorphoses* (London: Penguin Books, 1955).

32. It is worth noting that the myth of Atalanta had already entered this textual tradition via an episode in Boiardo's *Inamoramento*. In canto XXI of the first book, Leodilla tells her story to the knight Brandimarte, who has just rescued her from the giants who had taken her prisoner. Leodilla had resorted to the stratagem of the race in order to force her father to give her in marriage to her young suitor Ordauro, and to get rid of her old and wise lover, Folderico. Since she excels at running, she expects to defeat the old Folderico, but she is

defeated because she stops to collect the three golden apples he throws in front of her during the race (I, xxi, 48–68).

33. For a later example of this fantasy, see the episode of Clorinda's death in the *Gerusalemme liberata* by Torquato Tasso, canto XII, 52–69.

34. For an occurrence of the same subtext in the *Furioso*, see the duel between Bradamante and Rodomonte in canto XXXV. On the sexuality of weapons, see McLucas 1988.

35. Ascoli 1999a.

36. "Partirome di franza in tanta pace/ se consentir me vol la bella donna/ saro amico di Carlo verace/ Regina la faro e gran madonna/ perche viuo per lei in contumace/ et e della mia vita la corona/ portegli questo tutto quanto scripto/ e recha la risposta a me transcritto." [I shall leave France at complete peace: if the beautiful lady wishes to consent (to be my wife), I shall be a true friend to Charles. I shall make her a queen and a great lady, since I live for her, absent to myself, and she is the crown of my life. Take all this to him (Charlemagne), in writing, and bring me back his answer in writing (or: translated).]

37. "Che tanto manco ni fara piu guerra/ noi lhabiam a man salua in casa nostra/ non li lasiam tornar ne la sua terra/ da po che son venuti a far la mostra/ rispose orlando el to penser non erra/ come carlo vora nui faremo iostra/ in questo mezo lo re amansore/ la maza prese in man e poi se core." ["He is so beaten, he will not wage war (fight) any longer: we safely have them in our territory, let us not allow them to go back to their land, since they came to show off." Orlando replied: "You are not mistaken in this: if Charles wishes, we shall joust." Meanwhile King Almansor took his club and started running.]

38. On the crucial question of the representation of the role of women in society vs. the representation of the "essence" of women, see Desmond 1994, 15–17. On the importance of remembering that every description of women is a representation, see Biddick 1998, Scott 1999. I tend to see the warrior woman as a site of tension, a character in whom questions of gender identity and performance are conflated with, and often hidden by, strictly political concerns of conquest, expansion, and identity.

39. See Benson 1992, 155.

40. For the definition of "political unconscious," see Jameson 1981.

41. There is also a tradition of anonymous *cantari*, parallel to Andrea's version, of the "Gesta d'Aspromonte," to which I will refer throughout my study.

42. Andrea da Barberino, who lived in Florence between 1372 and

1433, was the author and possibly the performer of many epic-chi-valric works in prose, including the *Aspramonte*. For information on Andrea da Barberino's life and works, as well as for a thorough dis-cussion of textual attributions, see Allaire 1997. Allaire has worked tirelessly to offer new editions and new texts of Barberino's works. For a recent account of the *status quaestionis*, see Allaire 2006.

43. I am not prepared to rely on the truthfulness of such declara-tions, as Tomalin does (1992, 44). The composers of epic narrations (particularly prose epic, which is strongly linked to the chronicle tra-dition) often cite contrasting sources to give authority and add mys-tery to their accounts.

44. On the complex tradition of the *Chanson d'Aspremont* in Italy, see Andrea Fassò, *Introduzione* to his edition of the *Cantari d'Aspramonte inediti* (1981): ix–lvi. Fassò continues the work of his mentor, Marco Boni, who devoted many articles to this topic.

45. It is worth noting, in this instance, the presence of the motif of generosity and liberality—it is over their comparative liberality that the jester and the prince fight—and the centrality of the jester in the beginning of the text: these elements are both strongly present in the *cantari* tradition.

46. Barberino 1972, VIII, 44. All quotations are from the 1972 Cavalli edition, which reproduces the 1951 authoritative edition by Boni. I give the indication of the chapter, followed by page number. Translations are my own.

47. On the woman as gift-giver and intermediary in the circulation of objects and texts, see chapter 4.

48. To avoid incurring shame, Almonte has his servants remove the spear from Riccieri's back and put it in his chest. This stratagem, however, does not prevent Galiziella from discovering the truth. This episode further marks Almonte's descent into treachery.

49. Rajna 1975, 511–12.

50. The symbolism of the dream scene, where the pregnant Gali-ziella sees the outcome of another pregnancy, strongly links the risk of betrayal to the semantic field of generation. Also, compare this vision to Aude's dream in the Venetian version of the *Chanson de Roland*. The image of the fire from the womb is a topos that dates back at least to Ovid's *Heroides*, where Hecuba dreams that she will give birth to a fire (Paris) that will set the world ablaze (Ovid, *Heroides* XVI, 123–124). I am grateful to Ronald Martinez for pointing out this impor-tant textual precursor.

51. The motif of the pregnant warrior's death is a common theme in narratives of warrior women in the period. In the *Libro della Re-*

gina Ancroia, the protagonist Ancroia, pregnant with the twins of Malagise (who posed as Guidone), is killed and dismembered (*squartata*). The newborns almost disappear from the narrative, which becomes preoccupied with the magical and monstrous dissection of her body: four lions *in carne e osso* are wrapped around her heart. The lions are another topos connected with the warrior woman, like the character of Formosa in *Aquilante e Formosa*. On *Ancroia* and *Aquilante e Formosa*, see chapter 2.

52. The importance of this exogamous model for the *Furioso* will be the concern of chapter 5. A similar pattern of movement from pagan to Christian, on the female side only, is a founding principle of Tasso's *Gerusalemme liberata*, as studied by Zatti 1983.

53. See *Cantari del Danese*. On the potential connection to the prose text titled *Aquilante e Formosa*, see chapter 2.

54. *Li fatti de Spagna* (1951). The manuscript (Aldini 553) is preserved at the Biblioteca Universitaria di Pavia.

55. It is the portion entitled by Rajna *Castello di Teris*, according to a title found in the manuscript (MS. 1904, Florence, Biblioteca Riccardiana). See Rajna 1975, 379.

56. The first printed text of the *Danese* dates back to 1480, whereas its earliest manuscript was, at least in part, copied in the second half of the fourteenth century. On the textual tradition of the *Cantari del Danese*, see *I Cantari del Danese* 2003, edited by Furlati; Montanari 1997, 6; Villoresi 2005, 38–74.

57. I quote the text from Furlati's edition, preserving the italics used to indicate editorial integrations. Translations are my own.

58. The divinity Trevigante, always coupled with Mahomet, is spelled in a variety of ways in the Italian tradition. Spenser, in the *Faeirie Queene*, names it Termagaunt (see for instance VI.vii).

59. Here and throughout the book, I quote Boiardo's text from the Tissoni Benvenuti and Montagnani edition (1999), and the translation by Charles Stanley Ross 1989. The theme of the gift is also present here.

60. See Zampese 1994, in particular pp. 155–59, for a discussion of the Leodilla episode, as well as Battera 1987 and Searles 1902.

61. *Mambriano*, XIV, 97, 6. In this episode, Cieco parodizes the theme of the *amour de loin* and further ridicules the tradition of the old lover, which is apparent, for instance, in the episode of Boiardo's poem featuring Leodilla (discussed above). On the *Mambriano*'s treatment of the theme, see especially Everson 2006. I quote the text from the 1926 Rua edition, with my own translation.

62. Pinamonte sounds like a precursor of Cervantes's Quixote in his delusional (and book-induced) love frenzy.

63. It is likely that Marco Polo and Rustichello da Pisa—a traveler and a compiler of chivalric texts—wrote the *Devisement du monde* together, while held captive in a Pisan prison around 1298.

64. Marco Polo 1982, 618. In discussing the text, I use the standardized title *Devisement du monde*. Translations are my own.

65. Benson 1992 does not consider the elements of innovation that are present in these texts; for instance, she dismisses Galiziella by stating that "immediately after marriage, she gets pregnant and seems to give up fighting" (125). On the contrary, we have seen that the pregnant Galiziella plays a central role in the defense of Risa, and that her ambiguous disappearance from the text leaves her destiny open-ended.

66. There has been great critical interest in Amazons and women warriors in Italian literature. McLucas 1988 refines the idea that representing strong women warriors amounts to empowering all women; Allaire 1994 and Bendinelli Predelli 1994 collect a wealth of information on the various characters in medieval and early modern Italian literature; for Freccero 1995, the *Teseida* by Boccaccio enacts a strategy of containment and domestication over women warriors.

67. The debate over the rise of the modern novel, which has its milestones in the contributions of Hegel, Lukàcs, and Bakhtin, poses the rise of the individual as one of its central axioms. On the other hand, the same conclusion is reached by those who see the presence of a "modern" psychology of the characters as the trademark of the modern novel (See Girard 1966).

68. See Wiggins 1986.

69. Zatti 2001. It is likely for this reason that Tomalin and Benson, from very different perspectives, both see Bradamante as the realization of a more "realistic" character.

70. "Similmente non si confonderanno le donne guerriere colle gigantesse, le quali appartengono a una razza speciale, che in qualche modo si può dire intermedia tra l'uomo e la bestia." Rajna 1975, 47, emphasis added.

71. Boiardo, for instance, makes reference to Rinaldo's seizing of Belisandra (*Inamoramento de Orlando*, I, xxviii, 5 and notes).

72. The *princeps* of the text, printed by Georg Walch in Venice (1481) is conserved at the University of Pennsylvania (Van Pelt Library, Folio Inc. C-204). A second copy of this edition has recently surfaced at the Fondation Martin Bodmer, in Geneva (Inc. 156). The text was printed again in 1491, on February 12 in Bologna by Bazaliero de' Bazalieri (Parma, Biblioteca Palatina, Inc. Parm. 641, containing only the first nine cantos of the 1481 edition), and on July 31 in Venice by Dionigi Bertocchi (Milano, Biblioteca Nazionale Brai-

dense, Rari Castiglioni 35). Like most other texts in this tradition, the *Inamoramento* is anonymous and lacks a modern edition. I have consulted the copy of the *princeps* at the University of Pennsylvania and the 1491 edition preserved at the Braidense.

73. I use the expression in the sense given to it by Roland Barthes (1953), as the "neutral" or basic level of semiosis or meaning.

74. The same element is present, at least as a threat, in the case of Braidamonte in the *Danese*. In the *Inamoramento di Carlo*, Natasar, Calidonia's brother, cannot stand her betrayal and kills her: "Re agolandro hebe vista la figlia/ A cridar cominzava o macometo/ E natasar una lanza si piglia/ Disse: "Mia suora, che ha messo difetto,/ Mai non la portarà fra sua famiglia!"/ Con l'asta bassa corse per dispetto/ E sopra Calidonia el colpo dava/ Che morta in brazo a Rinaldo restava" (canto XXXIII) [King Agolandro, who had seen his daughter, started to cry "Oh Mahomet!" And Natasar took a spear, and said: "He shall never take my sister, who is now lost, into his family!" He ran, enraged, holding his spear, and he hit Calidonia, who was left dead in Rinaldo's arms].

75. On this figure, see Norma Alarcón, "Chicana Feminist Literature: A Re-Vision through Malintzin / or Malintzin: Putting Flesh Back on the Object," in Moraga and Anzaldúa, eds., 1981, 182–90, and Moraga 1986. On the Saracen queen, see Kinoshita 1995.

76. The figure of Clorinda in the *Gerusalemme liberata* presents interesting similarities, particularly because of her problematic religious status, brilliantly studied by Quint 1993.

77. Robinson 1985, 189.

78. Bradimonte plays only a marginal role in the *Inamoramento de Carlo*, and appears only in conjunction with other female warriors. The figure of the giantess presents an interesting variation, all Italian, on the giant theme. For an analysis of the cultural work done by giants, see Stewart 1984, Stephens 1989a, and Cohen 1999.

79. *Inamoramento de Carlo* VIII, 12–13. She proudly fights even with her legs cut off, but is finally defeated by Dudone (canto IX). The Christians celebrate her death as the destruction of the "mirror of the Saracens." Rovenza is the protagonist of *cantari* entirely dedicated to her, very similar to those named for the famous queen Ancroja. Rovenza's peculiar trait is that she has a hammer or a big stick as a weapon, as the titles of her stories point out: *Rovenza della falcia*, *Dama Rovenza del Martello*, and so on. On this figure, see *I cantari* 1984. On the textual tradition, see Harris 2003. Rovenza's weapon of choice and the fact that her defeat is connected to dismemberment provide an important link between these texts and the narra-

tives of exploration, such as Vespucci's *Letters from the New World*.
On Rovenza's textual history, see chapter 2.

80. A peculiar element of the *Inamoramento de Carlo* is that the
Christian heroes always try to convert the female giants, as was already the case with Rovenza: "Magna regina, se fai el mio conseglio/
Fate christiana, adora Yesue/ Ch'el mondo tuto cavoe de periglio"
["Oh great queen, follow my advice: become a Christian, adore Jesus,
who saved the world from danger"]. The attempt to convert the Saracen warrior is typical of the Franco-Italian poems (see, for instance,
the *Entrée d'Espagne*), where it is often coupled with a pseudo-theo-
logical argument on the part of the Christian warrior, who explains a
dogma (generally the Trinity). In the *Inamoramento de Carlo*, the addressees of such efforts are mainly the female giants.

81. See Halperin 1990, 113–152.

82. I would argue that what Schwarz 2000 terms "Amazon encounter" is a crucial component in the appearance of the Italian type
of the woman warrior. Women warriors, not unlike Amazons, say
less about women and their independence than about social boundaries: "As they intervene in male homosocial identifications, Amazon
encounters create an explicit and temporary illusion of sameness that
presumes its own exposure. Playing on misrecognition, such encounters suggest that there is something attractive about being so radically
wrong: female masculinity both sets up a mirror in which women
reflect men and translates the reflection into something else. Look-
ing at an image of idealized masculinity, men who confront Amazons
discover a body that can be incorporated into generative marriage.
By making narcissism the cause of a heterosexual effect, Amazon encounters seemingly ensure that the eroticism implicit in the privileg-
ing of likeness will consolidate homosocial power without implying
homosexual desire" (27).

83. I thus disagree with MacCarthy 2005, who sees the break of
the *Furioso* with the tradition in opposite terms: "Before Ludovico
Ariosto's *Orlando furioso*, women warriors of the Italian chivalric
romance tradition tended to become knights for a specific purpose.
Their aim was usually to escape danger, to aid or follow a lover, to
save personal honour or, simply, to provide comic relief to the reader."
For MacCarthy, Ariosto's Marfisa is the first woman warrior for
whom "chivalric identity is not just a temporary masquerade" (178).
On the contrary, my analyses of Boiardo's and Ariosto's predecessors
show that the traditional warrior women and giantesses are inherently
warriors. It is precisely Boiardo's and Ariosto's erasure of the destabilizing threats of this literary past that has distanced these female char-

acters from their textual "mothers." In the next chapter I will explore
the distinction between Boiardo and Ariosto in this respect.

2. AN AMAZONIAN PAST

1. The law, defined as "antiqua," ancient, and "crudele," cruel,
has the same marks as the other "cruel laws" of the poem, both
those introduced in the 1532 edition (Olimpia, Marganorre, Rocca
di Tristano) and those already present from the first edition ("L'aspra
legge di Scozia" of canto IV). On Ariosto's dichotomic view of the law,
see chapter 1.

2. "S'io ci fossi per donna conosciuta,/ so ch'avrei da le donne
onore e pregio;/ e volentieri io ci sarei tenuta,/ e tra le prime forse del
collegio." [If I were recognized for a woman, I know that the women
would honor and respect me; they would give me a ready welcome and
perhaps a position of eminence.] OF XX, 78, 1-4.

3. In both cases, the warrior women wave at their opponents the
violent threat of the sword. Bradamante is ready to defend her position: "E s'alcuno di dir che non sia buono/ e dritto il mio giudizio sarà
ardito, sarò per sostenergli a suo piacere,/ che'l mio sia vero, e falso
il suo parere." [And if anyone dares maintain that my judgement is
not good and sound, I am ready to sustain it against him any time
he chooses —mine is right, his is wrong!] (OF XXXII, 106, 5-8).
Marfisa could use her sword to cover up her perceived lack: "[E]t a
Marfisa non mancava il core,/ ben che mal atta alla seconda danza;/
ma dove non l'aitasse la natura,/ con la spada supplir stava sicura."
[Nor did Marfisa lose heart: she may have been ill equipped for the
second performance, but where Nature left her unaided she was confident of making good with her sword.] (OF XIX, 69, 4-8). The concept is further elaborated, with the same vocabulary of lack overcome
by violence, in octaves 73-74. Marfisa's companions fear she may not
be able to participate in the duel: "non disegnavan di Marfisa forte,/
stimando che trovar dovesse inciampo/ ne la seconda giostra de la
sera;/ ch'ad averne vittoria abil non era" [but they did not include
sturdy Marfisa, deeming that she would find an obstacle in the second joust, the night one, as she was not equipped to achieve a victory
here] (OF XIX, 73), and she promises to be able to "cut this Gordian
knot" with her sword. For a convincing interpretation of this episode,
of the image of the knot, and of Bradamante and Marfisa as central to
Ariosto's compromise between epic and romance, see Bateman 2007.
Ita MacCarthy 2007b reads this episode as anti-feminist mocking of
Marfisa's lacking female anatomy; see pp. 73–94.

4. It may be valuable to consider this factor from a pan-European comparative perspective, as does the volume *Playing with Gender*, edited by Brink, Horowitz, and Coudert (1991). Of particular relevance to my argument is the essay by Alison Taufer, "The Only Good Amazon Is a Converted Amazon: The Woman Warrior and Christianity in the *Amadís Cycle*," ibid., 35–51.

5. The female protagonists of Ferrarese history during Ariosto's times—Eleonora d'Aragona, Ercole's bride, their daughter Isabella, and Lucrezia Borgia, to name just a few—had an influence that would have been unthinkable fifty years earlier. Even though their power was dependent on that of the male figures they ultimately responded to, it was nonetheless very visible both within and outside their courts. On this subject in relation with the groundbreaking article by Joan Kelly, "Did Women Have a Renaissance?" (originally published in 1977, now in Kelly 1984, pp.19–50), especially regarding Isabella d'Este, see Shemek 2005c.

6. For the frescoes in the Manta Castle near Saluzzo and their relation with epic-chivalric literature, especially with *Le chevalier errant* by Tommaso di Saluzzo, see Meneghetti 1989.

7. On Carpaccio and this painting, see Mason 2000, 19. There is debate over the date of the work; Mason assimilates it to *cassone* paintings, on which see below.

8. Labalme, "Introduction" to *Beyond their Sex* (1980), 4–5. For the comparisons made by male humanists, see *Her Immaculate Hand*, edited by King and Rabil (1983), 123; Grafton and Jardine, *Humanism and the Humanities* (1986), 33–36; Baskins 1998, 38–40. Laura Cereta follows Boccaccio's *De claris mulieribus* in her praise of Marpesia and Lampedo ("Letter to Pietro Zecchi," in Cereta 1997, 68), as does Isotta Nogarola writing to Damiano dal Borgo in either 1439 or 1440 (Nogarola 2004, 99).

9. The press was that of Cristoforo de' Pensi de Mandello (fl. 1487–1503). It is worth noting that this is the same typographer who printed the 1498 edition of the *Ancroia*, preserved in Rome at the Biblioteca Apostolica Vaticana (BAV A- 235). On the *Ancroia*, see note 15 below.

10. The *Amazonida* was edited by Ernesto Spadolini (1908), and this edition was the object of a review by Rodolfo Renier in *Giornale storico della letteratura italiana* 54 (1909): 220–23. See Dionisotti, "Fortuna e sfortuna del Boiardo nel Cinquecento," in *Il Boiardo e la critica contemporanea*, ed. Giuseppe Anceschi (Florence: Olschki, 1970): 221–41, now revised as "Fortuna del Boiardo nel Cinquecento," in Dionisotti 2003a, 143–61. For the *Amazonida*, see in particular pp. 151–53. That Stagi was part of a circle at least known to the Gonza-

gas of Mantua is demonstrated by references in his text, in particular to the poet Marco Cavallo. For these connections, see Luzio and Renier 2005, 239. I consulted two extant copies of the 1503 edition of the poem, the one preserved at the Biblioteca Casanatense in Rome (RM0313) and the one owned by Harvard's Houghton Library (*IC. St136.503a), as well as the rare 1908 edition. I quote the text from the 1503 edition, and translations are mine. As Carlo Dionisotti noted in 1970, few scholars have studied this poem, which also had a limited history in print: only one edition followed the one that appeared in 1503, and its modern edition is rare. Verrier 2003 mentions the text as an important contribution to the Amazonian literature of the Renaissance (192–97).

11. See chapter 4 for a discussion of Ariosto's projected attempt to recover the deeds of Marfisa and Bradamante.

12. Nuovo 1998, 25; and Nuovo 2007, 353.

13. The letter to Giorgio Brognolo, dated September 24, 1491, is quoted in Luzio and Renier 2005, 8. Tissoni Benvenuti 1987 also quotes the letter (24–25). The *princeps* of the *Dama Rovenza* (Venice: Luca di Domenico, ca. 1482) is preserved at the Biblioteca Apostolica Vaticana in Rome (Inc. Ross. 1350), and this is the copy I consulted. For a review of the history of the *Rovenza* in print, see Harris 2003. On the text, see Antonio Pasqualino, "Dama Rovenza dal martello e la leggenda di Rinaldo da Montalbano," in *I cantari* 1984, pp. 177–98.

14. Nuovo 1998, 14–15; and Nuovo 2007, 353.

15. The 1479 edition (from the types of Filippo de' Petri) is the first known edition of the poem. It is preserved at the Pierpoint Morgan Library in New York, and this is the copy I consulted (PML 22108). Many other editions followed, including (just to mention the extant incunabula) Venice 1482, Venice 1485, Venice 1494, Venice 1498 (the one printed by the same typographer who printed the *Amazonida*, Cristoforo de' Pensi), and Venice 1499. On the *Ancroia*, see Montanari 1993, which provides interesting parallels with Boiardo's and Ariosto's poems as well as an excellent summary of the long poem, and Montanari 1995a. For the intertextual relations between the *Ancroia* and the *Danese*, as well as a great wealth of information on these poems, see Villoresi 2005, 38–74.

16. "Come quelle Amazzone veston maglia;/ son per natura coperte di vello,/ pilose, setolute, strane e brutte,/ ma molto fiere per combatter tutte" [They, like the ancient Amazons, wear mail,/ and are by nature horridly hirsute–/ ugly and hairy, very harsh and queer,/ but when they start to fight, they know no fear] (*Morgante* XXII, 158,

5–8). Pulci, notoriously ironic on the subject of the warrior woman—suffice it to think of the treatment he reserves to Merediana or Chiarella in battle—subjects his Amazons to male rule: they are the army of the evil lord Arpalista. On the episode in the *Morgante* (and its predecessor, the *Orlando*) as a source for the *Furioso*, see Rajna 1975, 297. Rajna himself argues that the scene is too commonplace in these texts to be able to trace a direct filiation.

17. Florence, Biblioteca Nazionale Centrale, MS. Panciatichiano 36.

18. Giovan Battista Ramusio's *Navigationi et viaggi*, published for the first time in 1550, is the first great collection of travel narratives of the modern era. I mention these accounts as symptomatic of this interest for Ariosto's contemporaries.

19. On Boccaccio's epic poem and its reception, see Everson 2001, 107–26. On its portrayal of the Amazon, see Freccero 1995.

20. I am grateful to Dennis Looney for bringing this element to my attention. Pier Andrea de' Bassi's *Commentary*, published for the first time in 1475 under Ercole's rule, is studied in Montagnani 2004, 3–49.

21. Rajna 1975, 513–17.

22. Florence, Biblioteca Mediceo-Laurenziana, MS. Med. Pal. 101 vol. 2. The text is studied in Vitullo 2000, 67–73.

23. See chapter 1.

24. On the *cassoni*, recently the object of monographic studies, see Hughes 1997, Baskins 2008, and Campbell 2009.

25. See Baskins 1998, 49. On chests featuring Amazons, especially derived from Boccaccio's *Teseida*, see pp. 26–49.

26. The adventures of Rinaldo, already mentioned in chapter 1, are the most interesting thread in the early epic-chivalric tradition of Italy, as well as one of the most abundant. Rajna, in his article "Rinaldo da Montalbano" (in Rajna 1998, 101–89), pointed to this corpus as one of the keys to the understanding of the Italian epic. On the Rinaldo traditions, see also Melli (1974, 1978) and Morosi 1978. Michael Sherberg has conducted a pioneering study of the Rinaldo tradition from the point of view of intertextuality and genesis of the chivalric character (*Rinaldo*, 1993).

27. *Libro della Regina Ancroia*, 1479. On the fact that Ariosto turns Guidone from Rinaldo's son into his brother, see Rajna 1975, 306, and Bigi, ed., (1982), 846.

28. In both cases, in keeping with the tradition, Guidone is Rinaldo's son, not his half-brother.

29. This is possibly another play with the tradition of the *poemi*

cavallereschi. In many texts, such as the *Ancroia,* the name of the knight is revealed only after long preambles. While this can be said of other genres as well, the character of Guidone seems to draw a direct connection with the *poemi cavallereschi.*

30. My translation.

31. My translation.

32. *Argonautica* I, 607.

33. Book II.

34. See Nuovo 1998, 183.

35. *OF* XXXVII, 36. On this specific passage, see Brand 1974, esp. 117–120, and Benson 1992, 143–44.

36. "Menie igitur fuere ex Iasonis atque Argonautarum sociis non minime nobilitatis splendidissime iuvenes." (*De claris mulieribus* XXXI, 3)

37. *De claris mulieribus* XVI.

38. For this pervasiveness of the model, see the discussion of Segre's term *vischiosità,* or stickiness, in the introduction and in chapter 1.

39. For Amazonian origins as necessarily "written out" of history, see Geary 2006, 26–42. For the Amazonian theme in Tasso, see Stephens 1989a.

40. Bestor 2005 and Looney 2005b, esp. pp. 16–17.

41. Bestor 2005, 52.

42. See Looney 2005b, who advances the hypothesis that "Ariosto's allusion to the myth may even reflect a local concern of the Ferrarese court with the issues of paternity and the legitimacy of succession among the members of the ruling family" (2).

43. Even though Bestor 2005 makes a convincing case for three literary texts.

44. The theoretical framework for my discussion of the Amazonian state as a state of exception is provided by Giorgio Agamben's reflection (*State of Exception,* [2003] 2005). I am particularly interested in the idea of the state of exception as a "threshold of indeterminacy between democracy and absolutism" (2–3). The episode of Alessandria in the *Furioso* is, in this sense, a profound reflection on the limits of the state and its laws. These laws, in particular, are all connected to the generative power of the citizens, making Alessandria a literary laboratory of biopolitics.

45. "Sì che, temprando il suo rigore un poco,/ scelsero, in spazio di quattro anni interi,/ di quanti capitaro in questo loco/ dieci belli e gagliardi cavalieri,/ che per durar ne l'amoroso gioco/ contr'esse cento fosser buon guerrieri./ Esse in tutto eran cento; e statuito/ ad ogni lor decina fu un marito" [So they tempered the law's rigour a little and

chose, over the course of four full years, out of all those who happened their way, ten handsome and bold knights who had proved their durability in the love-games. Matched, as they were, against a hundred women, it was decided that to every ten women one husband was to be allotted] (*OF* XX, 30).

46. "Per concepir di lor questo si fece,/ non che di lor difesa uopo ci sia" [This was done in order to conceive by them, not because we needed them to defend us] (*OF* XX, 51, 5–6).

47. "Tra noi tenere un uom che sia sì forte,/ contrario è in tutto al principal disegno" [To keep among us a man so powerful goes totally against our main objective] (*OF* XX, 52, 1–2).

48. On race, gender, and alterity in early modern literature, see Hendricks and Parker, eds. 1994; Ferguson, Quilligan, and Vickers, eds. 1986; Fradenburg and Freccero, eds. 1996; Goldberg, ed. 1994; Zatti 1998. On the Amazons, see discussion below.

49. In a recent study of Amazon encounters in the English Renaissance, Kathryn Schwarz has argued in favor of a different interpretation. The presence of Amazons in domestic contexts, she argues, is not subversive—rather, it impersonates contradictions recognized as part of society itself: "I want to suggest, perhaps somewhat counter-intuitively, that stories about Amazons are testing grounds for social conventions, playing out the relationship between homosocial and heterosocial systems of connection that produce an idea of the domestic." *Tough Love* (2000, 2).

50. In the *Furioso*, other than cantos XX–XIX and XXXVII, Amazons are mentioned in a number of other occasions. Bradamante describes herself as an Amazon to Fiordispina (XXV, 32); Marfisa is compared to an Amazon in canto XXVI, 69–70, and in canto XXVII, 52.

51. This connection is not sufficiently explored, probably because of Rajna's silence on the topic, coupled with the unlikely hypothesis that Marphisa was derived from a metathesis of Formosa, heroine of the above-mentioned Florentine prose text *Aquilante e Formosa* (Rajna 1975, 516). The commentary to the *Inamoramento* by Tissoni Benvenuti and Montagnani makes reference to the classical Marphesia (1999, 475), following Baldan 1981. For a linear account of a possible genealogy of the warrior woman, see Di Sacco 1996.

52. This passage is also quoted in Tissoni Benvenuti's introduction to the edition of the *Inamoramento* (1999).

53. Commentary to the critical edition of the *Inamoramento de Orlando*. On this, see also Montagnani 2005.

3. THE PARADOX OF HELEN

1. Chojnacki 1998, 84.

2. On rape as a representation of the foundational alliance, see Tylus 2007. Interesting suggestions on the theme are also to be found in Stephanie Jed, *Chaste Thinking* (1989). The connection between violent foundation and republican state is not convincing in Jed's book, but the comparison between representational violence in the foundation of the dynastic state and of the republican state deserves more critical attention, especially in a field, such as Renaissance studies, still founded on an opposition between Florence and the courts of the north. For a recent example of an effort to challenge this aspect of Renaissance and early modern Italian studies, see *Beyond Florence*, edited by Findlen, Fontaine, and Osheim (2003).

3. I do not mean to say that the classical versions of the story Ariosto tells are nonproblematic; they are, however, challenged and revitalized, at times reetymologized, through the combination with other narratives.

4. For a thorough exploration of the various versions of Helen, see Suzuki 1989.

5. An excellent example of the uncertainty surrounding Helen's will and responsibilities is in Boccaccio's *De claris mulieribus* (ch. XXXVI).

6. See in particular Javitch 1984, 1985, 1999.

7. See, for instance, Ascoli 1987, 45.

8. See the female genealogy of the Este in Pellegrino Prisciani's *Annales Ferrariae*, already quoted in the Introduction.

9. Ronald Martinez put forth the idea of characters in the *Furioso* as values on a "spectrum" in the unpublished essay "Ricciardetto's Sex and the Castration of Orlando: Anatomy of an Episode from the *Orlando Furioso*."

10. See Zatti 1990 on the "oggetti d'inchiesta"; see also Delcorno Branca 1973 on weapons as a component of the *entrelacement* technique.

11. On the importance of the passage from the "material *quête*" to the "knowledge *quête*," see Zatti 1990, 45–47.

12. This strategy is particularly common in the prologues: see, for instance, cantos XIV, XV, XVII, XX, XXXVI, XL, XLII, XLIV, and XLV.

13. "Troppo fallò chi le spelonche aperse,/ che già molt'anni erano state chiuse;/ onde il fetore e l'ingordigia emerse, ch'ad ammorbare

Italia si diffuse./ Il bel vivere allora si summerse;/ e la quïete in tal modo s'escluse,/ ch'in guerre, in povertà sempre e in affanni/ è dopo stata, et è per star molt'anni" [That man perpetrated the worst of crimes who opened the cave which had been closed for many a year: out came the stench and gluttony to pervade Italy and corrupt her. Happy days were at an end, and peace driven out. Ever since has Italy been steeped in wars, in poverty, and trouble—so to remain for years to come] (*OF* XXXIV, 2).

14. Rajna 1975, having claimed that the Lidia episode is a parody of the *Commedia*, adds that "it would be ludicrous [la più solenne delle corbellerie] to say that Ariosto wanted to ridicule the *Commedia*." However, he fails to substantiate his claim with a rational explanation; the reason for not riduculing the *Commedia* would probably be the respect accorded to Dante's authority. Even if we were to assume, as Rajna correctly indicates, that parody does not necessarily mean ridicule, the problem of determining Ariosto's seriousness remains. Rajna's subsequent remarks complicate the question even further: "Everyone seems to be convinced that Ariosto's intent is not to ridicule Dante. But then, why apply such different criteria of judgement to the relationship with the chivalric romances?" (537). The scholar, who accepts that Dante, like all the "classics," can only be a serious model for Ariosto, asks why the chivalric model is treated differently by critics. Why is it that the chivalric texts are only considered as the matter for nonserious rewritings? I will focus on this problem with an analysis of the Lidia episode.

15. For the sacrilegious voyage of the Senapo, see *OF* XXXIII, 109–110.

16. The Cerbero episode is in *If* VI, 1–33; Pluto appears in *If* VII, 1–15. We can imagine that a learned courtly audience would have appreciated the light reference to the *auctoritas* of Dante. It is difficult, though, to exclude the possibility that other, more polemical rereadings of the *Commedia* are at stake in this passage. See Javitch 1999, in particular 69–70.

17. The blending between the two traditions will be further expressed in St. John's explanation of the reasons for Astolfo's voyage. In the latter part of the canto, Astolfo leaves the underworld to visit the earthly paradise (48–67) and the moon, where he recovers Orlando's wits (68–92). St. John, his heavenly guide, will explain to the knight that he is not there by chance, or thanks to his own "virtù" or "sapere," but only due to divine will. "Disse: —O baron, che per voler divino/ sei nel terrestre paradiso asceso;/ come

che ne la causa del camino,/ né il fin del tuo desir da te sia inteso,/ pur credi che non senza alto misterio/ venuto sei da l'artico emisperio./ Per imparar come soccorrer déi/ Carlo, e la santa fé tor di periglio,/ venuto meco a consigliar ti sei/ per così lunga via, senza consiglio./ Né a tuo saper, né a tua virtù vorrei/ ch'esser qui giunto attribuissi, o figlio;/ che né il tuo corno, né il cavallo alato/ ti valea, se da Dio non t'era dato" ["O baron," he said, "who by God's will have ascended to the earthly paradise: as the cause of your journey and the object of your desire are equally hidden from you, your arrival here from the northern hemisphere is, believe me, not without highly placed help. It is to discover how you are to help Charlemagne and rescue the Holy Faith from peril that you have made so long a journey to come, all unawares, to consult me. You are not to attribute your coming here to your intelligence or courage, my son: neither your horn nor the winged horse would be of any use to you had not God given them to you] (*OF* XXXIV, 55–56). Ariosto turns upside down the traditional structure of the descent to the underworld, in which the hero normally undertakes the journey for a precise end (as in the *Aeneid*), and thus parodies the *Commedia*. Astolfo embarks on the journey out of sheer curiosity, solely to see what he expects to see in hell; to put it simply, he undertakes the journey for the sake of a literary convention. St. John's use of the term "desir," virtually a technical term in the *Commedia*, is an even clearer demonstration of Ariosto's parodic attitude.

18. This is a stylistic element proper to the *Purgatorio*, rather than to the *Inferno*. For this element, see note 35 below.

19. Rajna 1975 points to Anaxarete as a source for Lidia (541). See also Santoro 1989, 295-301. On this point, see below.

20. At this point, I would only like to note that this is a stratagem Ariosto employs quite often when discussing differences between men and women: at the beginning of canto XXVII, the narrator claims that women's sudden ideas ("i consigli") can be positive, while men's ideas need to be pondered with "alcun tempo e molto studio et opra" [mature deliberation and after the outlay of time and thoughtful rumination] (*OF* XXVII, 1).

21. Albert Ascoli has recently studied the episode, added in 1532, in connection with other "internal models." See Ascoli 1999a.

22. The words used by Lidia, "io di mai non l'amar fisso avea il chiodo" [I had made up my mind that I should never love him (the idea was fixed in my heart like a nail)] (XXXIV, 28, 8) are related to the semantic field of faith preserved against all obstacles (for the

vocabulary of faith in the *Furioso*, see Ascoli 2003). In this particular instance, the theme of faith is reversed: for Lidia, to keep her faith means to *avoid* performing an action, it means absence of love instead of constancy in it. The unbalancing of the equation of faith with consistent love is one of the sources of ambiguity in this episode, as well as of Ariosto's consideration of the theme of the "donna fedele,"

23. Once again, Lidia anticipates elements of characters who appear later in the poem. In canto XXXVII, Drusilla, forced to marry Olindro, Marganorre's son, kills both him and herself on their wedding day.

24. On faith as a central theme of the poem, see especially Saccone 1974, Ascoli 1987, Zatti 1990.

25. On the title of the romance, see Rajna 1975, 60–61. The text of the *Palamedès* used by Rajna in his work on the sources of the *Furioso* was preserved in a manuscript of the National Library in Turin. Unfortunately, the manuscript was seriously damaged by fire in 1904. The most complete study of the *Palamedès* is the study by Löseth (*Le roman en prose de Tristan*, 1891). See also Lathuillère 1966.

26. On the Estense library, see Bertoni 1903 and Tissoni Benvenuti 1987, 13–33. In particular, in the inventory of Niccolò III (1436) there is a "Gurone in francexe," and the most important inventories compiled during the reign of Ercole I (1471 and 1495) mention texts with the same subject.

27. Alberto Limentani, ed., *Dal "Roman de Palamedes"* (1962) has studied the independent diffusion of this episode in Italy.

28. I accept the composition dates proposed by Limentani 1962, p. xviii.

29. Paris, Bibliothèque Nationale, MS. fr. 12.599. See Limentani's description of the manuscript, pp. cv–cvii. The circulation of the Arthurian matter, fragmented into episodes, is in my opinion a crucial element for the development of genres such as the *novella* and the epic-chivalric poem.

30. Florence, Biblioteca Nazionale Centrale, MS. Banco Rari 45, formerly Magliabechiano II. II. 33. See Limentani 1962, cx–cxiii.

31. Limentani 1962 observes that the *volgarizzamento* is a rather basic rendering of the original text, and that the author of the *cantari* "si limitò a una versificazione del testo che gli serviva di canovaccio, al quale egli si attenne si può dire in tutto e per tutto; l'opera del cante-rino consistette principalmente nella costruzione delle ottave" [limited himself to versifying the text he had in front of him, which he fol-

lowed closely; the work of the *canterino* consisted mainly of rendering the text in octaves] (xviii–xix).

32. I am following the text of the *Cantari di Febus il forte* as edited by Limentani (1962). The text's first editor (Follini) had called them *Cantari di Febusso e Breusso*, the title also used by Rajna. In all likelihood, this was the title given to the *cantari* by one of the owners of the manuscript.

33. Translations of the *Febus* are mine, unless otherwise noted.

34. As demonstrated by Limentani, the *Commedia* is a model for the poet of the *cantari di Febus*.

35. For an example of this style in the *Commedia*, see Francesca's self-presentation in canto V of *Inferno,* and even more so *Purgatorio* V, 130–136 (self-introduction of the soul of Pia de' Tolomei); in this respect, even though Francesca's speech is clearly a model for Lidia, I see her as closer to a purgatorial figure than to an infernal one. Her punishment is lighter in comparison to those meted out in the *Inferno*—smoke itself is, in the *Commedia*, part of the penance for the wrathful in *Purgatorio* XVI; the tone of Lidia's confession and of her interaction with Astolfo is far from the harsh and conflictual tones of *Inferno*, including the emotional (but still conflicted) parenthesis of Francesca.

36. Ariosto also uses the *topos* of the "speaking" grave for Merlin in canto III and for Atlante in canto XXXVI.

37. Lydia is also the name of the protagonist in Matthew of Vendôme's *Comoedia Lydiae*, a source for Boccaccio in *Decameron* VII.9 (the tale of Lidia, Nicostrato, and Pirro). In the Latin text, the play on the name is an important element, and both for Matthew of Vendôme and Boccaccio, the tale consists of a power play between two young lovers and an elderly figure. In this power dynamics, we may be tempted to see a precedent for the negotiation that goes on in the *Furioso* episode. Additionally, the female protagonist in the *Comoedia* and especially the *Decameron* is explicitly in charge of the tricks played on her husband (and in the Latin text, she is therefore the object of mysogynistic attacks); Ariosto's Lidia is, as we shall see, at the center of a debate over female agency. On the *Comoedia Lydiae* and the *Decameron*, see Usher 1989 and Ascoli 1999b.

38. See Stallybrass 1986. For Stallybrass's discussion of the question of woman as territory, see in particular p. 127. One possible model for this passage is to be found in Boccaccio's *De claris mulieribus*, chapter X, "De Lybia Regina Lybie."

39. For a thorough discussion of the importance of the father in a narrative model, see Freccero 1991.

40. The only information provided about the three knights, engraved in their sepulchers, are their names and the remark that "a petto al padre loro non fuor valenti" [compared to their father, they were not valiant] (*Febus*, I, 48, 5).

41. The comparison between Adam, father of the mortals, betrayed by Eve, and Febus, father of the knights, betrayed by his beloved acquires further nuance if we examine it in the context of Ariosto's rewriting. Since the poet inserts this episode right before Astolfo's visit to the earthly paradise, many references to Adam and Eve surround Lidia's narration (*OF* XXXIII, 90, and XXXIV, 60); the only other reference to Adam in the poem (*OF* XLIII, 8) stresses the irreversibility of the original sin, a theme highly relevant to the *cantare* as well.

42. In the *cantari*, it is the daughter of the king of Norgalès who first rejects Febus; her rationale is the same as that later expressed by her cousin: Febus has killed her relatives: "(Da) poi che (lo) mio padre morto m'hai,/ amore di te né d'altro uom vo' giamai!" [Since you killed my father, I don't want you or any other man as lover!] (*Febus*, III, 11, 7–8). This literary strategy of stressing a particular theme through repetition is very common in the romances linked to the *Vulgata* cycle, and Ariosto himself recovers it and makes of it a principle of his narratorial strategy.

43. Quotations are taken from the edition of the *Aeneid* by Rosa Calzecchi Onesti (Turin: Einaudi, 1967).

44. Translations of the *Aeneid* are mine, unless otherwise noted.

45. *Aeneid* VI, 93–94.

46. The use of these Virgilian passages in the epithalamium Ariosto wrote for Lucrezia Borgia confirms that this aspect of the *Aeneid*, and its rhetorics of exogamy, was well present to the author at this point. On "externi thalami" and the uses Ariosto makes of this expression and of this concept in his epithalamium for Lucrezia Borgia, see chapter 5.

47. A completely different set of problems arise if we start to consider what *Aeneid* Ariosto uses, and whether he is influenced by the medieval readings of Virgil. On this and related issues, see in particular Hollander 1983 and Javitch 1984.

48. On the medieval representations of Dido, see Desmond 1994. Aeneas had a tormented history in the Middle Ages. The counter-legend of Aeneas as *impius*, as the traitor of Priamus and Troy, is already present in the classical tradition, from Livy (*Ab Urbe condita*, I, 1) to Horace, from Seneca to Tertullianus up to Servius and Donatus. The two archetypes of the medieval versions of this tradi-

tion are the Pseudo Dares of Phrygia's *De excidio Trojae* (CE 5th c.)
and the pseudo-Dictys Cretensis *Ephemeridos belli Trojani* (CE 4th
c.). Along with Antenor, the survivor of the war on the Trojan side
is accused of having betrayed his homeland and bought his freedom.
In the medieval tradition, epitomized by Benoît de Sainte-Maure's
Roman de Troie and reworked by Guido delle Colonne in his *Historia destructionis Troiae*, this element is present, even though less
prominent than the other criticism moved to the hero: the betrayal
of Dido's sincere love. The figure of medieval Dido, as it has been
studied by Marilyn Desmond (1994) and Margaret Ferguson (1994),
became the image of a certain claim of female right in opposition to
the necessities of history. In the *Aquila*, one of the only two *cantari*
printed in the fifteenth century on the stories of Troy, we see very
clearly the issue of the poets' lies. A third element of blame emerges,
though: Aeneas is illegitimate and of low birth. On the *Aquila,* see
Montanari 2004. Books on Trojan stories were very common at the
Este courts, and we find two *Cronicas Troianas* in Spanish, according to Luzio and Renier 2005 (280), in the inventory of the books
of Duke Federico Gonzaga of Mantua. A related topic is the iconography of Aeneas (and Dido) in Ferrara, especially in the Camerino
for Alfonso d'Este at the hand of Dosso Dossi. What is peculiar in
the representation of Aeneas is the conflation of three aspects within
the character of the impius Aeneas: traitor of his city, thief of kingdoms and women, and, last but not least, traitor against Dido. Furthermore, all these elements are connected, in the *Furioso*, with the
instability of poetic fame. There are many reasons why Aeneas becomes such a catalyst for all themes connected to infamy. It is peculiar, though, that this does not happen in the *Inamoramento de
Orlando*. I think that the crucial reason why all these references to
Aeneas coalesce in cantos XXXIV, XXXV, and XXXVI is that they
are building up to a theme Ariosto will expand upon in canto XXXVII: the *querelle des femmes*.

49. This "revision" of the character of Aeneas is clearly connected,
in the *Furioso*, with the theme of literature as a form of propaganda.
When St. John, in canto XXXV, challenges the value of the praise of
the patron, he starts by mentioning none other than Aeneas: "Non sì
pietoso Enea, né forte Achille/ fu, come è fama, né sì fiero Ettorre;/ e
ne son stati e mille e mille e mille/ che lor si puon con verità anteporre:/
ma i donati palazzi e le gran ville/ dai descendenti lor, gli ha fatto
porre/ in questi senza fin sublimi onori/ da l'onorate man degli scrittori." [Aeneas was not as devoted, nor Achilles as strong, nor Hec-

tor as ferocious as their reputation suggests. There have existed men in their thousands who would claim preference over them. What has brought them their sublime renown have been the writers honoured with gifts of palaces and great estates donated by these heroes' descendants.] (*OF* XXXV, 25).

50. On the end of the poem as an element of epic closure, see Fichter 1982, Zatti 1990, Sitterson 1992, Shemek 1998

51. I am here purposefully employing the two terms, *public* and *private*, to represent the sharp early modern division between these two spheres, precisely at the moment in which this distinction is forming.

52. As we shall see shortly, this element has important consequences for the construction of the female character, as well.

53. See Rajna 1975, 540–42. He observes that "a Lodovico piacque di ritogliere alla sua Lidia le giustificazioni, ossia di farla più simile ad Anassarete. Ed era ben naturale, se le pene eterne dovevano apparire giusto castigo" [Lodovico took away from his Lidia all justifications, thus making her more similar to Anaxarete. And this was only natural, if the eternal torments were to appear as a just punishment] (541). As I shall discuss below, I think that justifications for Lidia's behavior are not "taken away"; rather, Ariosto is negotiating the value of such justifications. Rajna also discusses the fact that Ariosto seems to recover Ovid, the original model, through the medieval imitation (of the French romance and the Italian *cantari*).

54. The theme of the burial together with the beloved is recuperated by Ariosto when describing the death of Fiordiligi: she decides to be buried with Brandimarte (*OF* XLIII). Fiordiligi is what we could call a "refraction" from and a model for Bradamante, like Lidia. For innovative insights in this direction on the figure of Bradamante, see in particular Martinez, "Ricciardetto's Sex and the Castration of Orlando: Anatomy of an Episode from the *Orlando Furioso*" (unpublished essay). Martinez suggests that "Bradamante, the destined progenitrix of the Estensi, is the focus of a discernible spectrum in Ariosto's distribution of sexual characteristics of women in the poem" (9). On this theme, also see, with different angles, Finucci 1992 and Shemek 1998.

55. It is worth noting the similarity between Organia, the place where Febus is sent, and Ircania, where Lidia sends Alceste (*OF* XXXIV, 36, 8). The various adventures Febus undertakes are synthesized in one octave of the *Furioso*: "E quando sol, quando con poca

gente/ lo mando a strane imprese e perigliose,/ da farne morir mille
agevolmente:/ ma lui successer ben tutte le cose; che tornò con vittoria, e fu sovente/ con orribil persone e monstruose,/ con Giganti a
battaglia e Lestrigoni,/ ch'erano infesti a nostre regioni" (*OF* XXXIV,
38) [I would send him off, sometimes alone, sometimes with a few
men, upon bizarre, dangerous missions, enough to kill any number
of others but not him—everything succeeded for him, and he would
come back victorious, though often he was faced with horrifying monsters, at grips with giants and cannibals which infested our land]. The
detail of the giants is a clear link to the world of the *cantari*: Febus
fights three giants in pagan lands.

56. "Po' che da lui ho avuta [co]tal*e* minaccia,/ dilletto di parlare
vo' darli alquanto,/ e di sua morte mi pensarò intanto" (*Febus*, V, 10,
5–8) [After he has uttered such threat, I decide to indulge him and talk
to him, and in the meantime I will plot his death].

57. This appears to be a very bleak aspect of the narrator's tendency to frustrate the readers' expectations, which has been consistently considered as one of the poem's most distinguishing—and playful—features, from Durling to Javitch.

58. In Boccaccio's *De claris mulieribus,* Helen is defined "hec, que
obsidioni causam dederat" [the one who had been the cause of the
siege]: 148–49.

59. It would also be worth considering how the Fury and the
Harpy in the Virgilian poem are connected to the Harpy in the
Furioso.

4. THE POEM AS A PROPHECY

1. Albert Ascoli has shown how this passage, echoing the *incipit*
of the poem ("le donne e i cavallier . . . "), stages the *Furioso* itself as
a poem/prophecy; see Ascoli 1987, 22–25, 385–93.

2. It is almost a critical commonplace that the *Furioso* is woven like a tapestry. Not only does Ariosto himself use this metaphor quite often for his own work but there has also been important
scholarly work on this aspect. See, for example, Wiggins 1986 and
Ascoli 1987.

3. Since Bronislaw Malinowski's studies on exchange in the Trobriand Islands, and Marcel Mauss's influential essay, the gift has been
a central theme of anthropological research. Mauss essentially saw the
gift as an altruistic alternative to the system of market exchange: in
his view, the primitive form of gift was destined to be supplanted by
the egoistic model of commerce. See Mauss [1923-24] 1990. Among

the most interesting phases of the debate, it is worth citing the following: Claude Lévi-Strauss's (1969) focus on the exchange of women as gifts between men; Marshall Sahlins's (1972) model of gifting based on the "spectrum of reciprocity," a range of gratuity and obligation; and Annette Weiner's (1976) revision of the dominant idea that gifts were exchanged only between men. Among the recent works by historians on the subject of gifts in the medieval and early modern periods, three books provide crucial theoretical frameworks and exemplar case studies: Natalie Zemon Davis, *The Gift in Sixteenth-Century France* (2000); Valentin Groebner, *Liquid Assets* (2002); and Gadi Algazi, Valentin Groebner, and Bernhard Jussen, eds., *Negotiating the Gift* (2003).

4. See Martinez 1994 and 1999.

5. In *The Gender of the Gift*, Marylin Strathern 1988 theorizes the gendering of the gift in relation to the gift giver, the receiver, and the type of transaction involved.

6. See chapters 1 and 3. I read Strathern's gendered gift theory through the lens of Gayle Rubin's influential revision of the theory of exchange of women, "The Traffic in Women" (1975). On the relevance of this theory of circulation to discursive practices, see Psaki 2004.

7. Esposito 2009, 4–12.

8. Ariosto uses the story of the daughter of the King of Norbelanda for the Lidia episode, and its frame (the fall into the cave and the genealogical vision/prophecy) for the Bradamante episode with the gender reversal. In so doing, the poet is probably making yet another statement on the "cruel lady" tradition of medieval romance. Bradamante is the victim of the betrayal (like Breusso), and the figure of the cruel lady (transformed into Pinabello) is eliminated. However, by transforming the cave into Merlin's "vocal tomb," Ariosto reintroduces the theme of the cruel lady: Merlin's undoing was at the hands of a woman, who locked him alive in the tomb he had prepared to share with her.

9. Critics have noticed the gender reversal, and in a few cases they have tried to explain it. Rajna 1975 justifies the reversal with Ariosto's "predilection" for his female characters and the female gender: "È accaduto uno scambio di sesso: nel romanzo francese era un uomo il tradito, una donna la traditrice. Ma come osservai altra volta, l'Ariosto in generale è molto benigno alle femmine, e tende a dipingerle infelici, pagate d'ingratitudine, oppresse" [A sex exchange has taken place: in the French romance the man was betrayed and the woman was the traitor. But as I have observed elsewhere, Ari-

osto is in general very benevolent toward women, and he essentially
represents them as unhappy, rewarded with ingratitude, oppressed]
(124).

10. Andrew Fichter 1982 addresses the topic of the gender reversal
in the course of his study of the Furioso as a dynastic epic along with
the *Aeneid*, Augustine's *Confessions*, Tasso's *Gerusalemme liberata*,
and Spenser's *Faerie Queene*. Unlike most critics, Fichter points to
the impact of the role exchange: "But what are we to make of the
most obvious of Ariosto's revisions of Virgil, the fact that it is Bradamante rather than Ruggiero who plays the part of Aeneas in this
episode?" (89). As well as underlining the change in respect to the *Aeneid*, Fichter calls attention to the fact that the role of addressee of the
prophecy is meant for Ruggiero. His explanation is only apparently
literary: he claims that Ariosto "has divided the role of Aeneas between Ruggiero and Bradamante" (89), thus shifting "the crisis of the
dynastic quest from the establishment of a new race and a new city
to the attainment of regenerate selfhood by the heroes" (90). According to this interpretation, Bradamante and Ruggiero, the "two halves
of an originally integral being," would be, at least in part, allegorical representations of the new, divided Renaissance subject seeking
reunion. Even though there is a clear division of roles between Ruggiero and Bradamante, there is no textual evidence to prove that their
union constitutes in any way a recomposition of the self. The psychology of the *Furioso* is a "collective psychology," in which characters
do not attain or seek consistency (Zatti 1990. See in particular the
chapter "La psicologia nel *Furioso*," 113–25). Moreover, as Albert
Ascoli has demonstrated, Ruggiero's education—which Fichter puts
at the center of his developmental structure—essentially represent
the failure of humanistic moral training (Ascoli 1987, 168–224). We
could also consider Wiggins's reading of Orlando as a "male Dido" as
part of a global gender shift in the poem (1986, 113). Everson 2001
underlines the gender shift and finds in the *Mambriano* a first model
for it, as we observed, but she finds that its liberating potential is contrasted by the need to conform Bradamante's behavior to the current
social norms (342–44).

11. The third character exposed to prophetic discourse and vision
is Astolfo, who receives knowledge on the voyages of discovery from
Andronica (canto XV), as well as being the protagonist of the lunar
episode, where St. John makes him see the "vello" destined to be Cardinal Ippolito.

12. It was Ruggiero who explained at length the future of the
House of Este to Bradamante, whom he had just met (*Inamoramento*

de Orlando, III, 5, 18–37). One of the elements differentiating the *I-namoramento de Orlando* from the *Furioso* is the fact that in the latter dynastic knowledge is always, consistently, presented through prophetic communication. This is not the case in Boiardo's poem, where the dynastic future is discussed as matter of fact, almost unrelated to secret and superior wisdom.

13. The theme of the astrologer unable to see his own destiny is a classical one (Virgil, *Aeneid* IX, 324–28). Ariosto uses it in this con frontation between Bradamante and Atlante, as well as in the episode of Cloridano and Medoro, closely derived from *Aeneid* IX. In *OF* XVIII, 174, the astrologer Alfeo is slain in his sleep by Cloridano: he had foreseen his own death in old age, in his wife's arms. As further proof of how deeply the *Furioso* is steeped in medieval romance, note that in the *cantare* of the *Ponzela Gaia*, Merlin is the one who cannot foresee his future; the *cantare* further proves the connection between Melissa and Merlin.

14. I have substituted *seed* for *womb* in Waldman's translation.

15. On this aspect see Jordan, "Writing beyond the *Querelle*"(1999), especially 297–99.

16. For a balanced account of the debate over female sperm and its generative power, see Cadden, *Meaning of Sex Difference in the Middle Ages* (1993), 117–34.

17. In what Laqueur 1990 calls a "one-sex model," which in his view dominated the medieval and early modern periods, female genitalia are but the inversion of male genitalia, and both men and women produce seed, even though the generative power of this seed is discussed.

18. On this, see Bell, *How to Do It* (1999), especially 25–26 and 60–61. On Renaissance medicine and on the function of seed in generation, see MacLean (1980) and Siraisi (1987). Valeria Finucci has reconsidered the problem from the point of view of literary production: see her *The Manly Masquerade* (2003); the problem of seed is treated in particular on pages 7–24.

19. We are far, one could observe, from the "search for the valiant seed" of Stagi's *Amazonida*, quoted in chapter 2.

20. Here I have substituted *seed* for *issue* in Waldman's translation. The translator's otherwise inexplicable changes to the original meaning of the text can be accounted for by the uneasiness caused by the terms normally associated with male paternity, which Ariosto attributes to Bradamante.

21. It is worth noting that this line echoes and manipulates the Evangelical passage which serves as the basis for the fourth line of the

Marian prayer *Ave Maria*: "et benedictus fructus ventris tui, Iesus."
See Luke 1:42: "et exclamavit voce magna et dixit benedicta tu inter
mulieres et benedictus fructus ventris tui."

22. "Conceived in you by Ruggiero's seed." Interestingly enough,
Waldman translates this passage leaving the original meaning of *seed*.

23. When Melissa, magically disguised as Atlante, scolds Ruggiero
for his hesitation to follow his destiny, she uses the vocabulary of generation and presents Bradamante as the sealed womb, to which Ruggiero denies conception: "Deh, perché il ventre eternamente claudi,/
dove il ciel vuol che sia per te concetto/ la glorïosa e soprumana prole/
ch'esser de' al mondo più chiara che 'l sole?" [Why do you eternally
seal the womb where, Heaven decrees, you are to conceive the glorious and superhuman progeny, which will be in the world more radiant
than the sun?].

24. In the *Furioso* itself, the terminology of the *seed*, gendered
male, as opposed to the *womb*, gendered female, applies to the birth
of Ruggiero and Marfisa from Galiziella (II, 32; XXXVI, 59) and to
the fraternal encounter of Rinaldo and Ruggiero in Lipadusa (XLIV,
5). For a similar approach, see for instance the discussion on Febus's
dynasty in the *Cantari di Febus il forte* in chapter 3.

25. Ascoli 1987 underlines the fact that she seems to represent the
"privileged reader who sees how the poem opens onto the self and its
place in history" (23). For this aspect, also see Jordan 1999, esp. 298.

26. In this light, other aspects of Bradamante's character become
more legible. For instance, the interpretation of her letters, confined
by the identification of the sole ovidian model, can be expanded in the
light of the character's epic-chivalric past.

27. Furlati, ed., *I cantari del Danese* (2003). Note that in the
Danese, Bradiamonte is a pagan (the daughter of the sultan) whose
brother is called Aquilante. This factor possibly establishes a connection with the prose *Aquilante e Formosa*. Whereas Bradiamonte falls
in love with Ulivieri in the *Danese*, in *Aquilante e Formosa*, Orlando
wants to marry Ulivieri to Formosa. In the *Castello di Teris*, belonging to the same tradition of *Aquilante e Formosa*, Braidamonte is married to Girardo, and it is Rovenza who pursues Ulivieri. Bradiamonte
clearly belongs to the same group as the giantesses, even though she
occupies a privileged and somewhat ambiguous position. On this, see
chapters 1 and 2.

28. For Ascoli, Bradamante's special position as a reader is seriously undermined, on the moral level, by the fact that she decides to
ignore the violent, deadly element of betrayal, represented in the tapestry by the infamous episode of the treachery of Ferrante and Giulio

d'Este (and paralleled, in and beyond the text of the *Furioso*, by the killing of Ruggiero at the hands of the Maganzesi). This suppression is not innate in Bradamante's character: the first time she had seen the "cruel couple," Ferrante and Giulio, in Merlino's cave, she had asked Melissa to explain their demeanor; but Melissa had silenced her curiosity: "Di ciò dirti più inanzi non accade./ Statti col dolcie in bocca, e non ti doglia/ ch'amareggiare al fin non te la voglia" [I shall tell you no further about this; leave with a sweet taste in your mouth, and do not complain if I refuse to turn it to bitterness] (*OF* III, 62, 6–8). For a discussion of the events surrounding the treachery of Giulio and Ferrante, see my introduction. For details on the historical event, see Bacchelli 1966.

29. Finucci 1992 argued that the choice of Bradamante as a privileged addressee of prophetic knowledge is not subversive; rather, it is a defensive move: "One reason to have women, rather than men, once again function as privileged onlookers to histories of men's valor is that they are outsiders and thus less likely to contest the representation. In other words, women are chosen to confirm male readings of dynastic genealogies because they have no recognized role in creating them" (250). Although I agree that Bradamante does not openly contest the prophecies, I would argue that the choice of this character as an addressee, coupled with the reflection on gender and genealogical politics in the poem, makes the prophetic discourse of the *Furioso* potentially subversive.

30. Ascoli 1987 indicates a similar direction of inquiry when, discussing the figure of Cassandra, he suggests that "by comparing himself to a woman artist, Ariosto is continuing the poem-long project of collapsing fundamental conceptual differences, including sex roles" (390).

31. To these *exphrases*, Rajna adds a fragment, containing the description of Ullania's shield, which was probably meant to fill the space assigned to the paintings in the Rocca in 1532. I will consider this fragment, as well as the Rocca di Tristano episode in the next chapter.

32. MacPhail, "Ariosto and the Prophetic Moment" (2001).

33. Dante Alighieri, *Divina Commedia*, edited by Giorgio Petrocchi (Florence: Le Monnier, 1988). The quotation is from *Inferno* II, 31–33: "But I, why come there? or who grants it? I am not Aeneas, I am not Paul. Neither I nor others believe me worthy of that" (translation by Durling and Martinez 1997).

34. In this sense, Bradamante's question anticipates Moderata Fonte's title *Il merito delle donne* (The Worth of Women), and not surprisingly so, given Fonte's deep knowledge of Ariosto's poem, amply demonstrated by her *Floridoro*.

35. For illuminating analyses of the lunar episode, see Durling 1965, 146–50; Quint 1977; and Ascoli 1987, esp. 284–304.

36. For a similar discourse on the praise of women, see the discussion of Andrea Stagi's *Amazonida* in chapter 2.

37. On Ariosto's treatment of his patrons, see Ascoli 1987, in particular 381–89.

38. Ariosto is probably referring to himself as the "new Virgil."

39. The poet was never in her service, but she played an important role in his life, encouraging his work. On the relation between Isabella d'Este and Ariosto, see Catalano 1931, II, 80.

40. Bigi, in his edition of the *Furioso*, comments: "Il paragone con Penelope acquista un curioso significato, se si tiene presente quanto l'Ariosto stesso dirà in XXXV 27, 8" (1982, 538) [The comparison to Penelope acquires an odd meaning, if we take into account what Ariosto himself will declare in XXXV 27, 8]. Lisa Regan 2005 has developed a very nuanced and original interpretation of Isabella in the *Furioso*. She convincingly argues that Isabella is the figure of the vulnerable patron, ambiguously mirroring the marginal condition of the poet and of poetry itself. I am also grateful to Lisa for sharing with me chapter 1 of her dissertation, "Ariosto and the Uses of Flattery."

41. There is obviously no reference to the lower, dominated classes. In both cases, Ariosto has in mind rulers, queens, and kings.

42. See Ascoli 1987 and MacPhail 2001.

43. The presence of a woman, the daughter of the king of Norbelanda, was a painful reminder of Febus's tragic demise.

44. The lord of the castle interprets the predictive frescoes painted by Merlin on the walls of the Rocca. This interpretation has come down to him through a line of ancestors, passed on from father to son (*OF* XXXIII, 25–26). On the impact of gender on the gift dynamics, see Strathern 1988.

45. For the Merlin tradition in France, see Zumthor 1943. For the Italian tradition, see Visani 1994 and Delcorno Branca 1998, 77–97. Delcorno Branca in particular has conducted groundbreaking research on the Merlinian tradition in Italy.

46. In a letter to her book finder Giorgio Brognolo, dated September 24, 1491, Isabella asks for a copy of *Merlino*, among other books. See Tissoni Benvenuti 1987, 24.

47. I consulted the 1480 edition at the Biblioteca Nazionale Braidense in Milan. Book 4, 2.

48. See above, note 28. *Aeneid* VI, 860–85.

49. Bigi provides an overview of the critical attempts at interpreting the emblem in his edition of the *Furioso* (1982), 1948–49. For an analysis of the image, see Ascoli 1987, 392. I distance my own interpretation from

Ascoli's inasmuch as I see betrayal as the constitutive opposite of the gift. Conor Fahy (1987, 106) observes that the emblem is present in the first two editions, and suggests that "the wood" was the property of Ariosto himself. The motto is present in all three editions, but in the 1532 edition it is not accompanied by this image. In three exemplars of the 1532 edition, the motto is replaced by an image that Fahy interprets as a sheep nursing a wolf cub, another rendition of the motto itself. See Fahy 1989, 111–16 and Beer 1987, 161-67. Jo Ann Cavallo discusses the theme of betrayal between Boiardo and Ariosto (*The Romance Epics of Boiardo, Ariosto, and Tasso*, 2004, 122). Alberto Casadei connects the motto to the biblical model. See *La fine degli incanti* (1997), 149–51. On Ariosto and emblems, see Farinella 2007. Masi discusses the emblem, remarking that it becomes part of the coat of arms of Rinaldo in the *Cinque canti* (2003, 80), a fact already highlighted by Ceserani 1988.

50. Remo Ceserani clearly sets up the state of the question on the emblem in the article "L'Impresa delle api e dei serpenti" (1988). See also Santoro 1989, 317-20.

51. Rajna 1975 points out the connection with Jove, indicating the account of Lactantius (130). Rajna also mentions the *Paradiso degli Alberti* as a possible source for the name, on which see below.

52. For a definition of donor, see Propp, *Morphology of the Folktale* (1958).

53. Jameson 1972, 195–205. I define *actant* as character-function, following Greimas 1970 and 1983.

54. Jameson 1981 gives as an example of this phenomenon the "character" of Heathcliff in *Wuthering Heights*, who "occupies in some complicated way the place of the donor in this narrative system: a donor who must wear the functional appearance of the protagonist in order to perform his quite different actantial function" (127).

55. See *Dosso Dossi*, ed. Humfrey and Lucco (1998), 114–18. For the identification of the subject, see also Zika 2002, n.1; and Wood 2006.

56. For a valuable summary of all the interpretations of the painting and a balanced approach to its interpretation, see Morel, "Mélissa et la magie noire," in *L'art de la Renaissance* (2006), 483–94, republished with revisions in Morel 2008, 232–56.

57. *OF* III, 22, 7–8. On the representations of demons in Renaissance art, see Cole 2002. The x-ray scan of the painting shows a large pentimento, where we see an armored figure standing, leaning over the seated figure (in Coliva 1998). It may be too daring to see Bradamante in this erased figure; still, the coincidences between the letter of canto III and some details of the painting may warrant further inquiry into the topic, outside the scope of this study.

58. See Morel 2008, 256.

59. The figure painted by Dosso is consistent with contemporary representations of the Sibyls (particularly in the head-gear and in the rich clothing), including a *Sibyl* painted by Dosso himself (see Humphrey and Lucco 1998, 184–87).

60. Ronald Martinez has offered brilliant analyses of cantos XLII and XLIII in connection with a variety of models, principally the *Fabula de Cefalo* by Niccolò da Correggio and the *Odyssey* ("De-Cephalizing Rinaldo,"1994, and "Two Odysseys," 1999). As suggested above, at the core of his argument is the opposition between the economy of tyranny and that of the gift, which has significantly influenced my reading of canto XLIII. Other readings of these episodes include the studies by Hoffman 1992 and Walter Moretti 1987, as well as the psychoanalytical reading by Juliana Schiesari, "The Domestication of Woman" (1991).

61. Internoscia 1948.

62. For the connections between Morgain and Mélusine, see Harf-Lancner, *Les fées au Moyen Âge* (1984); on the *ponzela*, see *Ponzela gaia*, edited by Amidei (2000); for a recent consideration of the monstrosity intertwined to the foundational aspect in the *Mélusine* story, see Huot, "Dangerous Embodiments" (2003). One could even point out that the snake and the bee, Manto and Melissa, are the two protagonists of the emblem of the poem discussed above.

63. Rajna mentions this element but disregards the fact that the priestesses in question were in Delphi (a site linked to prophetic knowledge and transmission). *Melissa* is also an epithet used for Demeter and Artemis.

64. The literary tradition on the qualities of bees is extensive, from book IV of the *Georgics* to the legend according to which Pindar had been fed by bees, to the Renaissance idea of imitation compared to the work of the bees, who make honey out of the nectars of different flowers.

65. On the representations of bees as a model society and on the shifts in the consideration of their genders, see: Haarhoff 1960, Roscalla 1988, Prete 1991, Mayhew 1999.

66. *Le api* was published posthumously in 1539. I quote from this edition.

67. Edited by Antonio Lanza (1975). Giovanni Gherardi da Prato, a judge, lawyer, and poet, lived in Florence between the second half of the thirteenth century and the first half of the following century. Rajna mentions the text as a potential source for the figure of Melissa, but further studies are necessary in order to determine a positive connection between the two texts.

68. On the tapestry as figure of the empire, see Fichter 1982, 104–108.

69. As Albert Ascoli observed, Cassandra herself receives the gift of prophetic ability. It is a bitter gift, however: since Cassandra refused to be taken by Apollo in exchange for the gift, she was doomed never to be believed (Ascoli 1987, especially pp. 390–393).

70. There is certainly a connection worth exploring between this circulation of prophecies as gifts and the representation of female patronage. The gratuity of poetic praise for the lady, as described for instance in canto XLII, could turn the relation between the poet and the female patron into a utopian site of altruistic exchange. In this context, an important parallel is provided by Alexander Nagel's analysis of the relation between Vittoria Colonna and Michelangelo, who established the innovative practice of presentation drawings, given as a gift from artist to friend. See Alexander Nagel, "Art as a Gift: Liberal Art and Religious Reform in the Renaissance," in Algazi et al., *Negotiating the Gift* (2003), 319–360, in particular 353–39.

71. It is, after all, her violent killing of Pinabello that sets in motion the chain of violence leading to Ruggiero's death.

5. *EXTERNI THALAMI*

1. Klapisch-Zuber 1985; De Giorgio and Klapisch-Zuber, eds. 1996, 119–303.

2. On the material culture surrounding weddings, see Baskins 1998 and 2008; for the case of Ferrara, see Bellonci [1939] 1994, Chiappini [1967] 2001, Gundersheimer 1973, Iotti 1997.

3. The event, related by Caleffini's chronicle *Diario Ferrarese*, is reported by historian Giovanni Ricci as an instance of the violent presence of youth in Renaissance society (2007, 18).

4. In 1933, Ezio Levi considered the *Orlando furioso* as a "nuptial epic," arguing that the marriage of Ruggiero and Bradamante is the central theme of the poem ("L'*Orlando furioso* come epopea nuziale"). Levi, a romance philologist and a medievalist, recovered the dimension of the *Furioso* as a *chanson de geste*, centered on the founding couple. Levi's aim was to historicize the poem in the context of the marriage politics of the House of Este, linking Ruggiero's adventures to traditional forms of genealogical narration. In particular, Levi demonstrated that the *geste* of Ruggiero have among their sources the Catalan chronicle by Ramon Muntaner, recounting the origins of the House of Aragon. This fact becomes particularly important when we consider, as Levi invites us to do, that the wedding of

Ercole d'Este and Eleonora d'Aragona, in 1473, played a crucial role in shaping contemporary Ferrarese culture. Levi convincingly argues for the influence of Aragonese genealogical narrations on the cultural milieu of the Este court, in particular on Boiardo and Tito Vespasiano Strozzi. Levi's article has not received much attention; an important exception is a 1984 article by Remo Ceserani, who developed some of Levi's insights ("Due modelli culturali e narrativi"). In particular, Ceserani focuses on the wedding theme as the fulcrum of one of the two "cultural and narrative models" of the poem. In the *Furioso* Ceserani finds two contrasting lines of development: "Da una parte c'è il mondo degli intrighi, delle illusioni, dei travestimenti, dei sogni . . . del desiderio ossessivo . . . il gran tema favoloso del desiderio e della 'devianza.' . . . Dall'altra parte c'è il mondo d'Ercole prodicio, delle scelte morali" (498) ["On one hand, we have the world of deceit, of illusion, of masquerade, of dream, of obsessive desire, and the fantastic theme of desire and 'deviation.' On the other hand, we have the world of Hercules, bearer of Justice: the world of moral choice"] (my translation). In the poem, the *fabula* of madness and desire is intertwined with that of moral choice. This is a widely accepted interpretation, one that we have discussed many times: a vision of the *Furioso* as a hybrid between *epos* and *romanzo*. What is particularly interesting in this analysis of the text is the foundation of one of the two cultural models on the theme of the wedding. In this move, Ceserani has followed Levi, but has not been followed himself, at least not to the full extent; the epic "pole" of the poem has been identified with its linear progression toward the dynastic end, in contrast to the text's novelistic digressions; the relevance of the wedding theme in this bipolarity, however, has not been studied.

5. Rajna 1975, 460.

6. Jane Everson provides an important direction of inquiry by combining these two approaches (2001, 342–44).

7. Recent studies on chivalric romance and other literary forms of the early modern period have insisted on the importance of kinship ties and the representation of marriage as ideologically central to the texts. Michael Harney, in his book *Kinship and Marriage in Medieval Hispanic Chivalric Romance* (2001), considers chivalric texts produced in the Iberian peninsula in the late Middle Ages, concluding that romances provide an image of marriage more favorable to women, and make space for the possibility of female freedom of choice as opposed to the constrictions of patriarchal necessity. Harney opposes the view expressed by Roberta Krueger and Ruth El Saffar, who analyze Old French and Spanish chivalric romance, respectively.

According to Harney, these two scholars envision the genre as "sexist or patriarchal" (239), simplifying a very complex issue in feminist scholarship: the relation between the representation of women in literature and historical ideologies about women's roles. This is a question of increasing importance ever since the publication of Joan Kelly's article "Did Women Have a Renaissance?" in 1977. Although Kelly's article proved groundbreaking in feminist literary and historical studies, it had two main limitations: it more or less openly identified sexuality with women, and it blindly relied on literary representations of women—for example, in French courtly lyric—to establish women's status in society. For a very clear reflection on Kelly's article, see Fisher and Halley's introduction to *Seeking the Woman in Late Medieval and Renaissance Writing* (1989): 1–17. Harney's conclusions about Spanish chivalric romances limit themselves to the consideration that, since women appear actively to pursue marriage with a husband of their choice against their parents' will, these texts are aimed "to please an audience in which women predominated morally if not numerically" (256). While agreeing that there are elements of escapist appeal for a female audience of these texts, I would observe that the opposition between the will of the parents and the will of the young couple is explained, at least in part, by a sociological model that is founded on the ascent of young nobles against the wishes of established families. Despite these differences of perspective, Harney provides a wealth of information on kinship ties in the chivalric romance. From a feminist perspective, Georgina Dopico Black has studied the figure of the wife in early modern Spanish literature as a site of anxiety in *Perfect Wives, Other Women* (2001). These texts' quixotic compulsion to control the body of the wife, she argues, both derive from and perpetuate a general anxiety over the body of the cultural other.

8. "Exogamy" is a term whose meaning varies widely over time. In the High Middle Ages the Church forbade marriages between relatives up to the seventh degree, and the prohibition was extended to "spiritual relatives." In 1215, the restriction was lowered to the fourth degree. Individual cities and states had different customs regarding the accepted degree of consanguinity between spouses. See Diane Owen Hughes, "Il matrimonio nell'Italia medievale," in De Giorgio and Klapisch-Zuber 1996, 5–61. On exogamy, see in particular 32–34.

9. Ibid., 32.

10. Molho 1994.

11. "Il matrimonio," 34. On the case of Venice, see the fundamental study by Stanley Chojnacki, *Women and Men in Renaissance Venice* (2000).

12. Dean 1988; Bestor 1992, 1996, 2000, and 2005; Iotti 1997.

13. Iotti 1997.

14. The term "hypergamy" denotes the practice of marrying into an equal or higher social class. On hypergamy as a trait of the marriage politics of the House of Este, see Chiappini [1967] 2001, Iotti 1997, Bestor 1996. It could be argued that when a limited number of reigning families continually intermarry, exogamy ceases to exist; this was the case among nineteenth-century European nobility, whose reigning families engaged de facto in endogamous intermarriage. This does not seem to be the case for noble families of the Italian peninsula throughout the fifteenth century.

15. Bestor 1992. Among the genealogical documents involving the House of Este and considered by Bestor, the *Furioso* and the *Inamoramento de Orlando* hold a marginal place, second to strictly genealogical texts, such as the famous *Genealogia dei principi d'Este* and standard local chronicles. The title Bestor uses for the *Genealogia* is *Iconografia Estense.* Her main contention is that these texts betray no consistent representation of genealogical structures, such as would reflect the influence of the prince, but rather condition their treatment of genealogical material individually and eccentrically.

16. Bestor sees them as participating in a "major ambiguity in the way the Este and other ruling houses thought about relations among kin." In her account, "the Este understood kinship bonds not given in blood to be made or 'contracted,'" while at the same time "they created such bonds because they were suspicious of contractual relations and the carefully delimited obligations and short-term interests they expressed" (1992, 444).

17. On the Este's aggressive marriage politics, see Chiappini [1967] 2001 and Iotti 1997. Levi, in the article on the *Furioso* as a nuptial epic quoted above, interprets Ruggiero's hypergamy in the *Furioso* as a reflection of the position of Ercole I in relation to his bride Eleonora d'Aragona.

18. Ariosto, *Opere minori* (1954).

19. Translations of the *Satire* by Wiggins (*The Satires of Ludovico Ariosto*, 1976), 127.

20. For the Borgias' fame, see Catalano 1930–31, Chiappini [1967] 2001, and Bellonci [1939] 1994. For a reconsideration of Lucrezia's myth, see Bordin and Trovato 2006 and Ghirardo 2008.

21. I follow Mario Santoro's edition of the oration, in Ariosto, *Opere*, vol. 3 (1989), 150–59. Translations are mine unless otherwise noted. Anthony D'Elia has studied the virtually unknown tradition of the humanistic wedding oration. He claims that humanists adapted

classical orations to the context of the Italian courts, giving voice to both traditional and innovative views on marriage, sexual pleasure, the position of women, and so on. See D'Elia 2002 and 2004. For a discussion of the violence of alliance through marriage in these orations, see below.

22. Even Ercole's reclamation of marshy land is glorified through the myth of Hercules defeating the Hydra: "ubi multiplicem Dux inclytus hydram/ contundit ignavis foedantem flexibus agros" (135–36) [where the glorious Duke vanquished the multi-headed Hydra, who polluted the fields with her lazy spires].

23. Francesco de Arquata Bertalono, *Oratio in laudem matrimonii*, MS Magl. VII 1087, Florence, Biblioteca Nazionale Centrale, fol. 131v. Quoted in D'Elia 2002, 394–95. D'Elia also quotes the Paduan humanist Egidio Guido, who makes a similar argument (395). The marriage is consistently defined as a "foedus," a pact, exactly as in Ariosto's epithalamium.

24. The treatise, written between 1506 and 1509, circulated in Rome shortly thereafter. Its modern edition was published in Rome in 1873 by E. Narducci. See Klapisch-Zuber, "An Ethnology of Marriage in the Age of Humanism," in her *Women, Family, and Ritual* (1985), 247–60. Jane Tylus also discusses Altieri's connection between rape and foundation in her article "The Rape of the Sabines" (2007), 105–108.

25. See chapter 2.

26. See *OF* XX, octaves 11 to 29, discussed at length in chapter 2. This passage presents a concise narrative in which the Trojan War is blamed for many illegitimate sons born to the Greek soldiers. These sons, after the war, form a platoon of "wayward men" who wander the Mediterranean Sea, bringing disorder and confusion. Ultimately, their mass abandonment of the Cretan women (whom they had taken from the island and brought to Puglia) impels the women to create a strong female society and revenge themselves upon men.

27. See chapter 2.

28. Guidone proudly introduces himself in canto XXXI: "Io son Guidone,/ concetto de lo illustre inclito seme,/ come ancor voi, del generoso Amone" (*OF* XXXI, 31, 2–4) [I am Guidone, conceived — like you—from the illustrious seed of noble Aymon]. Everyone greets Guidone like a brother, and compares him to his father for his prowess and courage (*OF* XXXI, 34).

29. The term "gagliarda" resonates with the qualifications of the women warriors discussed in chapter 2.

30. Ferrarese historiography consistently designates the daughters of Este as Este, and the wives of Este as Este.

31. *OF* XIII, 66–73.

32. For Casadei, the episode is the "least innovative" of the four great additions, from an ideological point of view (1988, 168 n.20). In the chapter devoted to the Rocca di Tristano, Charles Ross explores both the sociohistorical context and the political implications of the episode and of the innovative figure of Bradamante within it (Ross 1997, 58–80). The chapter appeared earlier as an article: "Ariosto's Fable of Power: Bradamante at the Rocca di Tristano," *Italica* 68 (1991): 155–75.

33. See in particular Finucci 1992, Benson 1983, Jordan 1999, Hairston 2000, and Deanna Shemek, "Gender, Duality, and the Sacrifices of History: Bradamante in the *Orlando furioso*," in Shemek 1988, 77–125.

34. This reading of the sequence does not eliminate the possibility of circularity in the definition of the self. Only a systematic analysis of gender construction in the *Furioso* could settle this problem. My reading, which confines itself to gender in relation to genealogy, should not be taken as a global interpretation of the *Furioso*.

35. Cantos XXXII and XXXVII, as well as the beginning of canto XXXIII, were written *ex novo* for the 1532 edition: the episode of the Rocca di Tristano and the episode of Marganorre are two of the four great additions Ariosto prepared for the last edition. The coupling of these two cantos is not arbitrary; rather, Ariosto himself provides a strong link between the two episodes in the person of the messenger Ullania.

36. The element of the choice of a mate based on his supreme physical prowess reminds us of the stratagem Bradamante will resort to in order to receive only Ruggiero as her husband; and in chapter two we have seen how this element is a component of the woman warrior persona throughout the tradition. If it is true that this is a typical trait of the chivalric tradition (the most beautiful lady must be paired to the most valiant knight), it is also important to observe that the competitive element links the prospective wedding of the queen to that of Bradamante, prefiguring the dynastic end.

37. Another possible intertext, which links the tale of the *femine omicide* and its protagonist, Guidone, with the *Rocca* episode, is the *Ancroia*: in the poem, Costanza gives to her son Guidone a pavilion with histories of heroes, as well as weapons with inscriptions. See Montanari 1993, 14. For the *Tavola ritonda*, I quote from Heijkant's 1997 edition. Translations are my own.

38. *Tristano Riccardiano* LIII (131–32). See the Parodi edition (1896).

39. This motif of excellence is typical of the *Tavola ritonda*. This text, which fully realizes the Italian version of the integration of Tristan within the cycle of the Arthurian Table, has a strong tendency to essentialize the superiority of Tristan and Iseult to any other couple. The rivalry-friendship with Lancelot and Guinevere becomes a topos: this is a defining trait of the Italian tradition.

40. "La donna, cominciando a disarmarsi,/ s'avea lo scudo e dipoi l'elmo tratto;/ quando una cuffia d'oro, in che celarsi/ soleano i capei lunghi e star di piatto,/ uscì con l'elmo; onde caderon sparsi/ giù per le spalle, e la scopriro a un tratto/ e la feron conoscer per donzella,/ non men che fiera in arme, in viso bella" (*OF* XXXII, 79). [Now Bradamant started to disarm. She set down her shield and drew off her helmet, but a golden band with which she concealed and contained her long tresses came off with the helmet, so that her hair fell loosely over her shoulders, all at once revealing her for a maiden no less beautiful than fierce in battle.]

41. *Inamoramento de Orlando* III, v, 40, 8; 41, 1–2.

42. Valeria Finucci claims that the emergence of Bradamante's beauty genders her, rendering her less active and "showing her as a properly feminized object for the onlooker" (1992, 249).

43. The *Tristan en prose* includes the encounter with the shepherd (here the protagonist is Tristano himself), and the episode echoes a long passage from the *Palamedès*, where the establishment of the custom is ascribed to King Uterpendragon (Rajna 1975, 487–502). These two models provide the basic structure of the adventure: in order to earn hospitality for the night, the knight must win a duel. In the case of the *Tristan*, the duel is with the host himself; in the case of the *Palamedès*, Guiron and his companion Danayn must joust with Brehus and Sir Lac. In this second version, the origin of the custom is narrated: Uterpendragon was defied and defeated by a "petit chevalier," and forced to leave the hostel for the night (495–97).

44. Rajna's hypothesis, that the theme could be a derivation from the episode of the *Passage perilleux* in the *Palamedès* (1975, 498), seems to depend on a merely generic comparison between the beauty of a lady and that of the wife of the jealous Dyodenas.

45. See Rajna (1975, 482), who also mentions historical episodes.

46. It would be possible to postulate the existence of only one text, either in Italian or in French, in which the episodes divided between the *Cantari di Febus il forte* and the *Tavola ritonda* are all present in the same narration. The similarities of the *Furioso* to the accounts of these two extant texts suggest such an archetype would probably have been Italian. Even without positing a single ur-text, however, we can

acknowledge that Breus and his adventures constitute a persistent intertext in the *Furioso*.

47. On the interpretation of the episode, I am in substantial agreement with Charles Ross, who has argued that "at the end of his life, in the final edition of his poem, Ariosto drew upon the old romance convention of the custom of the castle to dramatize the response of an individual to an institution that lacks integrity." In my opinion, the medieval text already posits itself in opposition to the lack of integrity of the custom, as I have tried to demonstrate by analyzing the use of the figure of Breus throughout the *Furioso*. See Ross 1997, 78.

48. See Finucci 1992, 249–50. Finucci interprets Bradamante's claims as potentially empowering for women, but she finds this potential ultimately to be frustrated by the ridicule imposed on the heroine.

49. See MacPhail 2001.

50. The original fragment was published by Santorre Debenedetti in his *I Frammenti autografi dell' "Orlando furioso"* (1937), with the title "Lo scudo della Regina Elisa." Finucci 1992 reads the exclusion of the shield as an omission of female prophetic power: the shield had been crafted by the Sibyl, and represents in Finucci's view the female version of history (251).

51. A key element links the Rocca di Tristano episode to the prophecy itself: France. The French custom of the castle is paired with a painted invective on the behavior of the French on the Italian battlefield. In this sense, the praise of negotiation becomes a praise of the little Ferrara, caught between France and the Empire, and always allied with the pope.

PRIMARY SOURCES

Manuscripts and Incunabula

Aquilante e Formosa. Florence, Biblioteca Mediceo-Laurenziana. Med. Pal. 101, vol. 2.

Castello di Teris. Florence, Biblioteca Riccardiana. MS. 1904.

Dama Rovenza. Venice: Luca di Domenico, ca. 1482. Rome, Biblioteca Apostolica Vaticana. Inc. Ross. 1350.

Fortunato. Florence, Biblioteca Nazionale Centrale, MS. Panciatichiano 36.

Historia di Bradiamonte sorella di Rinaldo. Florence: Francesco di Dino, 23 maggio 1489. Rome, Biblioteca Corsiniana, Cors. 51 B 41.

Historia di Bradiamonte sorella di Rinaldo. Brescia: Battista Farfengo, 1490. Milan, Biblioteca Nazionale Braidense, Rari Castiglioni 28.

Historia di Bradiamonte sorella di Rinaldo. Florence: Lorenzo Morgiani & Johannes Petri, ca. 1492. Yale University, Beinecke Library, 1979 632.

Inamoramento de Carlo Magno. Venice: Georg Walch, 1481. University of Pennsylvania, Van Pelt Library. Folio Inc C-204. T

Inamoramento de Carlo Magno. Bologna: Bazaliero de' Bazalieri, February 12 1491. Parma, Biblioteca Palatina. Inc. Parm. 641,

Inamoramento de Carlo Magno. Venice: Dionigi Bertocchi, July 31 1491. Milan, Biblioteca Nazionale Braidense. Rari Castiglioni 35.

Libro de l'Ancroia. Venice: Filippo de' Petri, 28 September 1479. New York, Pierpoint Morgan Library. PML 22108.

Libro de l'Ancroia. Venice: Cristoforo de' Pensi, 1498. Rome, Biblioteca Apostolica Vaticana. BAV A- 235.

Spagna in prosa. Florence, Biblioteca Mediceo-Laurenziana. MS. Mediceo-Palat. CI.

Spagna F. Ferrara, Biblioteca Ariostea. MS. c. II 132.

Stagi, Andrea. *Amazonida*. Venice: Cristoforo de' Pensi, 1503. Rome, Biblioteca Casanatense (RMo313); Harvard University, Houghton Library (*IC.St136.503a).

Ugieri il Danese. Venice: Luca di Domenico, 1480. Florence, Biblioteca Nazionale Centrale. Landau-Finaly 12.

Texts in Print

Alberti, Leon Battista. 1964. *Intercenali inediti*. Edited by Eugenio Garin. Florence: Sansoni, 1965. First published in "Venticinque intercenali inedite e sconosciute di Leon Battista Alberti." *Belfagor* 19: 377–98.

———. 2003. *Intercenales*. Edited by Franco Bacchelli and Luca D'Ascia. Bologna: Pendragon.

Ariosto, Ludovico. 1954. *Opere Minori*. Edited by Cesare Segre. Milan: Ricciardi.

———. 1960. *Orlando furioso*. Edited by S. Debenedetti and C. Segre. Bologna: Commissione per i testi di lingua.

———. 1974. *Orlando furioso*. Edited by Lanfranco Caretti. Turin: Einaudi.

———. 1976. *The Satires of Ludovico Ariosto: A Renaissance Autobiography*. Translated by Peter DeSa Wiggins. Athens: Ohio University Press.

———. 1982. *Orlando furioso*. Edited by Emilio Bigi. Milan: Rusconi.

———. 1989. *Opere*. Edited by Mario Santoro. Turin: Utet.

———. 1998. *Orlando furioso*. Translated by Guido Waldman 1974. Oxford: Oxford University Press.

———. 2006. *Orlando furioso secondo la princeps del 1516*. Edited by Marco Dorigatti and Gerarda Stimato. Florence: Olschki.

Barberino, Andrea da. 1951. *L'Aspramonte, Romanzo cavalleresco inedito*. Edited by Marco Boni. Bologna: Palmaverde.

———. 1972. *Aspramonte*. Edited by Luigi Cavalli. Naples: Rossi.

———. 2005. *Il Guerrin Meschino*. Edited by Mauro Cursietti. Padua: Antenore.

Bella Camilla. Poemetto di Piero da Siena. 1892. Edited by Vittorio Fiorini. Bologna: Romagnoli.

Boccaccio, Giovanni. 1941. *Teseida delle nozze d'Emilia.* Edited by Aurelio Roncaglia. Bari: Laterza.

———. 1980. *Decameron.* Edited by Vittore Branca. Turin: Einaudi.

———. 1998. *Tutte le opere.* Edited by Vittore Branca. Milan: Arnoldo Mondadori.

———. 2001. *De Mulieribus Claris. Famous Women.* Edited and translated by Virginia Brown. Cambridge: I Tatti Renaissance Library, Harvard University Press.

Boiardo, Matteo Maria. 1995. *Orlando innamorato.* Edited by Riccado Bruscagli. Turin: Einaudi.

———. 1989. *Orlando Innamorato (Orlando in Love).* Translated with an Introduction and notes by Charles Stanley Ross. Berkeley: University of California Press.

———. 1999. *Opere. L'inamoramento de Orlando.* Edited by Antonia Tissoni Benvenuti and Cristina Montagnani. Milan: Riccardo Ricciardi.

Cantari cavallereschi dei secoli XV e XVI. 1905. Edited by Giorgio Barini. Bologna: Romagnoli dall'Acqua.

Cantari d'Aspramonte inediti (Magl. VII 682). 1981. Edited by Andrea Fassò. Bologna: Commissione per i testi di lingua.

I Cantari del Danese. 2003. Edited by Sara Furlati. Alessandria: Edizioni dell'Orso.

Cantari del '300. 1970. Edited by Armando Balduino. Milan: Marzorati.

Cantari di Rinaldo da Monte Albano. 1973. Edited by Elio Melli. Bologna: Commissione per i testi di lingua.

Cantari fiabeschi arturiani. 1999. Edited by Daniela Delcorno Branca. Milan: Luni.

Cantari novellistici dal Tre al Cinquecento. 2002. Edited by Elisabetta Benucci, Roberta Manetti, and Franco Zabagli. Rome: Salerno.

Casola, Nicola da. *Attila. Poema Franco-Italiano.* 1907. Edited by Giulio Bertoni. Freiburg: Publications de l'Université de Fribourg.

Catullus, Gaius Valerius. 1957. *Poesie.* Edited and translated by Guido Mazzoni. Bologna: Zanichelli.

Cereta, Laura. 1997. *Collected Letters of a Renaissance Feminist.* Edited and translated by Diana Robin. Chicago: University of Chicago Press.

Cieco da Ferrara, Francesco. 1926. *Il Mambriano*. Edited by Giuseppe Rua. Turin: Loescher.

Debenedetti, Santorre, ed. 1937. *I Frammenti autografi dell'* Orlando furioso. Turin: Chiantore.

L'Entrée d'Espagne, chanson de geste franco-italienne. [1913] 1968. Edited by Antoine Thomas. 2 vols. New York: Johnson Reprint.

Falconetto [1483]. 2001. Edited by Andrea Canova. Mantua: Giulio Arcari Editore.

Li fatti de Spagna. Testo settentrionale trecentesco già detto Viaggio di Carlo Magno in Ispagna. 1951. Edited by Ruggero M. Ruggieri. Modena: Società Tipografica Modenese.

Fiore di Leggende. Cantari antichi. Series 1, *Cantari leggendari*. 1914. Edited by Ezio Levi. Bari: Laterza.

Folengo, Teofilo. 1991. *Orlandino*. Edited by Mario Chiesa. Padua: Antenore.

Gherardi da Prato, Guido. 1975. *Il paradiso degli Alberti*. Edited by Antonio Lanza. Rome: Salerno Editrice.

Limentani, Alberto, ed. 1962. *Dal* Roman de Palamedes *ai cantari di* Febus el Forte. Bologna: Commissione per i testi di lingua.

Montale, Eugenio. 1977. *Quaderno di quattro anni*. Milan: Arnoldo Mondadori Editore.

———. 1980. *It Depends: A Poet's Notebook*. Translated by G. Singh. New York: New Directions Books.

Nogarola, Isotta. 2004. *Complete Writings. Letterbook, Dialogue on Adam and Eve, Orations*. Edited and translated by Margaret L. King and Diana Robin. Chicago: University of Chicago Press.

Ovid (Publius Ovidius Naso). 1992. *Metamorfosi*. Edited by P. Bernardini Marzolla (1979), revised by Mario Ramous. Milan: Garzanti.

Pieri, Paulino. 1997. *La storia di Merlino*. Edited by Mauro Cursietti. Rome: Zauli.

Pius II. 2004. *Commentaries*. Edited by Margaret Meserve and Marcello Simonetta. Cambridge: I Tatti Renaissance Library, Harvard University Press.

Polo, Marco. 1982. *Il Milione nelle redazioni toscana e franco-italiana (Le divisament dou monde)*. Edited by Gabriella Ronchi. Milan: Mondadori.

Ponzela gaia. Galvano e la donna serpente. 2000. Edited by Beatrice Barbiellini Amidei. Milan: Luni.

Pulci, Luigi. 1955. *Morgante*. Edited by Franca Ageno. Milan: Riccardo Ricciardi.

Ramusio, Giovan Battista. 1978–88. *Navigazioni e viaggi*. Edited by Marica Milanesi. Vols. 1–6. Turin: Einaudi.

Le roman de Tristan en prose. 1987–97. Edited by Ph. Ménard. 9 vols. Genève: Droz.

Le roman de Tristan en prose. 1997 99. Version du ms. B.N. fr. 757. Edited by Jean-Paul Ponceau. Vols. 1–3. Paris: Champion.

Rucellai, Giovanni. 1539. *Le api*. Florence.

La Spagna. Poema cavalleresco del secolo XIV. 1939. Edited by Michele Catalano. 3 vols. Bologna: Commissione per i testi di lingua.

Stagi, Andrea. 1908. *Amazonida*. Edited by Ernesto Spadolini. Ancona: Stabilimento Tipografico Aurelio Fantoni.

Strozzi, Tito Vespasiano. 1977. *Borsias. Die Borsias des Tito Strozzi. Ein Lateinisches Epos der Renaissance*. Edited by Walther Ludvig. Munich: Fink.

Tasso, Torquato. 1961. *La Gerusalemme Liberata*. Edited by Lanfranco Caretti. Bari: Laterza.

La tavola ritonda. 1997. Edited by M.-J. Heijkant. Milan: Luni.

Tristano Riccardiano. 1896. Edited by E. G. Parodi. Bologna: Romagnoli-Dall'Acqua. 1991, reprint, with an introduction by M.-J. Heijkant, Milan: Luni.

Virgil. 1967. *Eneide*. Edited and translated by Rosa Calzecchi Onesti. Turin: Einaudi.

SECONDARY SOURCES

Agamben, Giorgio. [2003] 2005. *State of Exception*. Translated by Kevin Attell. Chicago: University of Chicago Press. Originally published as *Stato di eccezione*. Turin: Bollati Boringhieri, 2003.

Algazi, Gadi, Valentin Groebner, and Bernhard Jussen, eds. 2003. *Negotiating the Gift. Pre-Modern Figurations of Exchange*. Göttingen: Vandenhoeck & Ruprecht.

Alhaique Pettinelli, Rosanna. 1983. *L'immaginario cavelleresco nel rinascimento ferrarese*. Rome: Bonacci.

———. 2004. *Forme e percorsi dei romanzi di cavalleria*. Rome: Bulzoni.

Allaire, Gloria. 1994. "The Warrior Woman in Late Medieval Prose Epics." *Italian Culture* 12: 33–43.

————. 1996. "Portrayals of Muslims in Andrea da Barberino's *Guerrino il Meschino.*" In *Medieval Christian Perceptions of Islam*, edited by John Tolan, 243–69. New York: Garland.

————. 1997. *Andrea da Barberino and the Language of Chivalry.* Gainesville: University Press of Florida.

————. 2006. "The Narrative World of Andrea da Barberino," in *Firenze alla vigilia del Rinascimento*, edited by Maria Bendinelli Predelli, 11–20. Fiesole: Cadmo.

Ascoli, Albert Russell. 1987. *Ariosto's Bitter Harmony: Crisis and Evasion in the Italian Renaissance.* Princeton: Princeton University Press.

————. 1998. "Il segreto di Erittonio: politica e poetica sessuale nel canto XXXVII dell'*Orlando furioso.*" In *La rappresentazione dell'altro nei tesi del Rinascimento*, edited by S. Zatti, 53–76. Lucca: Pacini Fazzi.

————. 1999a. "Faith as Cover-up: Ariosto's *Orlando furioso*, Canto 21, and Machiavellian Ethics." *I Tatti Studies* 8: 135–70.

————. 1999b. "Pyrrhus' Rules: Playing with Power from Boccaccio to Machiavelli." *Modern Language Notes* 114: 14–57.

————. 2001. "Ariosto and the 'Fier Pastor': Structure and Historical Meaning in *Orlando furioso.*" *Renaissance Quarterly* 54: 487–522.

————. 2003. "Fede e riscrittura: il Furioso del '32." *Rinascimento* 43: 93–130.

————. 2010. "Like a Virgin: Fantasies of the Male Body in Orlando furioso." In *The Body in Early Modern Italy*, edited by Walter Stephens and Julia Hairston, 142–57. Baltimore: Johns Hopkins University Press.

Bacchelli, Riccardo. [1931] 1966. *La congiura di Don Giulio d'Este e altri scritti ariosteschi.* Milan: Arnoldo Mondadori.

Bakhtin, Mikail M. 1981. *The Dialogic Imagination.* Edited by Michael Holquist, translated by Carol Emerson and Michael Holquist. Austin: University of Texas Press.

Baldan, Paolo. 1981. "Marfisa: nascita e carriera di una regina amazzone." *Giornale storico della letteratura italiana* 158: 518–29.

————. 1988. *Metamorfosi di un orco. Un'irruzione folklorica nel Boiardo esorcizzata dall'Ariosto.* Milan: Unicopli.

Barbagli, Maurizio. 1984. *Sotto lo stesso tetto. Mutamenti della famiglia in Italia dal XV al XX secolo.* Bologna: Il Mulino.

Baron, Hans. 1955. *The Crisis of the Early Italian Renaissance: Civic Humanism and Republican Liberty in an Age of Classicism and Tyranny*. Princeton: Princeton University Press.

Barthes, Roland. 1968. *Writing Degree Zero*. Translated by Annette Lavers and Colin Smith. New York: Hill and Wang. Originally published as *Le Degré zéro de l'écriture*. Paris: Editions du Seuil, 1953.

Baskins, Cristelle. 1998. *Cassone Painting, Humanism, and Gender in Early Modern Italy*. Cambridge: Cambridge University Press.

——. 2008. *The Triumph of Marriage: Painted Cassoni of the Renaissance*. Boston: Gutenberg Periscope Press.

Bateman, Chimène. 2007. "Amazonian Knots: Gender, Genre, and Ariosto's Women Warriors." *Modern Language Notes* 122: 1–23.

Battera, Francesca. 1987. "Per una lettura di *Orlando Innamorato*." *Studi e problemi di critica testuale* 34: 85–103.

Beecher, Donald, Massimo Ciavolella, and Roberto Fedi, eds. 2003. *Ariosto Today. Contemporary Perspectives*. Toronto: University of Toronto Press.

Beer, Marina. 1987. *Romanzi di cavalleria: il* Furioso *e il romanzo italiano del primo Cinquecento*. Rome: Bulzoni.

Beissinger, Margaret, Jane Tylus, and Susanne Wofford, eds. 1999. *Epic Traditions in the Contemporary World: The Poetics of Community*. Berkeley: University of California Press.

Bell, Rudolph M. 1999. *How to Do it: Guides to Good Living for Renaissance Italians*. Chicago: University of Chicago Press.

Bellonci, Maria. [1939] 1994. *Lucrezia Borgia*. In *Opere*, vol. 1. Milan: Mondadori.

Bendinelli Predelli, Maria. 1994. "La donna guerriera nell'immaginario italiano del tardo medioevo." *Italian Culture* 12: 13–31.

Benson, Pamela J. 1983. "A Defense of the Excellence of Bradamante." *Quaderni d'Italianistica* 4: 135–53.

——. 1992. *The Invention of the Renaissance Woman. The Challenge of Female Independence in the Literature and Thought of Italy and England*. University Park: Pennsylvania State University Press.

Bertoni, Giulio. 1903. *La Biblioteca Estense e la coltura ferrarese ai tempi del duca Ercole I (1471–1505)*. Turin: Loescher.

Bestor, Jane Fair. 1992. "Kinship and Marriage in the Politics of an Italian Ruling House: The Este of Ferrara in the Reign of Ercole I (1471–1505)." Ph.D. diss., University of Chicago.

————. 1996. "Bastardy and Legitimation in the Formation of a Regional State in Italy: The Estense Succession." *Comparative Studies in Society and History* 38: 549–85.

————. 2000. "Gli illegittimi e beneficiati della casa estense." In *Il Rinascimento. Situazioni e personaggi,* edited by Adriano Prosperi, 77–102. Ferrara: Corbo.

————. 2005. "Marriage and Succession in the House of Este: A Literary Perspective." In *Phaeton's Children: The Este Court and Its Culture in Early Modern Ferrara,* edited by Dennis Looney and Deanna Shemek, 49–85. Tempe: Arizona Center for Medieval and Renaissance Studies.

Biddick, Kathleen. 1998. *The Shock of Medievalism.* Durham: Duke University Press.

Biondi, Albano. 1982. "Angelo Decembrio e la cultura del principe." In *La corte e lo spazio: Ferrara estense,* edited by G. Papagno and A. Quondam, 637–57. Rome: Bulzoni.

Bizzocchi, Roberto. 1995. *Genealogie incredibili: Scritti di storia nell'Europa moderna.* Bologna: Il Mulino.

Blasucci, Luigi. 1969. "La *Commedia* come fonte linguistica e stilistica del *Furioso.*" In Blasucci, *Studi su Dante e Ariosto,* 121–62. Naples: Ricciardi.

Bloch, R. Howard. 1983. *Etymologies and Genealogies: A Literary Anthropology of the French Middle Ages.* Chicago: University of Chicago Press.

Boiardo, Ariosto e i libri di battaglia. 2007. Edited by Andrea Canova and Paola Vecchi Galli. Novara: Interlinea.

Bologna, Corrado. 1998. *La macchina del* Furioso. *Lettura dell'*Orlando *e delle* Satire. Turin: Einaudi.

Bordin, Michele and Paolo Trovato, eds. 2006. *Lucrezia Borgia. Storia e mito.* Florence: Leo Olschki.

Branca, Daniela. 1968. *I romanzi italiani di Tristano e la* Tavola ritonda. Florence: Leo Olschki. *See also* Delcorno Branca, Daniela.

Brand, Charles Peter. 1974. *Ludovico Ariosto: A Preface to the* Orlando furioso. Edinburgh: University of Edinburgh Press.

Brink, Jean R., Maryanne C. Horowitz, and Allison P. Coudert, eds. 1989. *The Politics of Gender in Early Modern Europe.* Sixteenth Century Essays and Studies, vol. 12. Ann Arbor: Edwards Brothers.

————, eds. 1991. *Playing with Gender: A Renaissance Pursuit.* Urbana: University of Illinois Press.

Bruscagli, Riccardo, ed. 1983. *Stagioni della civiltà estense*. Pisa: Nistri-Lischi.

———, ed. 1987. *I libri di "Orlando Innamorato."* Modena: Panini.

———. 2003. *Scritti cavallereschi*. Florence: Società Editrice Fiorentina.

Butler, Judith. 1993. *Bodies that Matter: On the Discursive Limits of "Sex."* New York: Routledge.

———. 1990. *Gender Trouble. Feminism and the Subversion of Identity*. New York: Routledge. Reprint with a new preface 1999.

Cabani, Maria Cristina. 1988. *Le forme del cantare epico-cavalleresco*. Lucca: Pacini Fazzi.

———. 1990a. *Costanti ariostesche. Tecniche della rappresentazione e memoria interna nell'* Orlando furioso. Pisa: Scuola Normale Superiore.

———. 1990b. *Fra omaggio e parodia. Petrarca e petrarchismo nel* Furioso. Pisa: Nistri-Lischi.

Cadden, Joan. 1993. *Meaning of Sex Difference in the Middle Ages: Medicine, Science, and Culture*. Cambridge: Cambridge University Press.

Campbell, Caroline. 2009. *Love and Marriage in Renaissance Florence. The Courtauld Wedding Chests*. London: Courtauld Gallery.

Campbell, Stephen. 1996. "The Traffic in Muses: Painting and Poetry in Ferrara around 1450." In *Gendered Contexts: New Perspectives in Italian Cultural Studies*, edited by Laura Benedetti, Julia Hairston, and Silvia M. Ross, 49–68. Studies in Italian Culture Literature and History, vol. 10. New York: Peter Lang.

Il cantare italiano fra folklore e letteratura. 2007. Edited by Michelangelo Picone and Luisa Rubini. Florence: Leo Olschki.

I cantari: struttura e tradizione. Atti del Convegno Internazionale di Montreal, 19–20 March 1981. 1984. Edited by Michelangelo Picone and Maria Bendinelli Predelli. Florence: Olschki.

Carne-Ross, D. S. 1966. "The One and the Many: A Reading of *Orlando Furioso*, Cantos 1 and 8." *Arion* O.S. 5: 195–234.

———. 1976. "The One and the Many: A Reading of *Orlando Furioso*." *Arion* N.S. 3: 146–219.

Casadei, Alberto. 1988. *La strategia delle varianti. Le correzioni storiche del terzo* Furioso. Lucca: Pacini Fazzi.

———. 1993. *Il percorso del "Furioso." Ricerche intorno allle redazioni del 1516 e del 1521*. Bologna: Il Mulino.

———. 1996. "Il 'pro bono malum' ariostesco e la Bibbia." *Giornale storico della letteratura italiana* 173: 566–68.

———. 1997. *La fine degli incanti. Vicende del poema epico-cavalleresco nel Rinascimento.* Milan: Franco Angeli.

Catalano, Michele. 1930–31. *Vita di Ludovico Ariosto.* 2 vols. Geneva: Leo S. Olschki.

Cavallo, Jo Ann. 1993. *Boiardo's* Orlando Innamorato: *An Ethics of Desire.* Cranbury, N.J.: Associated University Presses.

———. 2004. *The Romance Epics of Boiardo, Ariosto, and Tasso: From Public Duty to Private Pleasure.* Toronto: University of Toronto Press.

Cavarero, Adriana. 2002. *Stately Bodies. Literature, Philosophy, and the Question of Gender.* Ann Arbor: University of Michigan Press.

Ceserani, Remo. 1984. "Due modelli culturali e narrativi nell'*Orlando furioso.*" *Giornale Storico della Letteratura Italiana* 161: 481–506.

———. 1988. "L'Impresa delle api e dei serpenti." *Modern Language Notes* 103: 172–86.

Chiappini, Luciano. [1967] 2001. *Gli Estensi. Mille anni di storia.* Ferrara: Corbo Editore.

Chojnacki, Stanley. 1998. "Daughters and Oligarchs: Gender and the Early Renaissance State." In *Gender and Society in Renaissance Italy*, edited by Judith C. Brown and Robert C. Davis, 63–86. London: Addison Welsey Longman.

———. 2000. *Women and Men in Renaissance Venice. Twelve Essays on Patrician Society.* Baltimore: Johns Hopkins University Press.

Cohen, Jeffrey Jerome. 1999. *Of Giants. Sex, Monsters, and the Middle Ages.* Minneapolis: University of Minnesota Press.

Cole, Michael. 2002. "The Demonic Arts and the Origin of the Medium." *Art Bulletin* 84.4: 621–40.

Coliva, Anna. 1998. "I Dossi della Collezione Borghese: Precisazioni documentarie, iconografiche e tecniche," in *Dosso Dossi. Pittore di corte a Ferrara nel Rinascimento*, edited by Peter Humfrey and Mario Lucco, 72–79. Ferrara: Ferrara Arte.

Crabb, Ann. 2000. *The Strozzi of Florence. Widowhood and Familiy Solidarity in the Renaissance.* Ann Arbor: University of Michigan Press.

Dalla Palma, Giuseppe. 1984. *Le strutture narrative dell' 'Orlando furioso.'* Florence: Olschki.

Dante Alighieri. 1966–67. *La Commedia secondo l'antica vulgata.* Edited by Giorgio Petrocchi. Milan: Mondadori.

————. *The Divine Comedy.* 1997–2010. Translated by Robert Durling and Ronald Martinez. Oxford: Oxford University Press.

Davis, Natalie Zemon. 2000. *The Gift in Sixteenth-Century France.* Madison: University of Wisconsin Press.

Dean, Trevor. 1988. *Land and Power in Medieval Ferrara: The Rule of the Este, 1350-1450.* Cambridge: Cambridge University Press.

DeConte, Mary Michelle. 2009. *Hopeless Love. Duiando, Ariosto, and Narratives of Queer Female Desire.* Toronto: University of Toronto Press.

De Giorgio, Michela, and Christiane Klapisch-Zuber, eds. 1996. *Storia del matrimonio.* Bari: Laterza.

Delcorno, Carlo. 1989. *Exemplum e letteratura: tra Medioevo e Rinascimento.* Bologna: Il Mulino.

Delcorno Branca, Daniela. 1973. *L'"Orlando furioso" e il romanzo cavalleresco medievale.* Florence: Olschki.

————. 1991. *Boccaccio e le storie di re Artù.* Bologna: Il Mulino.

————. 1998. *Tristano e Lancillotto in Italia. Studi di letteratura arturiana.* Ravenna: Longo Editore.

D'Elia, Anthony. 2002. "Marriage, Sexual Pleasure, and Learned Brides in the Wedding Orations of Fifteenth-Century Italy." *Renaissance Quarterly* 55: 379–433.

————. 2004. *The Renaissance of Marriage in Fifteenth-Century Italy.* Cambridge: Harvard University Press.

Desmond, Marilynn. 1994. *Reading Dido. Gender, Textuality, and the Medieval* Aeneid. Minneapolis: University of Minnesota Press.

Desole, Corinna. 1995. *Repertorio ragionato dei personaggi citati nei principali cantari cavallereschi italiani.* Alessandria: Edizioni dell'Orso.

Dionisotti, Carlo. 1967. *Geografia e storia della letteratura italiana.* Turin: Einaudi.

————. 2003a. *Boiardo e altri studi cavallereschi.* Novara: Interlinea.

————. [1968] 2003b. *Gli umanisti e il volgare fra Quattro e Cinquecento.* Milan: Five Continents Editions.

Di Sacco, Paolo. 1996. "Femmine guerriere. Amazzoni, cavalli e cavalieri da Camilla a Clorinda." *Intersezioni* 16: 275–89.

Donato, Eugenio. 1972. "'Per selve e boscherecci labirinti': Desire and Narrative Structure in Ariosto's *Orlando Furioso.*" *Barroco* 4: 17–34. Reprinted in *Literary Theory/ Renaissance Texts,* edited by Patricia Parker and D. Quint, 33–62. Baltimore: Johns Hopkins University Press, 1974.

Donnarumma, Raffaele. 1996. *Storia dell'*Orlando innamorato. *Poetiche e modelli letterari in Boiardo.* Lucca: Pacini Fazzi.

Dopico Black, Georgina. 2001. *Perfect Wives, Other Women. Adultery and Inquisition in Early Modern Spain.* Durham: Duke University Press.

Durling, Robert M. 1965. *The Figure of the Poet in Renaissance Epic.* Cambridge: Harvard University Press.

Erler, Mary, and Maryanne Kowaleski, eds. 1988. *Women and Power in the Middle Ages.* Athens: University of Georgia Press.

Esposito, Roberto. [1998] 2009. *Communitas: The Origin and Destiny of Community.* Translated by Timothy Campbell. Palo Alto: Stanford University Press. Originally published as *Communitas. Origine e destino della comunità.* Turin: Einaudi, 2006.

Everson, Jane. 1994. *Bibliografia del* Mambriano *di Francesco Cieco da Ferrara.* Alessandria: Edizioni dell'Orso.

———. 2001. *The Italian Romance Epic in the Age of Humanism.* Oxford: Oxford University Press.

———. 2005a. "Dall'*Attila* all'Ariosto: genealogia e mitologia nei poemi per gli Estensi." In *Les Chansons de geste: Actes du XVIeme congrès International de la Société Rencesvals,* edited by C. Alvar and J. Paredes, 215–30. Granada: Editorial Universidad de Granada.

———. 2005b. "The Epic Tradition of Charlemagne in Italy." *Cahiers de Recherches Médiévales* 12: 45–81.

———. 2005c. "Tradizione burlesca nei proemi ai canti del *Mambriano.*" In *Studi sul Rinascimento italiano/ Italian Renaissance Studies. In Memoriam Giovanni Aquilecchia,* edited by A. Romano and P. Procaccioli, 127–42. Rome: Vecchiarelli Editore.

———. 2006. "Sconvolgere gli stereotipi: la caratterizzazione del traditore e della donna guerriera nel *Mambriano.*" In *Diffusion et Réception du genre chevaleresque,* edited by J.-L. Nardone, 165–82. Toulouse: CIRILLS.

Fahy, Conor. 1987. "L'autore in tipografia: le edizioni ferraresi dell'*Orlando furioso,*" in *I libri di "Orlando Innamorato",* ed. Riccardo Bruscagli, 105–115. Modena: Panini.

———. 1988. *Saggi di bibliografia testuale.* Padua: Antenore.

———. 1989. *L'*Orlando furioso *del 1532. Profilo di una edizione.* Milan: Vita e Pensiero.

Farinella, Vincenzo. 2007. *Dipingere farfalle. Giove, Mercurio e la Virtù di Dosso Dossi: un elogio dell'otium e della pittura per Alfonso I d'Este.* Florence: Polistampa.

Fatini, Giuseppe. 1958. *Bibliografia della critica ariostea (1510–1956).* Florence: Le Monnier.

Faubion, James D., ed. 2001. *The Ethics of Kinship. Ethnographic Inquiries.* Lanham: Rowman and Littlefield

Fenster, Thelma, ed. 2000. *Arthurian Women.* New York: Routledge.

Ferguson, Margaret. 1983. *Trials of Desire: Renaissance Defenses of Poetry.* New Haven: Yale University Press.

Ferguson, Margaret, Maureen Quilligan, and Nancy J. Vickers, eds. 1986. *Rewriting the Renaissance: The Discourses of Sexual Difference in Early Modern Europe.* Chicago: University of Chicago Press.

———. 2003. *Dido's Daughters: Literacy, Gender, and Empire in Early Modern England and France.* Chicago: University of Chicago Press.

Ferrante, Joan. 1973. *The Conflict of Love and Honor: The Medieval Tristan Legend in France, Germany, and Italy.* The Hague: Mouton.

Ferretti, Francesco. 2008. "Bradamante elegiaca. Costruzione del personaggio e intersezione di generi nell'*Orlando furioso.*" *Italianistica* 37.3: 63–75.

———. 2010. "La follia dei gelosi. Lettura del canto XXXII dell'*Orlando furioso.*" *Lettere Italiane* 62: 20–62.

Fichter, Andrew. 1982. *Poets Historical: Dynastic Epic in the Renaissance.* New Haven: Yale University Press.

Findlen, Paula, Michelle M. Fontaine, and Duane J. Osheim, eds. 2003. *Beyond Florence. The Contours of Medieval and Early Modern Italy.* Stanford: Stanford University Press.

Finucci, Valeria. 1992. *The Lady Vanishes: Subjectivity and Representation in Castiglione and Ariosto.* Stanford: Stanford University Press.

———, ed. 1999. *Renaissance Transactions: Ariosto and Tasso.* Durham: Duke University Press.

———. 2003. *The Manly Masquerade: Masculinity, Paternity, and Castration in the Italian Renaissance.* Durham: Duke University Press.

Finucci, Valeria, and Regina Schwartz, eds. 1994. *Desire in the Re-*

naissance: Psychoanalysis and Literature. Princeton: Princeton University Press.

Firenze alla vigilia del Rinascimento. Antonio Pucci e i suoi contemporanei. 2006. Edited by Maria Bendinelli Predelli. Fiesole: Cadmo.

Fisher, Sheila, and Janet E. Alley, eds. 1989. Seeking the Woman in Late Medieval and Renaissance Writing. Essays in Feminist Contextual Criticism. Knoxville: University of Tennessee Press.

Foucault, Michel. 1969. L'archéologie du savoir. Paris: Gallimard.

Fradenburg, Louise, and Carla Freccero, eds. 1996. Premodern Sexualities. New York: Routledge.

Franceschetti, Antonio. 1987. "On the Saracens in Early Italian Chivalric Literature." In Romance Epic. Essays on a Medieval Literary Genre, edited by Hans-Erich Keller, 203–11. Studies in Medieval Culture, vol. 24. Kalamazoo: Western Michigan University.

Freccero, Carla. 1991. Father Figures: Genealogy and Narrative Structure in Rabelais. Ithaca: Cornell University Press.

———. 1995. "From Amazon to Court Lady: Generic Hybridization in Boccaccio's Teseida." Comparative Literature Studies 32: 226–43.

Gardner, Edmund G. 1930. The Arthurian Legend in Italian Literature. New York: Dutton.

Geary, Patrick. 2006. Women at the Beginning. Origin Myths from the Amazons to the Virgin Mary. Princeton: Princeton University Press.

Ghirardo, Diane Yvonne. 2008. "Lucrezia Borgia as Entrepreneur." Renaissance Quarterly 61: 53–91.

Giamatti, A. Bartlett. 1966. The Earthly Paradise and the Renaissance Epic. Princeton: Princeton University Press.

———. 1984. Exile and Change in Renaissance Literature. New Haven: Yale University Press.

Girard, René. 1966. Deceit, Desire and the Novel: Self and Other in Literary Structure. Baltimore: Johns Hopkins University Press. Originally published as Mensonge romantique et vérité romanesque. Paris: Grasset, 1961.

Goldberg, Jonathan, ed. 1994. Queering the Renaissance. Durham: Duke University Press.

Grafton, Anthony, and Lisa Jardine. 1986. Humanism and the Humanities: Education and the Liberal Arts in Fifteenth and Sixteenth Century Italy. Cambridge: Harvard University Press.

Greenblatt, Steven. 1980. *Renaissance Self-Fashioning. From More to Shakespeare*. Chicago: University of Chicago Press.

Greene, Thomas. 1963. *The Descent from Heaven: A Study in Epic Continuity*. New Haven: Yale University Press.

Greimas, Algirdas Julien. 1970. *Du sens*. Paris: Seuil.

———. 1983. *Du sens II – Essais sémiotiques*. Paris: Seuil.

Groebner, Valentin. 2002. *Liquid Assets, Dangerous Gifts: Presents and Politics at the End of the Middle Ages*. Translated by Pamela E. Selwyn. Philadelphia: University of Pennsylvania Press. Originally published as *Gefährliche Geschenke: Korruption und politische Sprache am Oberrhein und in der Eidgenossenschaft am Beginn der Neuzeit*. Constance, 2000.

Gundersheimer, Werner. 1973. *Ferrara: The Style of a Renaissance Despotism*. Princeton: Princeton University Press.

Haarhoff, T. J. 1960. "The Bees of Virgil." *Greece and Rome* s.s. 7.2: 155–70.

Haidu, Peter. 1993. *The Subject of Violence. The* Song of Roland *and the Birth of the State*. Bloomington: Indiana University Press.

Hairston, Julia. 2000. "Bradamante, 'vergine saggia': Maternity and the Art of Negotiation." *Exemplaria* 12: 455–86.

Halperin, David. 1990. *One Hundred Years of Homosexuality and Other Essays on Greek Love*. New York: Routledge.

Harf-Lancner, Laurence. 1984. *Les fées au Moyen Âge. Morgane et Mélusine. La naissance des fées*. Geneva: Slatkine.

Harney, Michael. 2001. *Kinship and Marriage in Medieval Hispanic Chivalric Romance*. Turnhout: Brepols.

Harris, Neil. 1986. "The 'Unicum' of the Second Edition of Boiardo's *Orlando innamorato* and a Forgery of the Last Century." *Rivista di letteratura italiana* 4: 519–36.

———. 1988, 1991. *Bibliografia dell'*Orlando Innamorato. Modena: Panini.

———. 1989. "Il Guerino o l'Ancroia a scelta in una silografia quattrocentesca." *La Bibliofilia* 91: 95–100.

———. 1993. "Marin Sanudo, forerunner of Melzi." *La Bibliofilia* 95: 1–37 and 101–45. Parts 1 and 2.

———. 1994. "Marin Sanudo, forerunner of Melzi." *La Bibliofilia* 96: 15–42. Part 3.

———. 2003. "A Mysterious UFO in the Venetian *Dama Rovenza* [c.1482]." *Gutenberg-Jahrbuch* 78: 22–30.

———. 2007. "Statistiche e sopravvivenze di antichi romanzi di caval-leria," in *Il cantare italiano fra folklore e letteratura*, edited by Mi-chelangelo Picone, 383–412. Florence: Olschki.

Hendricks, Margo, and Patricia Parker, eds. 1994. *Women, "Race," and Writing in the Early Modern Period*. London: Routledge.

Hoffman, Katherine. 1992. "The Court in the Work of Art: Patronage and Poetic Autonomy in the *Orlando Furioso*, Canto 42." *Quad-erni d'Italianistica* 13.1: 113–24.

Hollander, Robert. 1968. "Dante's Use of *Aeneid* I in *Inferno* I and II." *Comparative Literature* 20.2: 142–56.

———. 1983. *Il Virgilio dantesco: tragedia nella "Commedia."* Flor-ence: Olschki, 1983.

———. 1986. "Boccaccio's Dante." *Italica* 63.3: 278–89.

Hughes, Graham. 1997. *Renaissance Cassoni. Masterpieces of Ear-ly Italian Art: Painted Marriage Chests 1400–1550*. London: Art Books International.

Humfrey, Peter, and Mario Lucco, eds. 1998. *Dosso Dossi: Court Paint-er in Renaissance Ferrara*. New York: Metropolitan Museum of Art.

Huot, Sylvia. 2003. "Dangerous Embodiments: Froissart's Harton and Jean d'Arras's Melusine." *Speculum* 78: 400–20.

Internoscia, Donato. 1948. "Are There Two Melissas, Both Enchant-resses, in the *Furioso*?" *Italica* 25: 217–26.

Iotti, Roberta, ed. 1997. *Gli Estensi. Prima parte. La corte di Ferrara*. Modena: Il Bulino.

Irigaray, Luce. 1993. *Sexes and Genealogies*. Translated by Gillian C. Gill. New York: Columbia University Press. Originally published as *Sexes et Parentés*. Paris: Éditions de Minuit, 1987.

Jameson, Fredric. 1972. *The Prison-House of Language*. Princeton: Princeton University Press, 1972.

———. 1981. *The Political Unconscious. Narrative as a Socially Sym-bolic Act*. Ithaca: Cornell University Press.

Javitch, Daniel. 1976. "Rescuing Ovid from the Allegorizers: The Lib-eration of Angelica, *Furioso* X." In *Ariosto 1974 in America: Atti del Congresso Ariostesco*, edited by Aldo Scaglione, 85–98. Raven-na: Longo.

———. 1980. "*Cantus interruptus* in the *Orlando furioso*." *Modern Language Notes* 95: 66–80.

———. 1984. "The *Orlando furioso* and Ovid's Revision of the *Ae-neid*." *Modern Language Notes* 99: 1023–36.

———. 1985. "The Imitation of Imitations in *Orlando furioso*." *Renaissance Quarterly* 38: 215–39.

———. 1988. "Narrative Discontinuity in the *Orlando furioso* and Its Sixteenth Century Critics." *Modern Language Notes* 103: 50–74.

———. 1991. *Proclaiming a Classic: The Canonization of* Orlando furioso. Princeton: Princeton University Press.

——— 1999. "The Grafting of Virgilian Epic in *Orlando furioso*." In *Renaissance Transactions: Ariosto and Tasso*, edited by Valeria Finucci, 56–76. Durham: Duke University Press, 1999.

Jed, Stephanie. 1989. *Chaste Thinking. The Rape of Lucretia and the Birth of Humanism*. Bloomington: Indiana University Press.

Johnson-Haddad, Miranda. 1992. "Gelosia: Ariosto reads Dante." *Stanford Italian Review* 11: 187–201.

Jordan, Constance. 1987. "Boccaccio's In-Famous Women: Gender and Civic Virtue in the *De mulieribus claris*." In *Ambiguous Realities. Women in the Middle Ages and Renaissance*, edited by Carole Levin and Jeanie Watson, 25–47. Detroit: Wayne State University Press.

———. 1990. *Renaissance Feminism. Literary Texts and Political Models*. Ithaca: Cornell University Press.

———. 1999. "Writing beyond the *Querelle*: Gender and History in Ariosto's *Orlando furioso*." In *Renaissance Transactions: Ariosto and Tasso*, edited by Valeria Finucci, 295–315. Durham: Duke University Press.

Jossa, Stefano. 1996. *La fantasia e la memoria: intertestualità ariostesche*. Naples: Liguori.

———. 2002. *La fondazione di un genere: il poema eroico tra Ariosto e Tasso*. Rome: Carocci.

Kay, Sarah. 1988. *The Chansons de geste in the Age of Romance. Political Fictions*. Oxford: Clarendon Press.

———. 2007. *The Place of Thought. The Complexity of One in Late Medieval French Didactic Poetry*. Philadelphia: University of Pennsylvania Press.

Kelly, Joan. 1984. *Women, History and Theory: The Essays of Joan Kelly*. Edited by Catharine R. Stimpson. Chicago: University of Chicago Press.

King, Catherine E. 1988. *Renaissance Women Patrons. Wives and Widows in Italy c. 1300–1550*. Manchester: Manchester University Press.

King, Margaret L. 1991. *Women of the Renaissance*. Chicago: University of Chicago Press. Originally published as *Le donne nel Rinascimento*. Bari: Laterza, 1991.

King, Margaret L., and Albert Rabil, eds. 1983. *Her Immaculate Hand: Selected Works by and about the Women Humanists of Quattrocento Italy*. Binghamton: MRTS.

Kinoshita, Sharon. 1995. "The Politics of Courtly Love: *La Prise d'Orange* and the Conversion of the Saracen Queen." *Romanic Review* 86: 265–87.

———. 2002. "Fraternizing with the Enemy: Christian-Saracen Relations in *Raoul de Cambrai*." In *L'épopée romane. Actes du XVe Congrès international Rencesvals. Poitiers, 21–27 août 2000*, edited by Gabriel Bianciotto and Claudio Galderisi, 695–703. Poitiers: Université de Poitiers.

———. 2006. *Medieval Boundaries: Rethinking Difference in Old French Literature*. Philadelphia: University of Pennsylvania Press.

Kisacky, Julia M. 2000. *Magic in Boiardo and Ariosto*. Studies in Italian Culture. Literature in History, vol. 25. New York: Peter Lang.

Klapisch-Zuber, Christiane. 1985. *Women, Family, and Ritual in Renaissance Italy*. Chicago: University of Chicago Press.

Krauss, Henning. 1980. *Epica feudale e pubblico borghese*. Translated by Andrea Fassò. Padova: Liviana.

Kuehn, Thomas. 1991. *Law, Family, and Women. Toward a Legal Anthropology of Renaissance Italy*. Chicago: University of Chicago Press.

———. 2002. *Illegitimacy in Renaissance Florence*. Ann Arbor: Michigan University Press.

Labalme, Patricia, ed. 1980. *Beyond Their Sex. Learned Women of the European Past*. New York: New York University Press.

Laqueur, Thomas. 1990. *Making Sex. Body and Gender from the Greeks to Freud*. Cambridge: Harvard University Press.

Lathuillère, Roger. 1966. *Guiron le courtois. Étude de la tradition manuscrite et analyse critique*. Geneva: Droz.

La letteratura cavalleresca dalle "chansons de geste" alla "Gerusalemme Liberata." 2008. Edited by Michelangelo Picone. Certaldo: Pacini.

Levi, Ezio. 1933. "L'*Orlando furioso* come epopea nuziale." *Archivum romanicum* 17: 459–93.

Lévi-Strauss, Claude. [1949] 1969. *The Elementary Structures of Kin-*

ship. Translated by James Harle Bell, John Richard von Sturmer, and Rodney Needham. Boston: Beacon. Originally published as *Les structures elementaires de la parenté*. Paris: Presses universitaires de France, 1949.

I libri di Orlando Innamorato. 1987. Edited by Riccardo Bruscagli. Modena: Panini.

Loomis, Roger, ed. 1959. *Arthurian Literature in the Middle Ages: A Collaborative History*. Oxford: Clarendon Press.

Looney, Dennis. 1996. *Compromising the Classics: Romance Epic Narrative in the Italian Renaissance*. Detroit: Wayne State University Press.

———. 2005a. "Fragil arte: tradurre e governare nei volgarizzamenti boiardeschi ad Ercole I d'Este." In *Il Principe e la storia*, edited by S. Matarrese and C. Montagnani, 117–30. Novara: Interlinea Edizioni.

———. 2005b. "Ferrarese Studies: Tracking the Rise and Fall of an Urban Lordship in the Renaissance." In *Phaeton's Children: The Este Court and Its Culture in Early Modern Ferrara*, edited by Dennis Looney and Deanna Shemek, 1–23. Tempe: Arizona Center for Medieval and Renaissance Studies.

———. 2006. "Il mito di Fetonte ed altri miti luttuosi nel rinascimento ferrarese." In *Lucrezia Borgia. Storia e mito*, edited by Michele Bordin and Paolo Trovato, 151–61. Florence: Olschki.

Looney, Dennis, and Deanna Shemek, eds. 2005. *Phaeton's Children: The Este Court and Its Culture in Early Modern Ferrara*. Tempe: Arizona Center for Medieval and Renaissance Studies.

Löseth, Eliert. 1891. *Le roman en prose de Tristan, le roman de Palamède et la compilation de Rusticien de Pise. Analyse critique d'après le manuscript de Paris*. Paris: Bouillon. Reprint New York: Burt Franklin, 1970.

Luzio, Alessandro, and Rodolfo Renier. 2005. *La coltura e le relazioni letterarie di Isabella d'Este Gonzaga*. Edited by Simone Albonico. Milan: Edizioni Sylvestre Bonnard. Originally published in *Giornale storico della letteratura italiana*, 1899–1903.

MacCarthy, Ita. 2005. "Marfisa and Gender Performance in the *Orlando furioso*." *Italian Studies* 60.2: 178–95.

———. 2007a. "Ariosto the Traveller." *Modern Language Review* 102: 397–409.

———. 2007b. *Women and the Making of Poetry in Ariosto's* Orlando furioso. Leicester: Troubadour Publishing.

MacLean, Ian. 1980. *The Renaissance Notion of Woman. A Study on the Fortunes of Scholasticism and Medical Science in European Intellectual Life*. Cambridge: Cambridge University Press.

MacPhail, Eric. 2001. "Ariosto and the Prophetic Moment." *Modern Language Notes* 116: 30–53.

Marinelli, Peter. 1987. *Ariosto and Boiardo. The Origins of "Orlando furioso."* Columbia: University of Missouri Press.

Marsh, David. 1981. "Ruggiero and Leone: Revision and Resolution in Ariosto's *Orlando furioso*." *Modern Language Notes* 96: 144–51.

Martinez, Ronald. 1994. "De-Cephalizing Rinaldo: The Money of Tyranny in Niccolò da Correggio's *Fabula de Cefalo* and in *Orlando Furioso* 42–43." *Annali d'Italianistica* 12: 87–114.

———. 1999. "Two Odysseys: Rinaldo's Po Journey and the Poet's Homecoming in *Orlando furioso*." In *Renaissance Transactions: Ariosto and Tasso*, edited by Valeria Finucci, 17–55. Durham: Duke University Press.

———. N.d. "Ricciardetto's Sex and the Castration of Orlando: Anatomy of an Episode from the *Orlando Furioso*." Unpublished paper.

Masi, Giorgio. 2003. "The Nightingale in a Cage": Ariosto and the Este Court," In *Ariosto Today*, edited by Donald Beecher, Massimo Ciavolella, and Roberto Fedi, 71–92. Toronto: Toronto University Press.

Mason, Stefania. 2000. *Carpaccio: The Major Pictorial Cycles*. Milan: Skira.

Mauss, Marcel. [1923-24] 1990. *The Gift: The Form and Reason for Exchange in Archaic Societies*. Translated by W. D. Halls. New York: Norton. Originally published as "Essai sur le don. Forme et raison de l'échange dans les sociétés archäiques," *L'Année Sociologique*, n.s. 1 (1923–24): 30–186.

Mayhew, Robert. 1999. "King-Bees and Mother-Wasps: A Note on Ideology and Gender in Aristotle's Entomology." *Phronesis* 44.2: 127–34.

McLucas, John. 1988. "Amazon, Sorceress, and Queen: Women and War in the Aristocratic Literature of Sixteenth-Century Italy." *Italianist* 8: 33–55.

Melli, Elio. 1974. "A proposito dei *Cantari di Rinaldo da Monte Albano*." *Studi e problemi di critica testuale* 8: 73–81.

———. 1978. "Nella selva dei *Rinaldi*: Poemetti su Rinaldo da Mont'Albano in antiche edizioni a stampa." *Studi e problemi di critica testuale* 16: 193–215.

Meneghetti, Maria Luisa. 1989. "Il manoscritto Fr. della Bibliothèque Nationale di Parigi, Tommaso di Saluzzo e gli affreschi della Manta." *Romania* 110: 511–35.

Migiel, Marilyn, and Juliana Schiesari, eds. 1991. *Refiguring Women. Perspectives on Gender in the Italian Renaissance*. Ithaca: Cornell University Press.

Molho, Anthony. 1994. *Marriage Alliance in Late Medieval Florence*, Cambridge: Harvard University Press.

Montagnani, Cristina. 2004. *"Andando con lor dame in aventura." Percorsi estensi*. Galatina: Mario Congedo Editore.

———. 2005. "*Queste historie di fabulosi sogni son dipinte*: Boiardo, Ariosto e la genealogia degli Este." In *Il principe e la storia*, edited by Tina Matarrese and Cristina Montagnani, 157–79. Novara: Interlinea.

Montanari, Anna. 1993. "Il *Libro de l'Ancroia*." *Libri & Documenti* 18: 1–15.

———. 1995a. "Il *Libro de l'Ancroia* e il Boiardo." *Rivista di letteratura italiana* 13: 225–43.

———. 1995b. "Un precedente dell'episodio di Ruggero e Leone." *Giornale storico della letteratura italiana* 172: 415–21.

———. 1997. "Aquilante e Grifone. *Studi Italiani* 18: 5–25.

———. 2004. "'Sì come mi raconta el gran poeta.' Le storie di Enea nei cantari in ottave a stampa." *Libri & Documenti* 30: 1–17.

———. 2007. "Un repertorio per i poemi e i romanzi cavallereschi a stampa del Quattrocento." *Bibliologia* 2: 133–46.

Moraga, Cherríe. 1986. "From a Long Line of Vendidas: Chicanas and Feminism." In *Feminist Studies/ Critical Studies*, edited by Teresa de Lauretis, 173–90. Bloomington: Indiana University Press.

Moraga, Cherríe, and Gloria Anzaldúa, eds. 1981. *This Bridge Called My Back: Writings by Radical Women of Color*. Watertown, Mass.: Persephone Press.

Morel, Philippe, ed. 2006. *L'art de la Renaissance entre science et magie*. Rome: Académie de France à Rome.

———. 2008. *Mélissa. Magie, astres et demons dans l'art italien de la Renaissance*. Paris: Éditions Hazan.

Moretti, Franco. 2005. *Graphs, Maps, Trees*. New York: Verso.

Moretti, Walter. 1987. "Gli ultimi canti del *Furioso*: il viaggio dell'Ariosto nel mondo dell''avarizia.'" In *Studi in Onore di Lanfranco Caretti*, edited by W. Moretti, 25–43. Modena: Mucchi.

Morosi, Andrea. 1978. "Breve storia della 'Storia di Rinaldo.'" *Interpres* 1: 285–93.

Nuovo, Angela. 1998. *Il commercio librario a Ferrara tra XV e XVI secolo. La Bottega di Domenico Sivieri*. Florence: Olschki.

———. [1998] 2003. *Il commercio librario nell'Italia del Rinascimento*. Milan: Franco Angeli.

———. 2007. "I 'libri di battaglia': commercio e circolazione tra Quattro e Cinquecento." In *Boiardo, Ariosto e i libri di battaglia*, edited by Andrea Canova and Paola Vecchi Galli, 341–59. Novara: Interlinea.

Orvieto, Paolo. 1978. *Pulci medievale. Studio sulla poesia volgare fiorentina del Quattrocento*. Rome: Salerno.

Picone, Michelangelo, ed. 2008. *La letteratura cavalleresca dalle* Chansons de Geste *alla* Gerusalemme Liberata. Pisa: Pacini.

Praloran, Marco. 1990. *Maraviglioso artificio. Tecniche narrative e rappresentative nell'*Orlando Innamorato. Lucca: Pacini Fazzi.

———. 1994. *Tempo e azione nell'*Orlando furioso. Florence: Olschki.

Prete, Frederick R. 1991. "Can Females Rule the Hive? The Controversy over Honey Bee Gender Roles in British Beekeeping Texts of the Sixteenth-Eighteenth Centuries." *Journal of the History of Biology* 24.1: 113–44.

Il principe e la storia. Atti del convegno di Scandiano 18–20 settembre 2003. 2005. Edited by Tina Matarrese and Cristina Montagnani. Novara: Interlinea.

Propp, Vladimir. [1928] 1958. *Morphology of the Folktale*. The Hague: Mouton. Originally published as *Morfologija skazki*. Leningrad, 1928.

Psaki, Regina. 2000. "Chivalry and Medieval Italian Romance." In *The Cambridge Companion to Medieval Romance*, edited by Roberta A. Krueger, 203–17. Cambridge: Cambridge University Press.

———. 2004. "The Traffic in Talk about Women: Cultural Traffic in Medieval Texts and Medieval Studies." *Journal of Romance Studies* 4.3: 13–34.

Quint, David. 1977. "Astolfo's Voyage to the Moon." *Yale Italian Studies* O.S. 1: 398–408.

———. 1979. "The Figure of Atlante: Ariosto and Boiardo's Poems." *Modern Language Notes* 94: 77–91.

———. 1983. *Origin and Originality in Renaissance Literature: Versions of the Source*. New Haven: Yale University Press.

———. 1985. "The Boat of Romance and Renaissance Epic." In *Romance: Generic Transformations from Chrétien de Troyes to Cervantes*, edited by Kevin Brownlee and Marina Scordilis Brownlee, 178–202. Hanover, N.H.: University Press of New England.

———. 1993. *Epic and Empire. Politics and Generic Form from Virgil to Milton*. Princeton: Princeton University Press.

———. 1994. "The Death of Brandimarte and the Ending of the *Orlando furioso*." *Annali d'Italianistica* 12: 75–85.

Rajna, Pio. [1876, 1900] 1975 (reprint of the 1900 edition). *Le fonti dell' Orlando furioso*. Florence: Sansoni.

———. 1956. *Le origini dell'epopea francese*. Florence: Sansoni.

———. 1998. *Scritti di filologia e linguistica italiana e romanza*. Rome: Salerno.

———. 2004. *Due scritti inediti. Le leggende epiche dei Longobardi. Storia del romanzo cavalleresco in Italia*. Rome: Salerno.

Regan, Lisa. 2005. "Ariosto's Threshold Patron: Isabella d'Este in the *Orlando furioso*." *Modern Language Notes* 120: 50–69.

Rheubottom, David. 2000. *Age, Marriage, and Politics in Fifteenth-century Ragusa*. Oxford: Oxford University Press.

Ricci, Giovanni. 2007. *I giovani, i morti. Sfide al Rinascimento*. Bologna: Il Mulino.

Robinson, Lillian S. 1985. *Monstrous Regiment: The Lady Knight in Sixteenth Century Epic*. New York: Garland.

Roggero, Marina. 2006. *Le carte piene di sogni. Testi e lettori in età moderna*. Bologna: Il Mulino.

Romizi, Augusto. 1896. *Le fonti latine dell'Orlando furioso*. Turin: Paravia.

Roscalla, Fabio. 1988. "La descrizione del sé e dell'altro: Api ed alveare da Esiodo a Semonide." *Quaderni Urbinati di Cultura Classica* 29.2: 23–47.

Rosenberg, Charles M. 1997. *The Este Monuments and Urban Development in Renaissance Ferrara*. Cambridge: Cambridge University Press.

Ross, Charles. 1997. *The Custom of the Castle. From Malory to Macbeth*. Berkeley: University of California Press.

Rubin, Gayle. 1975. "The Traffic in Women: Notes on the 'Political Economy' of Sex." In *Toward an Anthropology of Women*, edited by Rayna Reiter, 157–210. New York: Monthly Review Press.

Saccone, Eduardo. 1974. *Il soggetto del 'Furioso' e altri saggi tra Quattro e Cinquecento*. Naples: Liguori.

Sahlins, Marshall. 1972. *Stone Age Economics*. Chicago: Aldine.

Sangirardi, Giuseppe. 1993. *Boiardismo ariostesco. Presenza e trattamento dell'*Orlando innamorato *nel* Furioso. Lucca: Pacini Fazzi.

———. 2006. *Ludovico Ariosto*. Florence: Le Monnier.

Santoro, Mario. 1973. *Letture ariostesche*. Naples: Liguori.

———. 1976. "La prova del 'nappo' e la cognizione ariostesca del reale." *Esperienze letterarie* 1: 5–24.

———. 1989. *Ariosto e il Rinascimento*. Naples: Liguori.

Schiesari, Juliana. 1989. "In Praise of Virtuous Women? For a Genealogy of Gender Morals in Renaissance Italy." *Annali D'Italianistica* 7: 66–87.

———. 1991. "The Domestication of Woman in *Orlando furioso* 42 and 43, or A Snake Is Being Beaten." *Stanford Italian Review* 10: 123–43.

Schwarz, Kathryn. 2000. *Tough Love. Amazon Encounters in the English Renaissance*. Durham: Duke University Press.

Scott, Joan Wallach. 1999. *Gender and the Politics of History*. Revised edition. New York: Columbia University Press.

Searles, Colbert. 1902. "The Leodilla Episode in Boiardo's *Orlando Innamorato* (I xx-xxii)." *Modern Language Notes* 17: 330–42.

Sedgwick, Eve Kosofsky. 1985. *Between Men. English Literature and Male Homosocial Desire*. New York: Columbia University Press.

Segre, Cesare. 1966. *Esperienze Ariostesche*. Pisa: Nistri-Lischi.

———. 1984. *Teatro e romanzo. Due forme di comunicazione letteraria*. Turin: Einaudi.

———. 1990. "Pio Rajna: le fonti e l'arte dell'*Orlando furioso*." *Strumenti critici* n.s. 5: 315–27.

Shemek, Deanna. 1998. *Ladies Errant: Wayward Women and Social Order in Early Modern Italy*. Durham: Duke University Press.

———. 2005a. "«Ci Ci» and «Pa Pa»: Script, Mimicry, and Mediation in Isabella d'Este's Letters." *Rinascimento: Rivista dell'Istituto Nazionale di Studi sul Rinascimento*, 2nd ser. 43: 75–91.

———. 2005b. "The Collector's Cabinet: Lodovico Domenichi's Gallery of Women." In *Strong Voices, Weak Histories*, edited by Pamela Joseph Benson and Victoria Kirkham, 239–62. Ann Arbor: University of Michigan Press.

———. 2005c. "In Continuous Expectation: Isabella d'Este's Epistolary Desire." In *Phaeton's Children: The Este Court and Its Culture in Early Modern Ferrara*, edited by Dennis Looney and Deanna Shemek, 269–300. Tempe: Arizona Center for Medieval and Renaissance Studies.

———. 2005d. "Isabella d'Este and the Properties of Persuasion." In *Form and Persuasion in Early Modern Women's Letters across Europe*, edited by Ann Crabb and Jane Couchman, 100–33. Brookfield, Vt.: Ashgate.

Sherberg, Michael. 1993. *Rinaldo. Character and Intertext in Ariosto and Tasso*. Stanford, Cal.: Anma Libri.

Sinicropi, Giovanni. 1981. "La struttura della parodia; ovvero: Bradamante in Arli." *Strumenti critici* 45: 232–51.

Siraisi, Nancy. 1987. *Avicenna in Renaissance Italy. The Canon and Medical Teaching in Italian Universities after 1500*. Chicago: University of Chicago Press.

Sitterson, Joseph. 1992. "Allusive and Elusive Meanings: Reading Ariosto's Vergilian Ending." *Renaissance Quarterly* 45: 1–19.

Solterer, Helen. 1991. "Figures of Female Militancy in Medieval France." *Signs: Journal of Women in Culture and Society* 16: 522–49.

Spiegel, Gabrielle M. 1993. *Romancing the Past. The Rise of Vernacular Prose Historiography in Thirteenth-Century France*. Berkeley: University of California Press.

Stallybrass, Peter. 1986. "Patriarchal Territiories: The Body Enclosed." In *Rewriting the Renaissance: The Discourses of Sexual Difference in Early Modern Europe*, edited by Margaret Ferguson, Maureeen Quilligan, and Nancy Vickers, 123–42: Chicago: University of Chicago Press.

Stephens, Walter. 1989a. *Giants in Those Days: Folklore, Ancient History and Nationalism*. Lincoln: University of Nebraska Press.

———. 1989b. "Saint Paul among the Amazons: Gender and Authority in *Gerusalemme liberata*." In *Discourses of Authority in Medieval and Renaissance Literature*, edited by Walter Stephens and Kevin Brownlee, 169–200. Hanover, N.H.: University Press of New England.

———. 2002. *Demon Lovers: Witchcraft, Sex, and the Crisis of Belief*. Chicago: University of Chicago Press.

Stewart, Susan. 1984. *On Longing. Narratives of the Miniature, the*

Gigantic, the Souvenir, the Collection. Baltimore and London: Johns Hopkins University Press.

Stoppino, Eleonora. 2001. "'Onde è tassato l'Ariosto'. Appunti sulla tradizione del romanzo nella *Gerusalemme liberata*." *Strumenti Critici* 16.2: 225–44.

———. 2007. "Bradamante fra i cantari e l'*Orlando furioso*: prime osservazioni." In *Boiardo, Ariosto e i libri di battaglia*, edited by Andrea Canova and Paola Vecchi Galli, 321–35. Novara: Interlinea.

Strathern, Marilyn. 1988. *The Gender of the Gift: Problems with Women and Problems with Society in Melanesia*. Berkeley: University of California Press.

Suzuki, Mihoko. 1989. *Metamorphosis of Helen. Authority, Difference, and the Epic*. Ithaca: Cornell University Press.

Tissoni Benvenuti, Antonia. 1987. "Il mondo cavalleresco e la corte estense." In *I libri di Orlando Innamorato*, edited by Riccardo Bruscagli, 13–33. Modena: Panini.

———. 1992a. "Note preliminari al commento *dell'Inamoramento de Orlando*." In *Il commento ai testi, Atti del Seminario di Ascona, 2-6 ottobre 1989*, edited by Ottavio Besomi and Carlo Caruso, 277–309. Basel: Birkhäuser Verlag.

———. 1992b. "Il terzo libro, ovvero *El fin del'Inamoramento de Orlando*." In *Tipografie e romanzi in Val Padana tre Quattro e Cinquecento*, edited by Riccardo Bruscagli and Amedeo Quondam, 29–44. Modena: Panini.

———. 1996a. "Rugiero o la fabbrica dell'*Inamoramento de Orlando*." In *Per Cesare Bozzetti. Studi di letteratura e filologia italiana*, edited by Simone Albonico, Andrea Comboni, Giorgio Panizza, and Claudio Vela, 69–89. Milan: Fondazione Arnoldo e Alberto Mondadori.

———. 1996b. "Una testimonianza parziale *dell'Inamoramento de Orlando*: il manoscritto Vat. Lat. 11255." In *Operosa parva, Per Gianni Antonini*, 113–21. Verona: Valdonega.

———. 1998. "Sul testo dell'*Inamoramento de Orlando*." In *Boiardo e il mondo Estense nel Quattrocento, Atti del Convegno Internazionale di Studi, Scandiano-Modena, Reggio Emilia - Ferrara, 13–17 settembre 1994*, edited by Giuseppe Anceschi and Tina Matarrese, 924–42. Padua: Antenore.

———. 2007. "Intertestualità cavalleresca." In *Tre volte suona l'olifante*, 57–78. Milan: Unicopli.

———. 2008. "I testi cavallereschi di riferimento dell'*Inamoramento de Orlando.*" In *La letteratura cavalleresca*, edited by Michelangelo Picone, 239–55. Pisa: Pacini.

Tomalin, Margaret. 1992. *The Fortunes of the Warrior Heroine in Italian Literature: An Index of Emancipation.* Ravenna: Longo Editore.

Tre volte suona l'olifante . . . (La tradizione rolandiana in Italia fra Medioevo e Rinascimento). 2007. Milan: Unicopli.

Tylus, Jane. 1988. "The Curse of Babel: The *Orlando Furioso* and Epic (Mis)Appropriation." *Modern Language Notes* 103: 154–71.

———. 2007. "The Rape of the Sabines and the Origins of Early Modern Theatre." In *Theatre without Borders: Early Modernities*, edited by Robert Henke and Eric Nicholson, 99–116. Aldershot: Ashgate.

Usher, Jonathan. 1989. "Rhetorical and Narrative Strategies in Boccaccio's Translation of the *Comoedia Lydiae.*" *Modern Language Review* 84: 337–44.

Verrier, Frédérique. 2003. *Le miroir des Amazones. Amazones, viragos et guerrières dans la littérature italienne des XVe et XVIe siècles.* Paris: L'Harmattan.

Villoresi, Marco. 1994. *Da Guarino a Boiardo. La cultura teatrale a Ferrara nel Quattrocento.* Rome: Bulzoni.

———. 1997. "Scaltrezza editoriale e formularità canterina: *La grande guerra et rotta del Scapigliato.*" *Libri & Documenti* 23: 73–81.

———. 1998. "Le donne e gli amori nel romanzo cavalleresco del Cinquecento." *Filologia e critica* 23: 3–43.

———. 2000. *La letteratura cavalleresca, Dai cicli medievali all'Ariosto.* Rome: Carocci editore.

———. 2005. *La fabbrica dei cavalieri, cantari, poemi, romanzi in prosa fra Medioevo e Rinascimento.* Rome: Salerno Editrice.

Visani, Oriana. 1994. "I testi italiani *dell'Historia di Merlino.*" *Schede umanistiche* 4: 17–61.

Vitullo, Juliann. 1994. "Contained Conflict: Wild Men and Warrior Women in the Early Italian Epic." *Annali d'Italianistica* 12: 39–59.

———. 2000. *The Chivalric Epic in Medieval Italy.* Gainesville: University Press of Florida.

Weinberg, Florence. 1986. *The Cave. The Evolution of a Metaphoric Field from Homer to Ariosto.* New York: Peter Lang.

Weiner, Annette. 1976. *Women of Value, Men of Renown: New Perspectives in Trobriand Exchange.* Austin: University of Texas Press.

Wiggins, Peter DeSa. 1986. *Figures in Ariosto's Tapestry. Character and Design in the* Orlando Furioso. Baltimore: Johns Hopkins University Press.

Wilkins Ernest Hatch. 1923. *The Trees of the* Genealogia Deorum *of Boccaccio*. Chicago: Caxton Club.

Wood, Christopher S. 2006. "Countermagical Combination by Dosso Dossi," *Res 49/50*: 152–70.

Zampese, Cristina. 1994. *Or si fa rossa or pallida la luna. La cultura classica nell'*Orlando Innamorato. Lucca: Pacini Fazzi.

Zatti, Sergio. 1983. *L'uniforme cristiano e il multiforme pagano. Saggio sulla* Gerusalemme liberata. Milan: Il Saggiatore.

———. 1990. *Il* Furioso *tra epos e romanzo*. Lucca: Pacini Fazzi.

———, ed. 1998. *La rappresentazione dell'altro nei testi del Rinascimento*. Lucca: Pacini Fazzi.

———. 2006. *The Quest for Epic: From Ariosto to Tasso*. Toronto: University of Toronto Press.

Zika, Charles. 2002. "Images of Circe and Discourses of Witchcraft, 1480–1580." *zeitenblicke* 1.1. http://www.zeitenblicke.historicum .net/2002/01/zika/zika.html.

Zumthor, Paul. 1943. *Merlin le prophète. Un thème de la littérature polémique de l'historiographie et des romans*. Lausanne: Imprimeries Réunies S.A..

INDEX

Italicized page references refer to illustrations.